THE WHITE

'LUCAS AND SUSANNAH WERE IN THE LIVING ROOM OF HIS APARTMENT...
standing at one of the big windows that looked down on the East River. As Lucas held Susannah in his arms and kissed her, she murmured, "If my father had the least idea what's going on . . ."

"I have to tell you something," Lucas said to Susannah. "Your father has threatened me with a nasty lawsuit."

"I wouldn't take that too seriously," she said. "Since I was a kid I can remember him always threatening to sue somebody about something."

"He's had the company auditors accuse me of misusing company funds years ago. They're talking about a million dollars or so."

"My father can't stand the possibility he might not be able to make you do what he wants you to."

Lucas held her close to him and caressed her hair. "I wish it didn't have to be like this, Susannah," he said.

She looked up solemnly into his face.

"So do I. But . . . I love you."' '

The White Knight

Carl F. Furst

NEW ENGLISH LIBRARY
Hodder and Stoughton

Copyright © 1986 by Pocket Books, a
division of Simon & Schuster, Inc.

First published in the United States of
America in 1986 by Pocket Books, a division
of Simon & Schuster, Inc.

First NEL paperback edition 1987

British Library C.I.P.

Furst, Carl F.
  The white knight.   (Harold Robbins
  presents)
  I. Title
  813'.54 [F]   PS3556.U76/

  ISBN 0-450-40415-3

Printed and bound in Great Britain for
Hodder and Stoughton Paperbacks, a
division of Hodder and Stoughton Ltd.,
Mill Road, Dunton Green, Sevenoaks,
Kent (Editorial Office: 47 Bedford
Square, London WC1B 3DP) by
Richard Clay (The Chaucer Press) Ltd.,
Bungay, Suffolk

HAROLD ROBBINS PRESENTS is a trademark of
Harold Robbins.

1985

Four Warm Days in May

_____ **1**

MAYBE TODAY, THIS so far unremarkable Thursday, will
turn out to be memorable, Timothy Bryan speculated
as he walked through the echoing cavern of Grand
Central Station and took an escalator up into the Pan
Am Building. Other associates in Wiltmeyer, Grayson,
Ruggiero & Hayes had come back with lurid stories of
their brief encounters with the formidable president of
HEST, Incorporated; but what little he knew of the
man was only from listening to others and reading
about him; he had never been called to the HEST
offices before. He checked his watch as he reached the
top of the second set of escalators and walked toward
the elevator bank. He was expected at three, so he had
ten minutes. In the elevator, in which he was alone, he
pulled his necktie tighter, shoved his shirt tail deeper
into his pants, and squirted his mouth with Binaca
breath spray. He was thirty years old, four years out of
Harvard Law, and intensely conscious of the nature of
the documents he carried in the scarred leather attaché
case that belonged to Foster Theisen.

The reception area he found when he left the elevator was a distinct disappointment. It was a small room,
furnished in shades of beige and brown, with only a
corporate logo on the wall to assure him he had reached
the right floor. The receptionist was a sour-faced,

middle-aged woman with a crisp, not entirely friendly air.

"Theisen," she said, as if the name of a senior partner at Wiltmeyer, Grayson, Ruggiero & Hayes meant nothing here. "Seeing General Fraser." That name, she made it plain, did mean something. She picked up her telephone and touched the buttons. "A Mr. Bryan here to see Mr. Theisen, who is supposed to be with General Fraser." After a moment, she nodded toward a pair of double doors. She pressed a button that buzzed the lock.

He stepped through the double doors into a cool, silent, two-story complex of big rooms. The white walls were hung with dramatically lighted modern paintings. The floors and stairway were carpeted in blue gray. The starkness was relieved by at least a dozen big trees and cacti growing in huge ceramic tubs—including one tall tree that shared the stairwell and grew more than twenty feet high. The pretty, English-accented receptionist rose from her desk to greet him. She led him into a large room where the tall windows faced the long, haze-obscured vista of Manhattan south of Forty-second Street: everything from the Empire State Building standing tall to the right, all the way downtown to the Trade Towers. He glanced only for a moment at the view, equally distracted by the art that covered the white walls and by the trim legs the receptionist showed below her short, tight skirt.

"I believe you have about five minutes' wait, Mr. Bryan," she said. "Would you perhaps like coffee or tea, or a soft drink, or a whiskey?"

"Well, maybe a diet Coke," he said.

She smiled knowingly and returned to her desk to order his drink. She looked up at him and smiled once again as he began a quick circuit of the room, checking

3

the names of the artists who had signed the paintings that caught his attention—Mondrian, de Kooning, Stella.

Major General Matthew B. Fraser (U.S. Army, retired), the president of HEST, Incorporated, was one of those men who attracted attention even when he did not want it. He was a big man, strong-faced, and handsome, which had been an asset to him at every step in his career. He stood three or four inches taller than most men, and he carried well the signs of late middle age. His eyes, set deep inside a circle of pronounced facial muscles and deepening lines, were pale blue; they suggested the cool, sharp eyes of the outdoorsman-model in a thousand cigarette and whiskey ads. His hair, which had been black—the color remaining in his eyebrows—was steel gray streaked with white. He obviously spent money on his clothes. The dark gray suit and blue shirt he was wearing were entirely unwrinkled in midafternoon and fit perfectly on his broad shoulders, big chest, and narrow waist. To shake hands with Tim Bryan, the general put a lighted cigarette aside in the ashtray on his desk. The cigarette, Tim noticed, was custom-made, with the general's initials printed on the cream-white paper.

"Go ahead," the general said. "Look around. Everyone wants to. We can spare a minute for you to look around."

One wall of the general's office was covered by three Japanese painted screens, centuries old, depicting historic battles fought on misty mountain landscapes by Samurai warriors—all so softly painted, in such stylized forms and colors, that only upon close inspection did one discover that the figures in the landscapes were fighting armies, marching and brandishing their weapons. In a glass case was displayed a suit of Japanese formal armor, in the Edo style. Another wall was hung with Japanese prints and scrolls, picturing grimacing Samurai, one using a spear to kill a fierce tiger, others fighting on foot or on horseback, still others simply displaying their elaborate armor and weapons. The furniture in the office was simple, set low and styled to complement the exquisite Japanese artifacts. Much of the polished oak floor was exposed, though the windows had all been covered to keep out any distracting view of the city. Hidden light fixtures filled the room with a warm, shadowless glow.

"I've offered drinks," said General Fraser. "Foster" —he meant Foster Theisen, the senior partner who had summoned Tim Bryan here—"has accepted a glass of chilled white wine. Jim"—meaning James Cahill, senior executive vice president of HEST—"is having a vodka martini, which he'll always accept, even for breakfast. And I'm going to inhale a Scotch on the rocks. You?"

Tim Bryan glanced at the senior lawyer. "Uh, a glass of wine, please," he said.

Cahill, of the four men in the room, was the only one who might be said to be relaxed. A tall, emaciated man, he had a smile that was too ready, too broad, revealing a hidden tenseness, but draped comfortably in one of the general's low chairs, he appeared ready to let the world hand him what it would. From time to time he pushed his horn-rimmed spectacles up and tangled them in his dark hair—as he did now. He was alone, too, in that he had left his jacket somewhere and sat in his shirtsleeves, with his collar unbuttoned and his tie pulled loose.

"You've brought all the crap?" asked Cahill.

"Uh . . . right," said Tim Bryan.

Foster Theisen reached for the attaché case, opened it, and began to scan the papers Tim had brought from the Wiltmeyer offices. "Yes," he said quietly. "Yes, sir." He put his finger on a sheet of paper and frowned over it. "Right. The changes have been made. With signatures, we can file. We're ready to go, Matt."

"'Half a league, half a league, half a league onward . . .'" said Cahill.

"Can that, Jim," snapped General Fraser. "We're going to win this thing."

Cahill shrugged. "'Tis a consummation devoutly to be'—"

"It's not a matter of wishes. We're going to *win*," insisted the general.

Foster Theisen pursed his lips and ran his hand across his mouth. "There are hazards," he said.

General Fraser turned on the flushed-faced lawyer. "You wouldn't guarantee me the sun will come up tomorrow morning, would you, Foster? You lawyers are all alike. Won't promise anything. Everything's 'if' and 'maybe.' Hell . . ." He pointed a finger at Tim Bryan. "How about you, young man? Is this deal going to work? Yes or no?"

Tim Bryan looked into the eyes of his senior, looking for a suggestion. Foster Theisen's red face was fixed and bland. Tim sighed. "Yes, sir," he said. "It looks to me as if you're going to win."

"*All right!*" said the general, clapping his hands. "That's what I want to hear."

"Rah, rah, siss-boom-bah," said Cahill.

"You son of a—"

"Barring an act of God," added Cahill. "Where're the drinks?"

6

"The notice of the meeting—" said Foster Theisen.

"Send it," said General Fraser. "Is there any reason to hold back?"

The lawyer shook his head. "You have the funding—"

"One-point-one bil, sure," said the general. "The consortium is committed. UNI can't resist. The cash it's going to get for its stock is going to save it from insolvency."

"The Fraser Tech bid will be . . .?"

"Twenty-eight and a half."

"Twenty-*eight* and a half? What happened to twenty-seven?"

"Jim's idea," said the general as he pressed the button to admit a young woman carrying a tray of drinks.

"You overreach on these things," said Cahill, "and you're just asking for it. Lucas Paulson's going to be in a fighting mood at any price. The point is to deprive him of allies. You haven't heard this, Foster, but it looks like Arthur Ringold will go along at twenty-eight and a half. With Ringold out of the fight, that leaves Paulson with nobody but Dave Berger and a few nickel-and-dime stockholders. It'll be hard for Paulson to yell squeeze-out when Ringold isn't yelling."

"What did Art say?" asked Foster Theisen, putting a sweating glass of cold white wine to his lips.

"You know Art Ringold," said the general, relaxing in his chair and throwing his feet up on his desk. "The old boy always needs money. But I put it to him frankly. Nobody is going to invest $100 million in reprogramming HEST unless the ownership and management can be consolidated in one aggressive company. He can hold on until somebody catches up, or he

7

can sell out for a fair price and enjoy his profits while somebody else carries the burden in future. If Paulson's smart, he'll see the merger as an opportunity to retire."

Cahill grinned. "I wouldn't count on that. He still thinks it's his baby. He wants his share of whatever it becomes."

The general swung his feet to the floor and tossed off his Scotch at a gulp. "I am the very first man," he said, "to acknowledge Lucas Paulson's contributions to this business. Those contributions do not, however, entitle him to a partnership in whatever HEST becomes."

"Besides which, we don't like him," said Cahill, sipping his martini.

"I'm going to admit that," said the general. "No, I don't like him."

"Don't you have some leverage with him, through his daughter's position with the company?" asked Foster Theisen. "Doesn't she have a pretty good job with HEST?"

"Melanie Paulson is not grateful for her job, and she feels no loyalty whatever to this company," said the general. "There is reason to believe she may already have violated the terms of her no-compete, no-disclosure agreement. She has all his ego and none of his middle-America conscience."

"All right," said Theisen. "The documents are ready for signature. Fraser Technologies, Incorporated will propose a merger with HEST, Incorporated. It will be a cash-out merger, with the HEST stockholders receiving $28.50 per share for their stock, instead of the stock for stock that is usual in a merger. You have all the votes you need—that is, a majority of the directors and a majority of the stock. UNI will vote its shares in favor, you and your associates will vote yours, Arthur Ringold will vote the Ringold shares, and some of the nickel-and-dime shareholders will go along, too. I have the SEC reports ready, and I see no problem there. All you really have to worry about is a lawsuit, and the worst I can see in that is delay."

"We've got the son of a bitch," said General Fraser, raising his glass—now containing nothing more than melting ice cubes. "Rid of UNI, rid of Ringold, rid of Berger, rid of Paulson. . . . By God, this business has a future!"

The papers were signed and the lawyers gone by 4:15. Jim Cahill sat for a while in the general's office, reviewing once again the strategy for the cash-out merger. Cahill, despite his casual air and his fondness for quips, was a meticulous executive who tied every string with three knots. Dick Morrison came in— another executive vice president—and they told him the papers had been signed and were on their way. General Fraser called his third executive vice president, Sid Huntington, in Washington, with the same news. The word to all of them was identical: that publicly they knew nothing, and further, that any statement about the merger was to come from General Matthew Fraser, president of HEST, and no one else.

Gail had a dozen calls waiting, and the general spent the next hour on the telephone. At six, she came in again. "Not much point in trying to return any more of these," she said. "They'll have gone home."

He glanced over the stack of telephone slips. "Except Duncan here, on the Coast. Get him for me, then we'll shut it off for today."

She nodded. "Uh . . . Joyce Milligan and her daughter are waiting."

"When I'm finished with Duncan," he said. "And thanks, Gail. See you tomorrow."

He was on the telephone with Duncan for twenty minutes. Bank of America had so far reached no decision about joining the consortium that would fund the cash-out merger of HEST and Fraser Tech; but Duncan was interested enough to call and ask how the process was going, which the general took for a good sign. Duncan was a friend. They spent their last five minutes reminiscing about evenings they had shared in Tokyo, twenty years ago.

When Duncan hung up, the general pressed the intercom button on his telephone. "Okay," he said. He buzzed the lock on the door between his office and Gail's.

Joyce Milligan opened the door and stood just outside for a moment, apparently waiting to be beckoned to enter. She was a woman about thirty-five: blonde, a little too generously proportioned to be stylish, a bit coarse of face and figure for his taste, but attractive overall and emphatically sensual in her air and manner. A lifelong Brooklynite, complete with accent, she had come to work for HEST as a clerk-typist, six years ago, and was now assistant office manager, responsible for mail, telephones, copying, and supplies.

"Come in, Joyce."

Joyce smiled faintly, uneasily, and turned to speak to her daughter, who had been out of sight and now stepped past her mother, into the office.

"This is Lisa," said Joyce. (She pronounced the child's name "Lee-suh.")

He stood. "Lisa," he said. "Come in."

Lisa had just had a birthday and was newly fourteen, as her mother had told him. She was a slender girl, with her mother's straw-colored hair and blue eyes but with delicate, little-girl features and a slight figure, wearing blue jeans and a white knit shirt. She paused just inside the door, turning her head from side to side, unself-consciously examining the office. She was curious, maybe even awed, but nothing captured her attention for very long. She worked her chewing gum in her mouth as her eyes passed over the screens and scrolls and prints, the suit of armor and the furniture, never stopping to look for more than an instant.

"Is everything all right?" the general asked Joyce.

"Yes, sir. It's all okay with her."

He extended his hand toward the girl, and she crossed the room toward him but did not give him her hand.

"Is that right, Lisa?" he asked. "It's okay?"

Lisa nodded. "Sure," she said.

He sat down on the black leather couch. "No problems?" he asked.

Lisa shook her head, shifted her chewing gum, and shrugged.

"You do understand that all of this is our secret," he said.

"Sure," she said, with more emphasis. "I know the score."

"You know I'm giving your mother a lot of money. And I have a present for you, too."

"Yeah?"

"Yeah," he said, grinning. "So . . ."

Lisa once more shifted her gum, making it possible for her to speak. "Wha' ya want me to do, strip?" she asked.

General Fraser nodded.

"*You* gonna?"

"No, I don't think so. Just you and your mother."

The girl glanced at her mother, just in time to see a surprised, puzzled expression. "You, too, Mom," she laughed.

11

Joyce Milligan blushed. She had, of course, been naked here before, but she had not understood anything was expected of her this time. She sighed and nodded in concession and began to unbutton her blouse.

Lisa pulled her shirt over her head, uncovering her tiny, newly-developing breasts. "What's Mom gonna do?" she asked.

"While you're doing your thing," said he, "she's going to lick my feet."

Lisa laughed again, glancing at her mother. "I got the best part of this deal," she said.

Joyce's face was hot red. She continued undressing, without a word.

The girl kicked off her shoes, then pulled down her jeans and then her panties. She became quite solemn for a moment, as she stood and dropped her eyes and studied her nakedness as if it were a surprise to her. She had lost her baby fat and had the trim, spare body of a new adolescent. Her breasts were as small as they could be and still be breasts, but her nipples were already dark and prominent. She had sparse pubic hair, but her mons and labia were defined and highly visible—it was perhaps her consciousness of them that embarrassed her.

Her mother finished undressing and sat down on the floor beside the couch, at the general's feet.

"Okay, Lisa," he said. "You know how to do it?"

She nodded. "Get it out."

He unzipped his trousers and reached inside and pulled out his penis. It was already hard, with swollen veins. The little girl sat down beside him on the couch, tipped her head to one side and for a moment regarded his penis curiously, as if something about it surprised her. Then she closed one hand around it and began to manipulate it.

"Joyce," said the general.

Joyce pulled off his shoes and then his socks. Still frowning and with her face still red, she began reluctantly to lick his toes.

"Use both hands, Lisa," he said.

Lisa obeyed. Affecting what she probably supposed was a casual air, she chewed her gum and worked on his stiff shaft, now and again glancing up into his face. He caressed her legs, her hips, and her breasts, which didn't seem to trouble her; but when he ventured a finger down into her crotch, she pressed her legs close together and kept him out. Joyce, on the floor, kept her eyes raised as much as she could. As she sucked his toes and licked his feet, she watched Lisa.

"How 'bout giving it a little kiss, Lisa," he suggested.

"Huh-uh."

"I'll do that, if you want," Joyce said quickly.

The general shook his head. "Lisa is doing fine. Hand her some of those tissues. Put those around it now, honey. We don't want to make a mess."

Although her mother had taught her how she would earn the money General Fraser was paying for this half hour, Lisa had no concept of the force with which the ejaculate would come. She gasped when it flew beyond her hands and the tissues, and she laughed when her mother scrambled for more tissues to wipe it off the general's pants.

Lisa and her mother dressed while the general was in his bathroom. "Here, Joyce," he said when he returned to his desk. From the center drawer he took an envelope, which he handed her. "And Lisa." From his jacket pocket he took five new twenty-dollar bills.

"That's for you, honey. That's extra, for being a good girl and doing a good job. You be sure to spend that on yourself, for something you like. Mother has hers."

Melanie Paulson drove a bright red Porsche Carerra, and on Friday morning she reached eighty miles an hour in the rain on the Cross Westchester Expressway, keeping a wary eye on her radar detector as she whipped past trucks and cars. She downshifted for her turns through the interchange and took brief pleasure in the growl of the engine as it decelerated and slowed the car. She turned into the wooded access road, shifted to third, and entered the HEST parking lot with the engine still growling impressively.

She was in a foul mood, a mood for the confrontations she felt sure would come this morning. She had seen the Friday-morning *Wall Street Journal*. The story told her nothing she had not known or suspected for some time, but its appearance brought the whole thing into the open, and it would be interesting to see what kind of pettiness it produced in the corporate bureaucracy.

The story was brief. It read:

> The recently rumored battle for control of HEST, Incorporated has been brought into the open. Newly formed Fraser Technologies, Inc. has notified the SEC that it is offering HEST shareholders $28.50 per share, cash, for stock in the high-technology company. The offer has been mailed to stockholders of record as of
> · April 30.
> Forty percent of the stock in HEST is owned by United Northeastern Industries, the basic-industries conglomerate. Ringold Corporation, formerly Ringold Aviation, a California-based company, owns another 15

percent, while Lucas W. Paulson and David Berger, the original partners who developed the HEST technology, own 5 percent apiece. General Matthew Fraser, president of HEST and president of Fraser Technologies, owns 2 percent, and the balance of the over-the-counter stock is publicly owned.

HEST is an acronym for Heuristic Ergonomic Speech Transcriber, a technology that converts the spoken word into printed text. Gross sales of the HEST service exceeded a quarter of a billion dollars in 1983.

It has been rumored for months that UNI might sell its interest in HEST. Recent operating losses in its other divisions and subsidiaries have been attributed by management to the state of the economy, but cash realized from such a sale could improve the company's debt position and place it in a better position to attract the capital it will require to modernize its foundry, milling, paperboard, and other heavy-industry facilities, a modernization the company has acknowledged it must achieve if it is to continue to compete in its traditional lines.

It has been rumored for some time, too, that General Matthew Fraser is impatient with UNI's insistence on dividends that sharply reduce the amount of capital available to HEST for research and development and that he has been anxious to gain control of the company for himself.

"Uh, there's a gentleman waiting for you—a Mr. Whitby," said the receptionist when Melanie stopped at the desk. "He had a nine o'clock appointment," she added reproachfully.

Melanie glanced at her watch. It was 9:08. "Did you get him coffee?" she asked brusquely. She would not be lectured to by any snip of a receptionist.

"He didn't ask for coffee."

"Did you offer?"

"Miss Paulson—"

"Better shape up, sis," said Melanie, turning abruptly and walking toward the Englishman who was sitting on the reception-room couch.

Henry Whitby was a London barrister, short and ruddy and jolly. He was in the United States looking at a variety of technologies that might be of interest to the British bar, and HEST was one of them. This appointment had been standing for two weeks, since a transatlantic call from him had been transferred to Melanie by George McConnell, manager for international sales.

"I'm sorry to be late, Mr. Whitby," she said.

"Oh, not at *all,* dear girl, not at all," said Whitby with an exaggerated smile. He rose and extended his hand. "It is indeed pleasant to meet you at last, Miss Paulson. I've heard something of you, as well as much of your father. I hope I may have the pleasure of meeting him as well before I return to London."

He was not subtle, and she was not unaware of his quick but intent examination of her big soft breasts, her little round belly, her broad hips—what she called, a little scornfully, her Catherine parts, though her father saw her late mother chiefly in Melanie's brown eyes and dark brown hair.

"Would you like some coffee before we go in to see the machine, Mr. Whitby?"

"Actually, I've had coffee this morning and was hoping our schedule would permit a pleasant lunch with a tot of gin."

"If it doesn't permit, we'll make it permit," she said. "I'm going to suggest we look in on the monitoring room first, where we can see what the system is doing this morning. Then I'll show you the hardware."

She had to sign three documents to gain access to the monitoring room. Even then, it was with manifest reluctance that the sober young man at the door let her take the British visitor inside.

"Our sales representatives," she said quietly to Whitby when they were in the monitoring room and out of the hearing of the grim little doorkeeper, "try to perpetuate the myth that it is technologically impossible for us to monitor the lines—that is, to see the transcripts the system is making. Of course, that's ridiculous. In our contracts we admit we can but promise we never do. The truth is, we look at the lines all the time. How else can we be sure the system is transmitting and receiving accurately?"

The monitoring room was a large, green-carpeted room where twenty operatives sat at twenty screens and watched transcripts being made.

Melanie introduced Whitby to the monitoring-room supervisor, a soft-spoken, courteous forty-year-old woman. Her name was Lucy Brady.

"We've got ninety-two quads up right now," said Lucy Brady.

"What we call a quad is a set of four telephone lines," Melanie explained. "One is a voice line that feeds the computer the talk from the courtroom or hearing room. One is a data line that sends the talk back in the form of words that appear on the screen before the operator in the courtroom or hearing room. Each line is backed up with a spare, just in case. She says there are ninety-two quads working. That means HEST is making transcripts for ninety-two trials or hearings right now."

"Uh . . ." said Lucy Brady, squinting at a printed sheet hanging off a small printer. "The Nuclear Regulatory Commission is in session. Uh, here's an FTC examiner taking testimony. Another one . . . the National Transportation Safety Board. And the rest of it is trials at the moment."

"How many can you handle?" Whitby asked.

"I guess that's confidential," said Lucy Brady. "But I can tell you we expect to have 350 quads going by noon."

"Can we look at one specifically?" asked Whitby.

"Certainly," said Lucy Brady. "We'd rather show you a trial than a hearing. Trials are public, so we couldn't possibly be breaching a confidence."

"And hearings may be private," said Whitby. "A trial would be my preference anyway. Have you a criminal case going?"

She scanned her printout. "Philadelphia," she said. "I'll put it up on my monitor here. Would you like to sit down?"

"Oh, thank you so much."

Lucy Brady pressed keys, and in a moment words began to appear in bright green on the black background of the monitor screen. "You understand," she explained, "that what you are seeing is exactly what the HEST operator in the courtroom is seeing. The words that appear on the screen were spoken in the courtroom at most one second ago, and they have come up here from Philadelphia on the line, have been processed by the computer, and are going back as printed words."

Whitby leaned forward and peered at the screen through the lower parts of his bifocals. This is what he saw:

MR. HIGGINS: WHEN WAS THAT?

MRS. DOVE: IN JANUARY, AS BEST I CAN RECALL.

MR. HIGGINS: JANUARY OF 1984?

MRS. DOVE: YES.

MR. HIGGINS: DO YOU REMEMBER THE MAN'S NAME?

MRS. DOVE: IT WAS *****PUTELLO***** (PITELLO?) AS BEST AS I CAN REMEMBER.

"Okay," said Melanie quickly. "HEST has checked its dictionary and doesn't recognize a name pronounced 'Putello.' It has the name 'Pitello,' so it's suggesting she might have said that. Now, see it goes on. The operator touched Pitello with his light pencil, and that's how the name will be spelled in the transcript."

The dialogue in the courtroom had continued while she was explaining, and the witness's response with the correction in it had by now rolled almost to the top of the screen. The witness mentioned Pitello again.

MRS. DOVE: WELL, MR. PITELLO—I THINK HIS NAME WAS PITELLO—SAID HE COULD DELIVER THE RADIO BY WEDNESDAY.

"You see," said Melanie. "It's still hearing 'Putello,' no doubt; but the operator touched 'Pitello' twice with his light pencil, and that told the system to take the name always to be Pitello."

The dialogue continued.

MR. HIGGINS: BUT HE DIDN'T, SO YOU CALLED?

MRS. DOVE: MR. DAMATO. (!!!)

THE COURT: I SEE SOMEONE IS SIGNALING AN ERROR ON THE TRANSCRIPT. MR. HIGGINS, WILL YOU SPELL THE NAME FOR THE REPORTER, PLEASE?

MR. HIGGINS: D—APOSTROPHE—A—M—A—T—O.

THE REPORTER: CORRECTION ENTERED.

MR. HIGGINS: YOU CALLED MR. D'AMATO. AND HE TOLD YOU?

Melanie explained. "Counsel have small monitors at their tables, and one of their assistants can watch the transcript being made. If they see an error, they touch it with their own light pencils. That's what produced the string of exclamation points."

Whitby continued to watch in rapt fascination for a quarter of an hour, after which, with effusive thanks to Lucy Brady, he pronounced himself curious to see the "machine that effects these marvels."

The hardware was housed in a separate building, which could be reached via a passage from the administration building. They passed through a security gate, which Whitby observed—correctly—looked like the grim barred gate of a prison cell block. Because many visitors came to see the computer center, a visitors' room was provided, with a glass wall that afforded a view both of the control room and the huge computer room. A dozen technicians in lab coats sat at the monitors in the control room, watching screens and signal lights. There was no one in the vast, brightly lighted expanse of the computer room itself.

"We'll go on in," Melanie said to Whitby. "But you can take an overall view from here."

"IBM?" Whitby asked, gesturing toward the banks of equipment.

"Some of it," she said. "The central processors are three Amdahl 470 V7A computers. The disk drives, which are, of course, the main memory, are Control Data units. The front end—that is, the communications ports—are IBM."

"Those printers," said Whitby, pointing at three printers running in the control room. "The paper from them seems to be moving directly into shredders."

Melanie nodded. "Right. Operations reports. Every second the system generates a status report, telling how many lines are active, which equipment is doing what,

what equipment is signaling it is on the verge of failure, and so on. If anything goes wrong, we have a printed record of how it happened and when, which tells us how to fix it and how to avoid a repetition. As long as everything is running smoothly, we just let the reports run into the shredders."

"Do you experience many breakdowns?"

"Almost none that interrupt the service," she said. "The system features total redundancy. If something fails, usually the system instantly switches itself to a backup, and it goes forward without a perceptible burp. Usually, the only people who are aware of the problem are the technicians at the monitors."

"Electrical power failure . . .?"

She shook her head. "On failure of outside power, the system switches instantly to battery power, which is enough to keep it going about five minutes. In those five minutes, two big diesel generators start up, and either one of those produces enough electrical power to keep the system optimal and keep the lights and air conditioning going in the administration building. We store enough diesel fuel for two weeks."

He wanted to enter the computer room itself, so she opened the door and took him inside, where their presence caused an urgent signal on the security monitor. She smiled and nodded at the technician who suppressed the intrusion signal, then she led Whitby through the room.

The cool, flat-lighted room was dead silent except for the low whir of the stacks of magnetic disks spinning in the memory units. Melanie opened a door on one of the Amdahls, exposing nothing but ranks of boards standing in slots—nothing glowing, nothing moving, nothing suggesting to the eye or ear that countless

21

billions of electrons, racing crazily through a tangle of circuits at almost the speed of light, were performing billions of complex tasks every second. Here was where the sounds of voices were sliced into sound-wave profiles every hundredth of a second, the profiles reassembled into mathematical models of the sounds heard, and those models matched to the system's huge inventory of models, to tell the computer what word or name to print on the monitor screen.

Melanie explained what was happening in the circuits.

"Amazing," said Whitby, sincerely respectful.

"The fact is, the system is obsolete," she said blandly, closing the door on the Amdahl.

"What?"

"HEST is too big, too expensive, and too central," she said. "It's going to have to be redesigned to run on the faster computers that are coming with wafer-scale integration. If you repeat that, they'll fire me."

"I should think so," he said solemnly.

Melanie looked up at Whitby and smiled. "I don't give a damn," she said.

Passing over the southern bluffs of Block Island at fifty-five hundred feet, Lucas Paulson squinted into the late-morning sunlight and identified the faint gray shoreline of Martha's Vineyard, some sixty miles distant and slightly to the left of his airplane's nose. Straight ahead, still not in sight but lying beyond on the Atlantic horizon, was Nantucket, his destination. Below his left wingtip lay the single runway of the airport on Block Island—his last landing field before the fifty-mile open-water passage to the Vineyard. He glanced at his instruments. The engine was running smoothly at twenty-three hundred rpm, burning thirteen gallons of fuel per hour, with temperatures in the green arc. He reached down with his left hand and switched from right to left fuel tank, noting that the engine did not miss a beat in the switch. His number-one VOR receiver had long since established a firm fix on Nantucket, and the needle indicated he was a mile or so to left of course. He adjusted the autopilot to bring the nose of the Bonanza a little to the right. Satisfied that everything was normal, he committed himself mentally to twenty minutes' flight over open water.

To his passenger, he said nothing of all this organized checking. She was comfortable, confident in him and the airplane. Likely, her thoughts were on the weekend they were about to spend together, which they had planned for a long time.

"Anyway, it was funny," she said. She had interrupted a story she had been telling him when she saw she had lost his attention as he scanned his instruments, switched fuel tanks, and adjusted his heading. "It's typical of him, though, isn't it?"

Lucas smiled and nodded. "I suppose it is," he agreed.

She nodded. "Daddy," she sighed.

She was Susannah Fraser—General Matthew Fraser's daughter. She had told her father and mother that she was spending the weekend on the Cape, visiting the family of a college girlfriend. General Fraser hadn't the slightest suspicion that Susannah was anything more than a casual acquaintance of Lucas Paulson.

"Is that a submarine?" she asked.

He peered over the nose and to the left at the long wake behind the thin black hull cutting the water. He nodded. The vessel was an atomic-powered submarine running on the surface, heading home, no doubt, to Groton, Connecticut. Except for a few white sails distinct on the gray water, the submarine was alone, majestic in its arrow-straight course.

He studied Susannah for a moment as she stared at the submarine. She was only nineteen years old, but she was wise and mature. She was only a girl in the blonde hair that hung straight down her back to her waist, perhaps also in the honest, toothy smile she showed so readily, certainly in the pride she took in matter-of-fact amorality. She was a woman in much else: her tall, long-legged body, the demonstrated accuracy of her judgments of people and things, her practiced yet restrained sense of humor, the perspective of experience that tempered her ideas.

She continued her story: "My father's French, you know, extends to sentences like, *'Pour le petit déjeuner je voudrais un demi-pamplemousse,' 'Je préfère le steak bien cuit,'* and *especially"*—her eyes brightened, and she smiled widely—*"'Il me faut encore du papier hygiénique.'"*

Lucas chuckled. "You are wicked, Susannah."

"So," she said, "when *Messieurs Quelque-chose* and *Autre-chose* were ushered into the party, it was apparent before five minutes had passed that I was the only person in the house who could carry on an intelligent conversation with them. No matter. When the time came for Daddy to escort them into the library and close the door, he took Cahill and Morrison—and nobody else."

"Into the library and close the door," said Lucas.

"You know the drill," she said. "Cahill and Morrison, leaving Springer standing there with his teeth in his

24

mouth, *and* McConnell, *and* Gustavson. McConnell actually turned pale, and his wife nearly cried, seeing her husband excluded and humiliated. But that's how Daddy operates. You know it better than I do."

"'I will be gracious to whom I will be gracious and will show mercy on whom I will show mercy,'" Lucas recited, shaking his head.

"Yeah, well he got it right in the butt this time," she said. "When they came out of the library, his jaw was set and his mouth was hard, and he was curt to Morrison. They couldn't cut the European deal because the two Frenchmen couldn't understand them, and they couldn't understand the two Frenchmen. In fact, I think it was worse than that. I think they offended each other."

"While his daughter, who is fluent in French, stands outside and isn't asked to help," said Lucas.

"He'd rather lose the deal than admit he needed help from me," she said grimly. She shrugged. "But you've seen it before. It's no surprise to you, is it?"

Lucas shook his head. "I don't want to spend the weekend running down your dad, Susannah," he said. He pointed ahead of the left wingtip. "Newport. And Providence. You can just barely make it out, up the bay."

He tuned his number-two radio to the transcribed weather broadcast for the Nantucket airport. Wind was nine-five at twelve, gusting to twenty. Altimeter was thirty-point-zero-eight. Clouds, scattered at five, broken at eleven. Visibility, twenty. Pilots were to expect a visual approach to Runway Six, caution light turbulence at three thousand and below.

Lucas eased off his power and trimmed the Bonanza for a five-hundred-feet-per-minute descent. He screwed

25

in a little richening of the mixture and watched his exhaust gas temperature as the airplane picked up speed and the altimeter began a steady downward turn.

"Too cold to swim, I suppose," said Susannah. "Can you swim close to your house?"

"Not really," said Lucas. "There's a violent riptide just offshore. You can walk on the beach, but to go out in the surf you have to drive to another beach."

Susannah smiled wickedly. "Well, I don't plan to get out of bed," she chuckled.

Lucas arrested the plane's descent and flew at two thousand feet as they paralleled the south coast of Martha's Vineyard. Nantucket, lying low in the Atlantic, was under a layer of cloud that appeared to hang lower than the five thousand feet mentioned in the broadcast. Under that layer the air was clear, though they began to feel the bumpy turbulence that had also been mentioned.

"Don't get sick, do you?" he asked.

She shook her head, but it was obvious the idea had occurred to her, too.

"Edgartown," he said, pointing to the town they could see on the Vineyard.

"Chappaquiddick?" she asked.

He pointed.

Twenty miles out, he called Nantucket tower and was told to make a left base for Runway Six. That brought them across the western tip of the island, and he descended to one thousand feet and lowered the landing gear. Cutting his power, he raised the nose and slowed the Bonanza to one hundred knots.

"Remember what Herman Melville said about Nantucket in *Moby Dick?*" he asked Susannah.

She shook her head.

"He said it was so barren they had to send boats over to Cape Cod and import weeds."

Susannah laughed. The island, spread out beneath them now, was flat and gray-green but not barren. The airplane bumped algng on the turbulence. Lucas reported to the tower and was cleared for his landing. As they crossed the beach on the approach to the runway, the wind shifted, and he was compelled to make a hard correction to keep the nose on the runway heading. He let the plane settle, making more quick corrections as the wind turned it or blew it to the left or right of the runway center. He put his left wing down into the prevailing wind, held the nose in place with the rudders, and pulled the throttle all the way back. The left wheel touched first, with a screech, then the right, and the Bonanza rolled down the center of the runway.

Susannah released her breath. "You're a pro, Lucas," she said. "Everything you do, you're a pro."

He taxied to the west ramp and turned the airplane into a tiedown spot. She helped him affix the ropes to the wings and tail; and when the line boy arrived in his Jeep, they were pulling their couple of bags out of the back and were ready to go. Susannah had brought almost nothing. She had come to Westchester Airport in her tennis whites, carrying everything she was bringing for the weekend in a nylon duffle bag to which two rackets were loosely strapped.

"Weekend, Mr. Paulson?" the line boy asked as he drove them toward the operations shack.

Lucas nodded. "Till Sunday afternoon," he said. "You can top off the tanks for me."

"Right. Want me to drop you at your car? I'll sign you in."

"Thanks, Burt."

They walked into the main terminal of the airport so Susannah could use the toilet before they went to his car. He noticed *The Wall Street Journal* on the newsstand counter; and he ignored it, though he knew the Friday-morning edition would carry the story of the Fraser Tech cash-out bid. There was nothing he could do about it over the weekend.

His car, waiting in the parking lot, was a yellow Volkswagen Beetle. It started easily, as always. He drove out of the airport and turned east on Milestone Road.

"Is *everything* built of gray shingles?" Susannah asked as they passed house after house along the road.

"Everything," he said. "It's required."

"Doesn't look rich," she said.

"It's Nantucket."

His little house on Nosegay Lane, in Siasconset, surprised her, too. It was small. It stood on brick pillars, and you could see underneath it. The weathered gray shakes were covered with a trellis that covered one entire side of the house and climbed the slope of the roof. The rose vines were just beginning to recover from the winter, but he told her they would fill the trellis to the top before the summer was far along and would cover the house with pink roses. What surprised her most was that all the little houses were so much alike. They all had rose trellises, and each one had a name, inscribed on a board. Lucas's house was called Beaten Retreat—which, he hastened to tell her, he had inherited when he bought the property.

Inside, he had a living room, one bedroom, a kitchen, and a bathroom. The furniture, too, he had bought with the house, and it reflected the former owners' taste for red maple, rough-textured, warm-colored fabrics, and rag rugs. Books and magazines were scattered

28

everywhere. He lighted the oil heater, which was too large for the modest area of the house, and the rooms were soon warm.

They made love on the couch in the living room, then again in bed—ecstatic that they had, for once, all the time in the world, no train to catch, no appointment to keep, no need to check their watches. If they had timed themselves, they would have realized that this time, with all the time they wanted, they took no more time for it than they had taken before, in his apartment in Manhattan; but this experience, with the luxury of unlimited time, seemed more satisfying than any love-making they had ever shared before.

Later they went out to buy groceries, and they had a midafternoon lunch. They went back to bed, fondled and snuggled and did not make love, and slept until six. Early in the evening he drove her into town. The summer places were not yet open, and they sat down in the cellar bar at the Jared Coffin House for drinks and dinner.

"Lucas," she said when there was a bottle of wine between them. She put her hand on his on the table. "You know my father is scheming to put you out of the business."

Lucas nodded. "He's had that in mind from the day I met him."

She sighed. "I've heard them talk about it. What's a cash-out merger?"

He closed his hand around hers and picked up his glass. They were drinking red wine, a good Bordeaux, a taste he had acquired over the years and made his substitute for almost every other kind of alcohol. "The usual merger," he said, "involves two companies that join together. Typically, it is a big company absorbing a smaller company; and, in that case, the stockholders of

29

the smaller company exchange their stock for stock in the big company. In a cash-out merger, the big company just offers cash for the stock in the small company. The stockholders in the small company may get the value of their stock in cash; but they are excluded, shut out of the company's future. They no longer own anything. They are, as the term is, cashed out."

"What if some of the stockholders of the small company refuse to sell for cash?"

"If the majority go along, the minority stockholders don't have much choice. They would be left with stock in a corporation that, in effect, no longer exists. They can go to court and complain that the price wasn't fair, and sometimes they win more money; but they do get shut out of the business, in any case."

"If they get their money, have they been cheated?" Susannah asked.

Lucas shrugged. "It depends on how you look at it. The new company, Fraser Technologies, Incorporated, will probably offer me the current cash value of my stock—something between twenty-five and thirty dollars a share. But I'll be shut out of the future of the business. A share now worth twenty-five or thirty dollars could, in ten years, be worth a thousand or more. So, have I been cheated? Maybe not. Maybe my twenty-five-dollar share will drop to a dollar fifty in the next ten years."

"The point is, you want to stay in and see," said Susannah.

Lucas smiled and nodded. "That is exactly the point. I've put a lot of years into this business, and being shut out does not appeal to me, no matter what the price."

She stared for a moment into the deep red of her own glass of wine; then she glanced around the warm cellar room: at the stone walls, the beamed ceiling, the burning candles that provided most of the light. "What's it going to do to *us?*" she asked.

"Nothing," he said. "Seriously, Susannah, the business is irrelevant to the way you and I feel about each other."

Susannah drew a deep breath. "My father will say you seduced me to hurt him."

"Melanie has raised that point," said Lucas. "I mean, she has urged me to examine my motives very objectively, to be sure I am not doing just that."

"And . . .?"

He shook his head. "I thought of it first. When I thought of it, I still could have stopped seeing you."

"Before we went to bed?"

"Yes, before that."

"Lucas . . ." she whispered.

"I am forty-five years old, Susannah," he said firmly.

"I know that," she said. "You have reminded me too many times. And your daughter is three years older than I am. I'll say what I've said before—I don't give a damn."

Lucas smiled at her and for a moment withdrew and looked at her—again reaching for a perspective. Susannah had carried nothing much with her in her bag and was wearing a pair of blue jeans and a Smith College sweat shirt. She wore no cosmetics, no jewelry, not even a watch. Her face was unblemished and undamaged. She was—as he was acutely aware— nineteen years old and had another year to go before she graduated from Smith. She had spent last summer and the first semester of this college year at the University of Luxembourg, honing her French to a conversational level. She was acquiring what Melanie scornfully called "a leisurely education."

She stared at him, over her wineglass. Lucas was a

man of medium height and medium build. He played tennis occasionally and swam when he could, but he resolutely refused to jog or run or to engage in what he called "the physical jerks," so was trim and solid and still a little paunchy. The flesh around his jaws was a little loose, and his hair, though thick and strong, had been white for the past five years. He was wearing blue jeans, too, and a white shirt, a dark blue cashmere sweater, and Gucci loafers.

"It is easy to love you, Susannah," he said quietly. "It is very easy. Maybe it's too easy."

"I don't think you have any idea of how easy it is to love *you*, Lucas," she said.

"Many have resisted," he said with a little smile.

"They were fools," she said. "Anyone who ever saw you smile . . . If you have a fault, it is your chronic want of self-confidence."

"Actually," he said with mock gravity, "I've been told my self-appraisal is egomaniacal."

Susannah's quick peal of laughter attracted a moment's attention from nearby tables, and she faced Lucas and grinned. *"I love you!"* she whispered, and it was distinct enough for some of those who had turned toward them to understand. A young woman her age at the next table raised her hands and silently applauded.

"Well, I love you, too," he said softly. "Very much. More than I could have thought possible."

"Then we'll be married," she said flatly.

"After you graduate," he said.

"No. That's the conventional thing to do, but we're not conventional. Anyway, I can finish at Columbia."

Lucas picked up his glass, swirled his wine, and sipped. He frowned. "Next summer you'll be twenty," he said.

"And you'll be *forty-six*," she whispered shrilly.

"And we'll have spent a year apart, wanting to be together." She shook her head. "No, Lucas. No. Why waste a whole year?"

He lowered his eyes. "A powerful argument," he said.

Susannah sighed. "Anyway, they'll find out. Sooner or later, my father and mother are going to find out about us. I don't mean six months or a year from now. Look around. How do we know someone in this room won't call my father tonight to tell him we are here? And when he finds out—" She shook her head. "I'd rather have it all over, Lucas. All at once. *Fait accompli.*"

"I'm going to be in the middle of a fight, honey. No time for a wedding trip—"

"I don't care about that. I want to be *with you* while the battle is going on. I don't want to be out in Westchester, living with my father and mother, having to pretend I want to see them beat you."

Lucas reached across the table and touched Susannah's cheek. "How would you like a Nantucket wedding?" he asked. "We can stay over Monday and apply for the license."

He awoke before dawn on Saturday morning and lay quietly beside Susannah, savoring the warmth of her slender naked body stretched all along the length of his. She slept, faintly snoring. He caressed her, and she murmured but did not awaken.

Her father would want to kill him. He'd had his chance once, and it was not too strong a description of the incident to say that he had tried. The ironic thing was, General Fraser did not remember.

1965–1985

Twenty Years

2

November 1965

THE RIVER LOOKED like a sewer and smelled like a sewer. The sluggish water was black with rotting vegetation, and its surface was streaked with a slime like a thin oil slick that reflected a pale spectrum of colors. Seepage oozed down the banks and into the water. The air was still and damp and filled with jungle stench, and it was hot, unbearably hot.

Every few seconds the point man stopped, and everyone behind him stopped. Everyone listened. They heard nothing each time: nothing but the hum of insects and occasionally the slithering sound of some small reptile in the nearby undergrowth. They strained to listen, but they heard nothing more. Then they would set out again, moving as quietly as they could but well aware that their equipment jangled, that their boots thumped on exposed rocks, that they sloshed and splashed through the knee-deep water, that even their heaving breath was an intrusive sound in the silence of the jungle.

The third man in the line was Lucas Paulson: First Lieutenant Lucas Paulson, commanding Second Platoon, Able Company. He stopped and waited, letting five men pass him; then he fell in beside a big black soldier, the platoon sergeant. "Whatta ya think, Kilbourne?" he asked.

"Too fuckin' slow," said the sergeant.

Paulson nodded. "We got another mile, as best I can figure. That's assuming the ville is where the map shows it."

"They're not around, Lieutenant. They'll let us know if we catch up."

"Yeah."

Paulson splashed ahead, passing the men ahead of him until he reached the point man. "Step it up, Porter," he grunted. "We don't want to be in this goddamn hole after dark."

"Yes, sir," said Porter resentfully, leaving unspoken what was in his mind, that as point man he would take the first fire and that it was easy for an officer from back along the line to order less caution.

Paulson dropped back and resumed third position, and Porter obeyed orders, stopping only half as often. He glanced back at the line maintaining standard separation behind him. Paulson guessed that Porter wondered why they sounded like a troop of cavalry in a John Wayne western.

Two years of ROTC was mandatory at Oklahoma University. Like everyone else, he had slouched his way through it without enthusiasm. On the other hand, he had gone through all the required motions, dutiful at least in appearance; he had seen no point in trying to make some kind of adolescent protest. No one could have been more surprised when he was called in by the army major in charge of the program and asked to sign up for the non-compulsory two years. He thought about it. The Korean War was over, and it was difficult to imagine a President sending American troops into another one like it. If, however, it happened—so the rationalization went—it would be better to go as an officer than as a private. Anyway, his father had liked the idea. Lucas had signed up.

He had arrived at Da Nang in August.

Small-arms fire didn't sound as dangerous as it was. It sounded like corn popping and like someone tearing up a newspaper. "Ambush!" Porter screamed, and he fired a burst in the direction from which he thought the firing came. He went down then, hit. The platoon dispersed to both sides of the little river and in an orderly, almost casual way began to scythe the bush to the left of the stream with a deadly concentration of fire. Chopped leaves and wood filled the air.

"Slow fire! Slow fire, f' God's sake!" Paulson yelled; and his words were echoed in a somehow more authoritative bark from Platoon Sergeant Kilbourne.

The fire trailed off, then stopped since nobody was shooting at a target. It was likely they had loosed several hundred rounds at just one VC, and it was very unlikely they had hit him. Probably one VC had been left behind the party they were supposed to be trailing, and probably he had fired one magazine and taken off.

Porter groaned. Paulson ran forward. The man had taken a big flesh wound in the right leg above the knee. He was a Texan; and, lying on his back in the ooze, clutching his leg with both hands, he yelled, "Shee-it! Aw, shee-it!"

In seconds, four men were around him.

"Don't make a committee, for Christ's sake!" Paulson told them. "One burst would get all of you. Tucker. Hackford. Carry him back. The rest of you, get away."

They poured sulfa powder into the deep and ugly wound and wrapped it in gauze. They gave Porter a shot to quiet him, and they made a litter and carried

him. You couldn't send a couple of men back with him.
Two men carrying a litter could be ambushed by a child
or an old woman. Porter's only safety was in being
carried along. When the platoon found and destroyed
the ville, as ordered, they would carry him back. The
only other option was to abort the mission because of
one man's wound.

Porter was wounded, but other men were sick. There
was no way a platoon could walk knee-deep in putrid
water for three miles in this heat and men not get sick.
Paulson could see it in their faces. In two months he
had learned the strengths and weaknesses of most of
these men, and for most of them he had a measure of
respect—for some, in fact, he had a great deal of
respect—but he knew their limit. He wondered if they
could reach the ville. He wondered if they would find
any rest there.

Corporal Clemente, leader of First Squad, was the
new point man. In spite of what had happened to
Porter, Clemente set a faster pace. The way he figured
it—as Paulson well understood—you couldn't hear the
VC and there was no point in cocking an ear for them;
it was better to get where you had to go as fast as you
could and so reduce the amount of time you were
exposed. Clemente was a veteran. He had been in
Indochina six months.

Lucas Paulson was married. Catherine was at home
in Kansas City, working in her family's restaurant,
saving money as she wrote. They had been living in
Columbia, Missouri, when he was called—he finishing
his second year of law school at the University of
Missouri, she working part-time as a secretary and
caring for their two-year-old child. One of his law
professors had advised him to apply to J.A.G.—the

Judge Advocate General's department—and become an army lawyer. He thought about it, but actually the option had never been open to him. He had met his reserve obligation and was regarded by the army as fully trained and qualified in small-unit tactics. What was more, he was older, conspicuously more mature, than most of the lieutenants called up with him.

He had sweated through two months of exercises before he was flown to Da Nang—whether to refresh him in infantry tactics, as they said, and to teach him what the army was learning in Indochina, or to toughen him physically, he was not certain. What he learned, chiefly, was dramatic proof that something he had heard from a law-school wise ass had been, in fact, a bit of wisdom. "Hell," the boy had said, "you'll pass the bar exam; of course you'll pass the bar exam. Look at the practicing bar. Look at the idiots who *have* passed it." And similarly, in the army. He looked at the captains and majors. He didn't know how good he was, but he was as good as any of them.

Somebody else thought so, too. A colonel in Da Nang set him to work inventorying supplies, chewed him out unmercifully for having filled out the forms wrong, and then recommended his promotion to first lieutenant and sent him out to Able Company. The lieutenant in command of Second Platoon had just been promoted to company commander.

"ROTC, huh?" a major had said to him somewhere along the way. "Well now, by God, Paulson, you're gonna find out what it was all about."

"Lieutenant." His radio man trotted forward. "We're recalled. Battalion wants Able Company back at Peyton Place by 1400."

"What about the ville?"

"Fuck the ville, is what the man said. The choppers are taking us out of the area at 1400."

"Never make it," said Paulson.

They didn't make it. There was no way they could slosh their way back the three miles they had come and reach the helicopter landing area called Peyton Place by 1400 hours. It was 1445 before they reached the clearing.

An angry lieutenant colonel strode across the clearing, ducking under the helicopter blades. "Where the hell you been, Mister?" he demanded of Paulson.

"We were more than three miles away, Sir, and in the river, when the order came."

"Three fuckin' miles in a whole fuckin' hour? I don't buy that, Mister."

"In the river, Sir. We had to march in the river. Otherwise, we'd have had to cut our way through the brush with machetes."

"Well, get your ass in gear, Lieutenant. You're holdin' up the whole goddamn operation."

The colonel stalked away toward one of the helicopters.

"Who's that asshole?" Paulson asked his company commander, Captain Exeter, who had come up as the colonel walked off.

"That asshole, Paulson, is the battalion commander, Lieutenant Colonel Fraser. Don't get on his shit list. If you do, you'll wish you hadn't."

The operation for which they had been recalled from the river was an assault on a wooded rise called Fox Ridge. The battalion commander believed a hundred or more VC were on the ridge, in the woods, and that they could be trapped there by assaulting the ridge from two sides with two companies. Able Company was to assault from the southeast, while Baker Company assaulted simultaneously from the northwest. Helicopters would carry the two companies to clearings from where the assaults would be launched. It was to be, as Colonel Fraser put it, "a textbook operation," which would result in the elimination of a lot of Charlies—which was, after all, why they were in Indochina in the first place.

The choppers took everyone first to an assembly area at the rear, where Porter was handed over to the medics and flown away in an evac helicopter. Preparation continued. Ammunition and rations were checked and augmented. Signals were reviewed. An officers' briefing took half an hour. By 1630 the two companies were ready to board the choppers again, but by then Paulson was not the only junior officer nervously eyeing the sun and wondering if the assault could be accomplished in daylight. At 1700 word was passed that the operation had been postponed to 600 hours tomorrow.

The battalion commander ordered the company commanders to establish a tight defense perimeter around the area. Second Platoon of Able Company was ordered to dig latrines.

During the night a steady popping of small-arms fire—sniping—from all around the perimeter hit no one but disabled one helicopter. Shortly before dawn six mortar rounds landed, blowing another helicopter to bits. At 630 the helicopters began to lift off, carrying the two companies to Fox Ridge.

The flight took a quarter of an hour, mostly over dark green jungle. Fox Ridge, when they sighted it, was a finger of lighter green. The landing zones were clearings where perhaps Vietnamese villages had recently stood and had been burned out—they were barren fields now. As the choppers started down toward the landing zones, they came under fire from the ground. Men were sick with fear of the kind of wound you would take from a round punching up through the belly of the chopper. They took off their flak jackets and sat on them.

Lieutenant Paulson leaped gratefully from the chopper as soon as it touched, glad to be on the ground where a man could scramble for cover. He dashed for the south edge of the clearing and dropped to his belly in the edge of some tall, coarse grass. The platoon followed him. Shortly they were spread out and reasonably well covered against the harassing fire from the surrounding woods. With the platoon communications man beside him, Paulson waited for the order to move toward the ridge.

They waited the better part of an hour, while other choppers passed overhead and dropped on the other side of Fox Ridge. "If Charlie didn't have us figured out, he does now," said Sergeant Kilbourne to Paulson. During the wait, sporadic fire wounded two men, neither of them in Second Platoon.

The base of the ridge was half a mile away, across wooded land. At this higher altitude the land was not a jungle but heavily wooded, with small trees and tangled brush. Paulson wondered if the VC had mined the approaches to the ridge. He wondered if Fox Ridge had any significance besides a chance to kill a hundred Charlies. Anyway, it would be, as the colonel had said, a textbook operation, a frontal assault, the kind ROTC and his subsequent training had supposedly taught him to do.

The order came. They rose and, in the infantryman's characteristic crouch, began to move. Able Company was spread out along a half-mile line, crashing noisily through the brush. They did not return the fire from the

43

ridge. How could they? They couldn't see where it was coming from. They continued forward, and Second Platoon took no casualties. In ten minutes they reached the base of the ridge and started up. First Platoon was firing, but Second Platoon still had no targets. Maybe they had been lucky. Maybe their sector of the ridge was undefended.

Platoon Sergeant Kilbourne was beside Paulson, trudging forward, using his sleeve to wipe sweat from his broad black face. Suddenly he stopped, looking up. The air above was hissing, at first faintly, then more loudly. "Jesus Christ!" breathed the sergeant, and he dropped to the ground. The hissing sound grew in seconds to a deafening terrifying screech, and then a hundred yards ahead the woods boiled up in a confusion of flying earth and trees. The shock and sound of the explosion hit their ears like a hard punch. Another hiss grew. Men pressed themselves as close to the earth as they could. Another shell howled overhead and detonated on the ridge above them.

"Fuckup!" yelled Sergeant Kilbourne to Paulson. "They gone send in the 155s they shoulda sent before, before we got halfway up the goddamn ridge."

It was a minor exaggeration. They were not halfway up the ridge. But they were too close to the target area. If anything fell short, the assault could be wiped out by the barrage sent to support it. No one had told them the assault would be accompanied by a furious bombardment. The timing was crucial—if they had moved up the slope five minutes earlier they would have been in the middle of the target area—but no one had told them. Paulson could not disagree with Kilbourne's assessment. It was a fuckup.

They clung to the earth and waited out the bombardment. At least a hundred heavy shells fell on the crest and upper slopes of the ridge, each one hurling jagged-steel shrapnel howling through the air, each one blasting an immense hole in the earth. Holdren, a nineteen-year-old private from Illinois, was hit by shrapnel, Second Platoon's first casualty. Paulson wondered about the VC who had been sniping at the two companies—what could it be like to be the target of that kind of fire? He wondered, too, if the artillery would silence the machine guns and mortars they expected to be used against them as they mounted higher on the ridge.

The bombardment ended. Captain Exeter appeared from somewhere and ordered them forward. Paulson rose and led Second Platoon up the ridge. The air seemed to have been corrupted by the ton or more of explosives that had been detonated here, and it burned in their throats and lungs as they trudged over churned-up earth and among shattered trees. They saw their first Charlies: mangled bodies. Some of the new boys, recently sent to the platoon, had never seen anything like it before and were sick. Paulson's stomach churned, and he fixed his eyes determinedly ahead and strode a little faster.

No one fired at them. There wasn't a sound of firing anywhere on Fox Ridge. In ten minutes they reached the crest and met men from Baker Company coming up from the other side.

"Shit," grumbled a lieutenant from Baker Company. "If there was twenty Charlies up here, I'd be surprised."

They returned to the landing zone to wait for the choppers. The assault on Fox Ridge had cost Able and Baker Companies six wounded—four by enemy fire, two by the bombardment. Someone said they had captured three VC; Paulson did not see them. He did see four Russian SKS carbines that had been picked up.

Lieutenant Colonel Fraser jumped down from the second helicopter. That he was angry was obvious, but in the confusion of the landing of more helicopters and of assembling his men to be taken aboard for the flight back, Paulson did not see him for half an hour. Then, abruptly, the colonel was in front of him, curtly giving him orders.

"Second Platoon, right?"

"Yes, Sir."

"I want bodies, Lieutenant. I want 'em stacked right here, like cordwood."

The colonel was a tall, handsome man, with cold blue eyes. He wore his silver oak leaf on a sweat-stained fatigue cap, and he wore paratrooper boots and a .45 hung from a web belt. If he had planned this operation, he was a first-rate fuckup; but he had the *look* of command, the air of it; and maybe that was what counted.

"I doubt there's a cord of them up there, Sir," Paulson said. "I only saw six or seven, and two of those may have been the separated pieces of one man."

"Well, you go look for 'em, Mister," snapped the colonel. "And you bring 'em down here. Bring me pieces if that's what you find. I got a general coming out here in an hour, and I'm gonna show him bodies. I mean in an hour, Lieutenant. And don't tell me you gotta wade in a river to get up there and bring down bodies."

They carried along extra tent halves to make litters to carry down the shattered corpses. Half a dozen men from First Platoon volunteered to go along, to allow Paulson to relieve a few of his boys whose bellies revolted at the very thought of picking up and carrying the kind of oozing human remains they had seen. Climbing the ridge again, Paulson tried to conceal his anger. Enough other men were showing it.

They reached the top of the ridge and began to wrap the bodies and parts of bodies in canvas. He sent one squad to search for more, and in a little while Clemente returned saying they had found two more. They would be able to give the colonel eight, or maybe nine Charlie corpses.

"How's he gonna explain?" asked Sergeant Kilbourne. "Either there was never more than a dozen Charlies up here or a whole lot of 'em got away. Shee-it, there wasn't even a machine gun or a mortar up here."

They had been on the crest for twenty minutes. Maybe there were more bodies, half buried, but the colonel had been more than emphatic that Second Platoon was to return within an hour. Paulson put Clemente in charge of carrying and dragging the grisly bundles down the slope and sent them on ahead, figuring they would be slowed by their burden and that the rest of the platoon would catch up with them. With Kilbourne, Paulson ventured a little way down Baker Company's side of the ridge, thinking maybe they would find another body or two. The colonel might get off his ass if he could come back with a few more.

"Looka this," said Kilbourne crisply. He pointed to the ground at an ugly, wet, fly-blown object. It was a piece of human intestine. It marked a faint trail of blood that was indistinctly visible on the ground and leaves. "Torn open and crawled off," said Kilbourne.

Paulson shook his head. "Enough's fuckin' enough," he said. "Let's haul ass outa here."

The sound of a full-automatic weapon was like a deep cough, immeasurably louder. It sounded once, then again. Then another one joined the first. A crackle of M-14 rifle fire seemed like a weak reply to the two machine guns. A grenade exploded.

Paulson and Kilbourne sprinted for the top of the ridge to rejoin the squads that remained there. Bullets howled past them as they ran, until they threw themselves on the ground among the heavily engaged men.

"Guess Charlie likes this ridge," said a private named Earhart. "He's come back."

It was true. The VC had come up the northwest slope, abandoned only an hour ago by Baker Company, which had returned to its landing zone and was probably away by now. If there had been only a dozen or twenty here before, more than that were coming now. Second Platoon was not dug in. Half its men were down the southeast slope, carrying bodies. Here on the crest, two men were wounded already.

"Battalion," said the communications man, handing Paulson the handset.

"What the hell's going on up there, Lieutenant?" It was the voice of Colonel Fraser, angry as always. "What are you doing?"

"Charlie's up here, Sir. In force."

"Of course he is. 'Cause some sons of bitches didn't clear him out when they were sent up there to clear him out."

"Half my platoon's on its way down with the bodies, Sir. I'm outnumbered up here. And outgunned. I've got wounded, too."

"Clear out, Lieutenant. Get off there. I'm gonna call in the 155s again."

"Give me ten minutes, Sir."

"Ten minutes, Mister. Haul ass."

Sergeant Kilbourne, with five men, took responsibility for the wounded, now three. He crawled off and set

48

to work dragging them down the slope. Paulson ordered five men to accompany him into a shallow defile—the only semblance of cover within reach—and set up covering fire to allow the rest of his men to begin their retreat. He took grenades from those who were going, and he and his men began pitching them down the northwest slope.

In this kind of war you saw your enemy. The VC advanced steadily, crawling, jumping up to run a few steps, sprawling. They seemed to have plenty of ammunition and kept up a steady fire—most of it fortunately whistling well overhead. Paulson saw two Charlies torn to pieces by a grenade he had thrown at them. He shot another one with his Colt.

He lost one of his men. A North Carolinian named Harrison was hit in the face and killed instantly. An Arizonan named Hernandez pulled the bandoleer from Harrison, to have his ammunition. Behind them the rest of the platoon made an orderly retreat, and in a little time—it could not have been more than three or four minutes—Paulson could order Hernandez to make his break. Hernandez crawled out of the defile and down the slope. Paulson sent another one. Finally, when only three of them remained, they pitched grenades to set up a shield of explosions and backed out of the defile. Another man was wounded, but only superficially, and he scrambled down the slope unimpeded.

The men of Second Platoon lost contact with each other on the way down. They knew another bombardment like the one they had seen this morning was coming, and they ran when they could. When Paulson felt he could stand, he was alone. He looked up at the crest. The VC had taken it. They were standing, boldly firing at the scattered Americans running away from them. One of them fell as Paulson watched. Someone in Second Platoon had kept his wits and had had the courage to shoot back.

He didn't like this headlong retreat. He didn't know what Colonel Fraser would say of it. But he'd been given no options. He ran in a crouch, looking around him as he made his way down, trying to be sure his men were making it.

There was Kilbourne. He was lying on his back with one knee drawn up. He had been hit.

"Gotta move, Sergeant," said Paulson as he dropped beside the big black man. "The 155s are coming in any minute."

"Can't make it, Lieutenant," gasped Kilbourne.

The wound was in his belly. He had been hit in the back by a high-velocity slug, which had torn through his guts and blown a hole the size of two fists out of his abdomen just to the right of his navel.

Paulson stripped off his fatigue jacket. He wrapped it around Kilbourne's middle and knotted the sleeves tightly as the sergeant groaned in agony. The idea was to slow the leakage of fluids and flesh. Paulson struggled then to lift the big man to his feet. Kilbourne screamed, but he put his feet down and tried to help. Paulson squatted in front of him, circled his legs with his arms, and let Kilbourne settle forward on his back. Paulson stood, surprised he was strong enough, and staggered forward.

"Can't do it, Lieutenant," Kilbourne breathed.

Paulson did not respond. Straining to carry the man's weight, he stumbled down the slope.

"I'm checkin' out anyway," Kilbourne groaned. "Go on! The 155s will—"

"Shut up, Elvin," Paulson growled. "Goddammit . . ."

He tried not to jostle the man too much. He could

50

feel the blood and whatever else was coming out of him, wetting his back where the wound was pressed to it. Kilbourne moaned and seemed to slip in and out of consciousness. He could not hold on, and Paulson had to clutch his hands in his own to keep the man from falling off. He stumbled down the slope, fighting for his balance every step.

The hiss and whine of incoming shells began. The first one split the air directly above their heads and blasted the earth no more than fifty yards behind them. The shock nearly knocked Paulson over. "Ten minutes!" he yelled. "Goddamn, *ten!*"

Shrapnel from the next shell—fortunately its force nearly spent—hit him in the back of his right leg, above the knee. He fell forward, and Sergeant Kilbourne fell on top of him, now unconscious. Paulson pressed his face to the earth. Although the earth and everything on it were shaking violently, he managed to fix his eyes on his watch. "I had two more minutes, you fuckin' idiot," he muttered. "Two more goddamn minutes."

When a party from First Platoon found them, Lieutenant Paulson was sitting on the ground, softly weeping, still pressing a wad of jacket into the hole in Sergeant Kilbourne's belly, still trying to stop the seepage he was sure had killed him.

Sergeant Elvin Kilbourne survived. He was flown back to the States, spent a year in a military hospital, and was discharged with a disability pension.

Paulson was flown to Da Nang, where he spent five weeks in a hospital. After that he spent two weeks in Saigon, on leave. Seven weeks after the battle for Fox Ridge he returned to the command of Second Platoon, Able Company, in which capacity he served for the balance of his tour of duty.

Captain Exeter recommended Paulson for the Silver Star. The battalion commander would have none of that, and the recommendation stopped on his desk. Paulson received his Purple Heart, dropped off by a second lieutenant who distributed them in the hospital at Da Nang, and nothing more was said.

When Lucas Paulson next met Matthew Fraser, years later, he was amused at how Fraser pretended not to remember him. He was even more amused when he realized it was no pretense. Matt Fraser did not remember.

3

"I GUESS YOU won't take offense if I suggest you wouldn't mind saving a buck," said Professor David Berger to Lucas Paulson as they waited to recover Paulson's bag.

"I wouldn't mind at all," said Lucas. "The bar association committee agreed to pay my expenses, but they weren't enthusiastic about it."

"What I figured," said Berger dryly. "You can move in with me if you don't mind sleeping on a mattress on the floor. I told you about my living quarters."

Lucas grinned. "You told me."

"You've slept worse places," said Berger.

"Let's not put it that way. I appreciate the invitation, and I accept."

"Fine. If United Airlines ever gives up your bag, what I propose is that we go straight to the computer lab. Then we can go out to the house, and this evening we'll find a good place for dinner and spend the money you saved by not putting up in a hotel."

Some of the people waiting around the baggage carousel were inspired to curiosity by the contrast between the two men and were unsubtle in their repeated glances. Paulson looked like the Kansas City lawyer he was, wearing a gray suit, white shirt and tie,

53

and black shoes, carrying a raincoat over one arm. Berger wore faded blue jeans with a hole at one knee, an equally faded checkered wool shirt, and buckskin shoes with thick rubber soles. He was clean-shaven, but he wore small gold-rimmed eyeglasses.

Berger had a comment on Paulson's appearance: "You're going to damage my reputation on campus. Word'll be all around that I'm consorting with a CIA agent."

"People who'll think that have obviously never seen a CIA agent," said Lucas quietly.

Berger drove them to the Berkeley campus in his tiny, battered Renault, thoroughly frightening Lucas. Threading the minuscule car through the freeway traffic, he jammed the car into a narrow parking place, jerked Paulson's bag out of the back, and led him across the campus toward the computer-science laboratory of the University of California at Berkeley.

"I scheduled us half an hour," said Berger when they were in the computer center. "We're late, but our program is still up."

Lucas surveyed the computer room: the control console with its characteristic blinking lights, the big IBM mainframe in a blue steel cabinet, the jerking tape drives, the whirring disk drives. He had seen the like before. What he had not seen before were barefoot technicians, male and female, uniformly clad in worn-soft jeans, confidently attending and managing the multimillion-dollar machine.

"Doc Hallowell's star program goes up in fifteen minutes, Dave," said one of the attendants.

"Gotcha," said Berger. "Judy, meet Lucas Paulson. He's a lawyer from Kansas City. Represents the Missouri Bar Association. Flew all the way out here to see the speech transcriber."

"It's working," said the intense, flat-chested young woman. She extended a hand to Paulson. "Glad to meet you."

Berger sat down at the console and touched some keys. A printer to the side clacked and spewed up a line of green-and-white printout paper. It had printed: READY.

Berger handed Lucas a small black microphone. "Numbers only, Lucas. Give it four or five numerals."

"Six-oh-six-one-one," said Lucas.

The printer clacked. 60611.

"Seven-seven-four-two," said Lucas, a little faster. 7742

"Eleven," said Lucas.

ULEVUN

"Well . . ." said Berger. "You didn't take long to fool it."

"No, I like it," said Lucas. "Phonetic."

The printer clacked as both of them broke into a grin. He had spoken again into the microphone, and Berger had not deactivated the program.

NO EYE LIKE IT FONETIK appeared on the paper.

Lucas glanced at Judy, then at Berger, put the microphone close to his mouth and said, "I ate eight steaks."

"You bastard!" Berger laughed.

EYE 8 8 STAKES

"Some whores raise hell," said Lucas.

SUM HORSE RACE HEL

Berger sighed. "You see the problems," he said. "It only takes half a minute."

"You're ahead of the Chicago group," said Lucas, handing back the microphone.

"Grammar algorithms," said Berger. "If it can be programmed to parse a sentence, so it knows it is

55

looking at a place where a verb logically should be, then it can choose 'ate' instead of 'eight.'"

"But that won't help it choose 'I' instead of 'eye' or 'steak' instead of 'stake,'" said Lucas. "The system is going to require a human operator, constantly supervising."

"It would overwhelm him," said Judy. "No human operator could keep up with it, making decisions and making all the corrections." She shook her head.

"He can if you program the system heuristically," said Lucas,

"Meaning?" she asked.

"Program it to learn from its own mistakes," he said. "The human operator corrects an error once, corrects it a second time to confirm, and thereafter the computer corrects that error itself. Let it build a huge file of its own errors, to which it can refer and make 95 percent of its own corrections."

"Wow . . ." said Judy.

"How *about* this?" said Berger to her, nodding. "We got a goddamn lawyer from Kansas City telling us how to program our goddamn computer." He looked up at Paulson. "Trouble is, he's right. Of course, he hasn't the remotest notion how difficult it would be to write a heuristic program. . . ."

"We could get it done in this century," said Judy with a little scorn.

"Five years," said Lucas. "Here or somewhere."

They arrived at the ramshackle Edwardian house about six. Berger had already explained that if the people living there constituted a commune, they were one of the most restrained communes in the Bay area—only a group of professors and graduate students sharing the house, sharing a style of living that was perhaps eccentric but certainly was not wildly radical.

They left Lucas's suitcase at the bottom of the stairs; Lucas folded his raincoat over it. Berger led him into the big living room.

"Meet Gabe Lincoln," Berger said, introducing a young man with a bushy beard, dressed in frayed shorts and a white T-shirt. "Gabe's on his way to a doctorate in mathematics, specializing in computer science. I've told him your idea about programming heuristically. And his friend there is . . .?"

"Tersa," said the young man.

Gabe Lincoln was sprawled over a sagging, old sofa, with a slight young woman in a voluminous pink dress sprawled over him. They were sharing a joint. She was taking two or three drags to his one and looked up at Lucas from a dreamy haze. Lincoln held the joint out toward Lucas and Berger, and both shrugged and shook their heads.

"But you'll take Scotch, as I remember," said Berger. "I'll get us a couple of drinks. Have a seat."

Lucas lowered himself a little reluctantly onto a pile of cushions—the only kind of seat in the room besides the couch.

"Too big, man, too big," said Lincoln.

"What?"

"Mainframes, man. Too big. Wait till we have computers we can carry around, computers we can take home. That's when they'll really mean something."

"Well . . ." said Lucas tentatively. He squirmed around, trying to make himself comfortable on the cushions, trying also not to drag his pants legs through the dust on the floor.

"We build 'em small enough to shoot into space,"

57

Lincoln went on. "Why not build 'em small enough so every man can have his own?"

"Why not?" Lucas shrugged.

"I mean, like, you can't run your heuristic program on a dumb terminal. You want to use the speech transcriber in a courtroom, the operator is going to have to have a smart terminal, a little computer right there in front of him—I mean, if he's going to make the corrections. Right?"

"Right," said Lucas, suddenly more respectful of Gabe Lincoln.

"Dave told me about your schoolteacher girl who had to sit in jail for seven weeks while the reporter typed up the transcript of her trial. I don't understand that, but—"

"I couldn't appeal her case without the transcript," said Lucas. "The court of appeals had to have the transcript of the trial so it could see the mistakes the trial judge had made."

"And it took seven weeks to type it?"

"No, it took two weeks to type it; but it was five weeks before the reporter's office could assign a typist to her transcript. The typing staff was swamped with other cases."

"I was in the slammer once," murmured Tersa. "Jus' two days. Seven weeks . . . Jeez!"

"She wasn't guilty, either," Lincoln said to her. "That's what blew the man's mind."

Tersa shook her head. "Neither was I."

Berger returned carrying two drinks in peanut-butter jars. "Hey," he said. "Look who's here."

"Lela!" said Lincoln. "Have a drag."

"Lela Reese, meet Lucas Paulson," said Berger.

The young woman nodded at Lucas, accepted a quick drag on the joint, and settled on the floor and crossed her legs. She accepted, too, a sip from Berger's Scotch and water, while regarding Lucas Paulson skeptically with calm hazel eyes. Her jeans were faded, stained, and holed at both knees; her feet were bare, their bottoms black with dirt; and her breasts jiggled amiably inside a man's ribbed-cotton vest undershirt.

"What would happen to the world, I wonder, if there were no lawyers?" she asked quietly.

"What would happen to the world if there were no professors?" Lucas retorted.

"Like, wow," she said blandly and seemed to withdraw from any dialogue her question might have started.

"Lela's finishing her Ph.D. in international economics," said Berger.

Lucas was unable to conceal his surprise. "Oh," he said.

"Counselor Paulson's here to teach us how to redesign the speech transcriber," said Lincoln.

"Really?"

"Heuristically," said Berger. "It's an interesting idea. It could be our breakthrough."

Lela Reese cocked her head to one side and showed Lucas a little smile. "Well, I suppose it's a mistake to judge people by their shoes," she said.

Lucas returned her smile. "Or by the bottoms of their feet," he agreed.

She laughed. "Like, wow," she said again. "You brought home a real one, McDonald."

"Want to join Lucas and me for dinner?" Berger asked her.

"Why not? Fisherman's Wharf?"

Lucas could not conceal his surprise, even his dismay, when he discovered that, for Lela, dressing for dinner meant slipping on a pair of sandals. He was even more surprised when he discovered that her jeans and undershirt were no impediment to their being welcomed in a handsome restaurant and conducted to a candlelit table.

They ordered abalone. Lela said every visitor to San Francisco should eat it once and then forget it. They shared two bottles of chilled white wine, which was enough to take the hard edges off their conversation. Lucas relaxed and enjoyed the dinner and the evening.

"Lela knows a little something about computers," Berger said as they were nibbling bread and butter and sampling their first glasses of the wine.

"From pillow talk," said Lela casually.

"She's seen the speech transcriber," Berger went on. "Did a job on it, about like you did."

"What do you think of my heuristic idea?" Lucas asked her.

She shrugged. "By the time the words are printed out and the operator reads them and makes the corrections, whoever is talking will have changed the subject."

"That's a matter of computer power," said Berger. "With more power we could run faster."

"How fast can you print?" she asked.

"You don't," said Lucas. "You don't print until you're finished."

"Come again?"

"You communicate to the operator on a CRT," said Lucas. "A cathode-ray tube, a screen. The operator identifies the error by touching a light pencil to it, then he taps in the correction on the keyboard. Also, if things are developing too fast for him, he can just dump a screen into a buffer—that's a little bit of memory on the side—and recall it later when there's time to work with it."

"Wow, McDonald," said Lela to Berger. "Sounds like the man's been *thinking.*"

"Oh, he can think," said Berger. "He's a whole lot deeper'n he looks."

Lela tipped her head and regarded Lucas with a critical eye. "Let's hope so," she said. "He looks like a Holiday Inn."

After the meal, Berger went to the men's room, and Lucas sat alone with Lela. Lulled by the superb food and drink, both of them were at ease. She had said to him a moment before that he was obviously reluctant to put the world aside; and now he consciously relaxed and tried to savor the moment.

"Why do you call him McDonald?" he asked her, inclining his head in the direction in which Berger had gone.

She grinned. "Because he's a burger," she laughed. "You get it? Berger . . ."

Lucas laughed heartily. "God, Lela, what are you going to call me?"

For a moment she studied him speculatively. "Doc," she said. "For Doc Holiday. Holiday Inn . . ."

He laughed again. "I could have done worse."

They fell silent. He tried not to stare at her, but he was fascinated with her. Certainly she was no chic beauty—she had too much nose and jaw, and her uncombed, mousy-brown hair afforded her face only an indistinct frame—but he appreciated her bold wit and her air of amused optimism.

"Dave expects you to raise money to reprogram the speech transcriber," she said suddenly, injecting a different note into the conversation.

"I hope I can," he said simply.

She drew a deep breath. "You'll never make it with

61

government grants and gifts from law firms," she said. "You're talking about a *business,* Doc. I can see you guys spending five million to make this thing work—"

"Five—"

"And I can see it becoming a business that generates five million revenue a year," she went on.

"You're the economist," he said.

"And you're a realist. Getting a little schoolteacher out of jail seven weeks sooner is a noble motive, but you'll never raise the money to reprogram the speech transcriber on that premise. The money will come from the big firms, man—the big firms and their clients, who generate tens of thousands of pages of transcript in, like, one antitrust litigation. There's where your revenue will come from. Five million, did I say? If you can make it work, you'll have individual cases that will produce five million."

"Is it that clear to you, Lela?" he asked. "It isn't to some of the lawyers I talk to. And they should know."

"Forgive me," she said, "but your profession is not known for progressive thinking."

"Well, I've thought in the same terms you are," he said. "In a big, multimillion-dollar litigation, a trial may last a year. The lawyers want each day's transcript overnight, so they can be armed the next day with a record of the exact words said the day before. They pay immense fees to the people who take the record on Stenotype each day and type it up overnight. A machine that could produce that record directly off the microphones in the courtroom—"

"Will snatch every dollar of those fees," she said. "I thought that's what you had in mind."

"*And* will speed up the course of justice," he added quickly. "Which is what interests the bar association."

Lela nodded and smiled. "Mixed motives," she said.

"A social conscience made more acute and determined by the chance to make a fortune in a big new business. Not bad, Doc. I like it."

"I—"

David Berger, returning, interrupted Lucas's response. He summoned the waiter. "Seems to me it's time we went home," he said. "Lucas is scheduled to see some people tomorrow. We'll give the program a more thorough run-through. Mama, you want to take the boy for a drive around the Bay tomorrow afternoon? You got time?"

"Sure," she said. "I've got time."

"Hey, you don't have to—"

"You two know each other pretty good?" Berger asked.

Lela nodded. "He's deep, like you said."

The waiter put their check down on the table—and before Lucas could touch it, Lela had grabbed it and handed it back to the waiter with her American Express card.

Berger lifted his glass and took a final sip of the wine. "Well, then," he said. "Where's he sleeping, Lela? With you or me?"

Lela shrugged. "Maybe *he's* got something to say about that."

Berger spoke with mock earnestness to Lucas. "Don't miss the chance if she's giving it to you," he said.

"You married, Doc?" Lela asked.

"Divorced," he said, frowning and uncertain.

"Okay," she said. "I wouldn't mind getting to know you better. Anyway, McDonald snores."

The big house was quiet when they returned. Lela's room had been the master bedroom, apparently—it was on a front corner, with a wide bay window over-looking the street. Berger handed Lucas his suitcase at the door of the room, and Lela welcomed him with a quick gesture. She did not switch on the lights, and the only light in the room was the orangish glow of the city, reflected from low-hanging clouds. He could tell the room had but little furniture in it. Her bed was a mattress on the floor. It was surrounded by shadowy heaps of books and papers. He could see a typewriter, too, on the floor.

"Doc . . . plan to sleep in your clothes?"

She had already shrugged out of her jeans and undershirt and had sat down on the mattress, quite naked.

"Of course I'm not," he said. "I'm gonna rape you."

She laughed. "That remains to be seen."

He undressed. It took him a couple of minutes to remove a necktie, jacket, shirt, pants, shoes, socks, undershirt, and shorts. He knelt, finally, on the edge of the mattress.

"Ah!" she exclaimed. She had reached for his penis and held it in her hand. "Damn, Doc, you're not Jewish."

"Required?"

Her laugh was guttural. "Required, hell. But I never touched one, never saw one, with the skin still on."

"Best kind," said Lucas.

"Remains to be seen." She rolled over on her back and spread her legs. "C'mon. First time, quick. Let's see if it's the best kind."

She coupled with clumsy enthusiasm—laughing, grunting, moaning, wrapping her long legs around his backside and her arms around his shoulders as if she were afraid he would break away from her in mid-ecstasy. Her maladroit vigor was new to him. It left him satiated but also exhausted and his penis even a little raw. She insisted on what she called a second performance before they fell asleep in each other's arms.

Lela's room had its own adjoining bathroom—and was the only room in the big old house that did. Lucas awoke early Friday morning, put on his pants and went in the bathroom to brush his teeth and shave. As he stood at the basin, shaving, Lela wandered in, yawning, heavy-lidded, naked. To his utter amazement, she sat down on the toilet and, giving him an affectionate pat on the hip, noisily urinated.

She returned to the mattress, and he followed her. She stretched, massaged her calves, rubbed her breasts, and even ran her fingers sensually through her crotch—all with the nonchalance of a cat, hardly noticing how he stood watching her. She handed him a little coffeepot and told him to get some water from the bathroom, so she could make coffee on the hot plate by the wall. While she made coffee and they drank it, nibbling on some day-old doughnuts, Lela remained naked—as he was to learn she almost always would remain when she was in her room. An uncircumcised penis, she told him, was something every girl should experience.

Lucas had arrived in San Francisco on Thursday afternoon and was supposed to fly back to Kansas City Saturday morning. To Dave Berger's vast amusement, he stayed over until Monday, to give him two more nights with Lela.

She found him a pair of jeans and a shirt and sandals. He admitted to her that he had never before worn blue jeans except as work clothes, when he had a messy job to do. By Saturday, when she took him walking in Muir Woods and later ambling casually through the streets of

Sausalito, no one glanced at them as an oddly matched couple.

She was busy converting her doctoral dissertation into a book that would be published next year by the University of Chicago Press. Everything she needed for her work was in reach from her mattress—her portable electric typewriter, and books and papers, which she insisted were not scattered higgledy-piggledy but were organized so she could find anything she wanted, a hot plate on which she brewed strong black coffee, a few cups and bowls and a can opener and some cans. Lela lived without non-essentials and usually without distractions.

Her gawky nakedness both amused and fascinated him. She was peculiarly graceless. Her pale, rawboned, angular body, spread out on the mattress, looked like a doll made of Tinker Toys. She bathed every day, but she did not shave her armpits and she declined to smear them with what she called chemicals. He found he liked the honest redolence of her sweat. He didn't like his own and continued to spray his armpits, but she did discourage him from splashing after-shave lotion on his face. She discouraged him, too, from pulling on even a pair of underpants in the morning. "I mean, after all, I like to look at yours, too."

That was another surprise. She liked to look at his penis and would reach for his foreskin and knead it between her fingers and thumb, laughing over how his shaft would swell and throb. The sight would stimulate her, and she would roll over on her back and beckon him to cover her. "Hey, c'mon, Doc. That makes me really feel like it," she would say. On the street or on the campus, she might put her face up to his ear and whisper: "You horny as I am?" She didn't realize she was talking to a man whose wife had never acknowledged receiving any satisfaction from copulating. ("He came home and just had to have it," Catherine would say. "So I gave it to him. I let him have it Monday night, too.") Lucas was not an innocent, but he had never known a woman like Lela.

She had another surprise for him on Saturday morning, when suddenly she switched off her typewriter, bent over him, and took his penis into her mouth. "I love the taste of a good, clean, stiff dick," she murmured. Her fascination with his foreskin continued. She sucked at it, nibbled it, licked it, and said it tasted different from the exposed head of a circumcised shaft. Lucas hardly heard her. He had never experienced oral sex before.

She asked him lots of questions about himself, about his family, his marriage, his little daughter who missed a Sunday afternoon with him because he stayed over with Lela. She said little about herself and would not be cross-examined. She was interested in his law practice and in the idea of the speech transcriber. They talked about organizing a corporation to own the software and raise the money for the extensive new programming. He read parts of her dissertation—he hadn't time to read it all. He thought it was brilliant.

On Sunday evening, his last night there, they had an early dinner with Dave Berger. They met him downtown, on the Wharf, and when he came up to them, they were strolling, holding hands, happily chatting about nothing much.

"Oh, ho-ho," said Dave. "What do I see? You two . . .?"

"I've been thinking seriously, Dave," said Lucas. "I think this business is going to require my spending a lot of time in San Francisco."

_____ 4

December 1969–March 1970

"I'LL FIND YOU something nice for Christmas in San Francisco," said Lucas Paulson to the dark-haired little girl who held his hand as they walked through the terminal at the Kansas City municipal airport.

"I know where San Francisco is," she said. "It's in 'Nam."

"No," he said. "Not nearly that far away. Daddy's not going back there, not ever. I won't be gone long. I'll be home by the middle of next week."

Melanie nodded solemnly, obviously not at all convinced.

Lucas glanced into the earnest, lined face of John D'Annunzio, Melanie's grandfather. "A weekend and Monday and Tuesday," he said to Melanie. "That's not long, is it, Granddad?"

"No," said the spare, beak-nosed Italian. "Daddy won't be gone long at all."

Lucas checked his bag and got a seat assignment. They stood near a window then, where Melanie could see the big airplane that would fly her daddy to San Francisco. He lifted her up and held her in his arms the last couple of minutes.

"Would you like to go flying on a plane like that sometime?" her grandfather asked Melanie.

She nodded.

"You wouldn't be afraid?" Lucas asked.

Melanie shook her head. "The Blessed Virgin would be watching over me," she said.

The two men exchanged troubled glances. Melanie didn't see Lucas wince or John D'Annunzio shake his head and frown.

Melanie lived with the D'Annunzios. Lucas had agreed to it. They had a big, warm home, and they were simple, generous people. His own family, his father and mother, had suggested she could live with them, but he doubted they would easily adjust to having a six-year-old move in with them. Lucas expected to provide a home for her himself before long, but for the immediate future he knew he couldn't. He was, in fact, living with his parents, and his business travel promised to become more frequent and extended.

The point was, Catherine was dying. The cancer that had been found six months ago was racing through her body, invading every organ. When they found it in her bone marrow, the doctors told her family there was no longer any chance. She had begged Lucas, out of any love he had ever felt for her, to cooperate in having Melanie reared as a devout and practicing Catholic. He had agreed. He had offered to move back into the small house he provided for her and Melanie, to help her through her ordeal and to be there with Melanie. Catherine's angry response had been that she would soon have to atone for her sins in purgatory and that he might have the decency to remember that for a man and woman no longer married to resume living together was a heavy sin, for which she would be punished.

Filled with somber thought, Lucas stared vacantly at the snowswept gray plains spread out beyond the wing of the TWA 707. He no longer loved Catherine, but it was painful to watch what was happening to a woman he had once loved. Almost as painful was to endure her consistent rejection of his sympathy.

He accepted two Scotches from the hostess and tried to relax. He looked forward to lying on Lela's mattress, in the middle of that spare, rationally cluttered room, and giving himself up to whatever her erotic imagination might suggest.

The next morning—Saturday—Dave Berger awakened Lucas and Lela by his ten-o'clock knock on their bedroom door. Lela, who opened the door to let him in, covered her nakedness less than adequately with Lucas's white shirt; and Lucas, to Berger's surprise, troubled himself only to the extent of pulling on a pair of Jockey shorts. He sat yawning on the mattress, unshaven, his hair falling over his eyes.

"I brought bagels and cream cheese," said Berger, handing Lela a brown paper bag. "You got coffee?"

"We will when we make it," she yawned. "Wanta put some water in the pot, Doc?"

"What news?" Berger called after Lucas as he shuffled into the bathroom to fill the coffeepot with water.

"If you're talking about the bar association grant, rotten news," said Lucas over his shoulder.

"Grant?" Lela asked.

"The Missouri Bar Association gave its committee on law and technology five thousand dollars to study technologies for managing big transcripts," said Berger. "We were hoping to get that money."

"We get half of it," said Lucas from the bathroom. "Maybe."

"Half? Where's the rest of it go?"

"To the study of microfiche, you'll be intrigued to hear," said Lucas, returning. "When the committee

met, one of the senior members made a speech saying
the best approach was to have transcripts typed in the
usual way, the pages reduced to microfiche, and an
index machine used to call up the proper microfiche for
scanning on a reader."

"Oh, shit," said Lela. "Why not cuneiform tablets?"

"Microfilm technology is one of the crosses computer
technology has to bear," said Berger. "The world is still
full of people who think libraries of the future will be
on little snips of film, not in the memories of computers."

"Anyway," said Lucas, "he got half the money for
microfiche. Frankly, I'm an associate in a medium-sized
law firm, and I didn't have enough clout in the committee to prevent it."

"I told you guys a month ago," said Lela, "to forget
grants—and I don't care if you're talking about government grants or bar-association grants—and go after
investment capital."

"That's going to be a little tough," said Lucas. "How
can we ask anybody to invest in a project we haven't
even defined? I mean, we don't know exactly how the
transcriber is going to work. We don't know what it's
going to cost or how long it's going to take to build it.
Prospective investors are going to ask a lot of tough
questions, and we don't have answers."

"Well, *get* the answers," she said impatiently.

Berger settled a condescending smile on her. "It
takes a lot of *work* to come up with the answers, Lela,"
he said. "The answers to those kinds of questions are a
long way down the road."

"Cut the academic horseshit, McDonald," she said.
"Don't play professor with me. You guys have got to go
out and face the world—either that or forget the whole
idea."

Berger sighed loudly. "How do we start, economist?"

Lela closed her eyes and shook her head. "With a goddamn business plan, of course," she said. "Elementary. You put together the information you have in some rational form. From that you *project.* And you build a plan. You tell people, *this* is what we're going to do."

"Oh? And what about the information you don't have? How do you project from that?"

"You *invent,* for Christ's sake," she snapped. "What do you suppose?"

"In other words," said Berger scornfully, "you fill in the gaps with lies."

She smiled and nodded. "Precisely. Elementary business planning. It doesn't take an MBA to do it, either."

Berger allowed an ironic little smile to come to his face. "Not much different from a grant application, when you think of it," he said.

Lucas did not smile. "We'll have to form a corporation," he said.

Squatting on the mattress in Lela's room, scribbling page after page of notes on sheets from five yellow legal pads, the three of them wrote, during that one weekend, the first business plan for the company they decided to name Electroscript. Twice they called in Gabe Lincoln to discuss with Berger the feasibility and the possible cost of some element of the design—telling Lincoln he was the company's first consultant. Another graduate student summoned by Berger squatted in a corner, doing calculations on a desk calculator and looking—as Lela described him over dinner on Saturday night—like some mountain guru drunk on the obscurity of his own philosophy.

Berger and Lincoln defined the design more precisely than Berger had ever taken the trouble to define it before. Of Lucas's insistence on a heuristic program, Lincoln remarked that no computer could be programmed to learn something from nothing. If it were to learn from a wrong guess, the wrong guess could not be a random guess but had to bear some logical relationship to the correct answer. The heuristic element of the program had to work, in other words, as an overlay, built onto a substantive system. The substantive system was not yet good enough, and they bent themselves to estimating how much time and cost would be involved in designing a system infinitely more powerful and sophisticated than the one they were running in the Berkeley lab.

Lucas and Lela defined the market. They made projections of how many contracts the new company might expect to get in the first year after a working system was ready to offer. They made a wild guess—the best guess they could—as to what fee Electroscript would have to charge for an hour's time on the transcriber. They projected forward five years and estimated that in the fifth year, after the introduction of a practicable, working system, it might generate gross revenues of ten million dollars.

An essential element of the business plan was a résumé of each of the chief participants in Electroscript. Lela agreed to be listed as a participant, and it was only when she handed him the yellow sheet with her résumé scribbled over it that Lucas learned that Lela Reese was the daughter of Jacob Riis, the owner of a chain of discount department stores that covered the West Coast from Seattle to San Diego. She was a graduate of UCLA and in February would be awarded her doctorate in international economics from Berkeley. She had accepted a position next fall as an instructor in economics at Case Western Reserve University in Cleveland.

They agreed to form Electroscript as a five-hundred-dollar corporation, to be incorporated in Delaware with five hundred shares of common stock. Lucas bought three hundred shares for three hundred dollars, and Dave Berger and Lela Reese invested one hundred dollars apiece. The three of them were the initial stockholders, directors, and officers of Electroscript— William Lucas Paulson, president and treasurer; David E. Berger, vice president; Lela S. Reese, second vice president and secretary. The corporation would attempt to sell ten thousand shares of preferred, non-voting stock at one hundred dollars a share.

In the lightheaded optimism of Monday night, they agreed to decline the twenty-five-hundred-dollar grant from the Missouri Bar Association.

Lucas returned to Kansas City. On Christmas morning he carried Melanie's presents to the D'Annunzios', where the little girl laughed and played in innocent delight; and Catherine, wrapped in a blanket on a couch, watched in unconcealed anguish and resentment.

Lucas's law firm, Huggins, Dodd & Drake, was engaged in the formation of a new insurance company, and the paperwork demanded his time and attention for eight weeks of twelve-hour days. Even so, he managed to file the papers to form Electroscript, Incorporated. What was far more difficult and complex, he completed the necessary filing with the Securities and Exchange Commission to allow the corporation to sell its preferred stock.

"The business in which the company expects to engage," he wrote in the prospectus, "has never before been successfully pursued, and investment in the company's stock must be regarded as highly speculative."

The partners at Huggins, Dodd & Drake agreed to listen to his first sales presentation, and on a March evening gave him thirty minutes on the agenda of a partners' meeting. He asked the firm to buy a hundred shares of the Electroscript preferred stock. The partners agreed to buy twenty-five. The senior partner offered to accompany Lucas to partnership meetings of the other large firms in the city, to introduce him and endorse his proposition. In ten days he sold 145 shares. He bought a ticket for San Francisco, to take to Dave Berger and Lela Reese—in person—the news that Electroscript had $14,500 in the bank. He flew out the third weekend in March.

Dave Berger picked up Lucas at the airport. He was shocked by Lucas's appearance. Lucas strode tensely toward him, looking jerkily around, probably for Lela, not seeing Berger. He was dressed in his lawyering suit, as Lela called his dark Ivy League suits, but this one seemed to hang loose on him.

"How is Catherine?" Berger asked him.

"Hospitalized," said Lucas. "She won't see me."

"I'm sorry, old man," said Berger. He had met Catherine Paulson for a brief moment on his one visit to Kansas City eight months ago and remembered her as a young woman whose soft beauty was spoiled by her curt hostility to Lucas and anyone who seemed to be his friend. As he thought of it now, maybe she had already known she was dying, even then, which would have accounted for her demeanor. "I know it's tough for you."

"Melanie says her mother has gone to what she calls 'Nam. Whenever anyone's gone for what she thinks is a long time, she says they've gone to 'Nam—which also means she's not sure they're coming back."

"Doesn't she see her at the hospital?"

"No. It's too late. She won't see her again."

"I'm sorry, Lucas."

"Thanks, Dave."

They walked out of the terminal, toward Berger's car in the lot. "Lela has a proposition," he said.

"Which is?"

"She's about ready to fold up here, you know. She's moving on to Cleveland to take her faculty position; and she'd like to spend a weekend with you somewhere but in her room here, somewhere but on that mattress."

"I love the room with the mattress," sighed Lucas.

"Her father owns a seaside chalet out in Marin County. She wants four of us to spend the weekend there. I'm afraid it's pretty much arranged, old man. I've invited a girl to go with me."

Lucas shrugged. "So be it then," he said dully.

Lela kissed him warmly as he arrived on the porch of the commune and suggested he leave his lawyering clothes in what she called "our room." He gladly slipped into the jeans she kept for him, and a sweat shirt she had picked up somewhere. She had packed a few things in a duffel bag and encouraged him to stuff his toiletries and underwear in it. In half an hour they were on their way in her Oldsmobile, and Berger saw Lucas relax as the miles sped by.

Berger's date was a graduate student in microbiology

—a tall, slender blonde girl from Michigan, named Norma. Her hair was sleekly styled, probably just for this weekend with Professor Berger; her makeup had been carefully and subtly applied, and she was wearing a pink knit minidress. On the drive across the bridge and out into the county, she was manifestly uncomfortable—unable to conceal what Berger imagined was apprehension that she had misunderstood the invitation and was committed to a weekend very different from what she had expected.

The redwood chalet, at the end of a lane that turned for half a mile through fragrant evergreen woods, sat on a rocky point above the ocean, with a spectacular view of the rough Pacific coastline. A large deck overlooked the steep fall to the rocks where the surf rumbled. A stone fireplace dominated the living room. Each of the four bedrooms had its own bath, and the fully equipped kitchen was large and airy. There was no television in the house, and no radio. The one telephone was in the kitchen. Norma's apprehension was immediately eased by her first exploration of the chalet.

Someone had prepared it for their visit. The refrigerator was crammed with food, including a stack of thick steaks, and with a dozen bottles of French champagne. The wine closet was filled. A bin by the fireplace was filled with firewood and kindling. The living room and bedroom tables were heaped with books and current magazines.

"See the trail?" Lela said, pointing, as they stood on the deck. "It goes down to a sheltered cove where you can go swimming if you feel like a polar bear. Personally, I feel like having a glass of champagne. You want to do the honors, McDonald?"

When Berger returned from the kitchen with the

77

champagne and glasses, Lela had tossed aside her clothes and was lying nude on a chaise on the northern corner of the deck, where it was solidly fenced to make a windbreak. Lucas sat beside her, without his sweat shirt but still wearing his jeans. Norma, the only one of them who had brought a bathing suit, had gone in to change.

"I asked my father to invest in a little of the stock," Lela said without opening her eyes, which were closed against the sun. "He'll take 250 shares."

Berger was surprised at Lucas's disapproval. His glance was so hard that for a moment Berger thought he was going to tell Lela he would not accept the $25,000—not as a gift, not as a financial prop from her wealthy father. His silence alone was expressive; Lela even opened her eyes and looked at him curiously.

"Okay, Doc?" she said.

"Does he think it's a reasonably sound speculative investment?" Lucas asked.

She nodded, but the hurt, comprehending look that for a moment clouded her eyes drew Berger's sympathy.

"I've got every nickel spent," said Berger quickly. He wanted to put the cruel moment behind them. "We're going to have to buy computer time off campus."

"Has the university evicted us?" Lucas asked.

Berger shook his head. "No, but it understands we are launching a commercial enterprise. We can't use university facilities indefinitely."

He poured the champagne while Lucas silently mulled over this news. It meant, of course, that the $25,000 from Jacob Riis, plus the $14,500 from the Kansas City firms, would not go far. Lucas had said he

meant to reimburse himself for some of his expenses—
travel, filing fees, printing letterhead for Electroscript,
secretarial assistance—from the money he had raised.
Maybe this meant he couldn't do it.

Norma's return interrupted their somber silence. She
was wearing a tiny white satin bikini and sunglasses.
She accepted a glass of champagne and cast a quizzical,
almost comical look at the thought-filled Lucas and
Berger—then an appraising glance over the stretched-
out naked body of Lela, who had gulped her champagne and again lay back with her eyes closed.

"I know where we can go," said Berger. "There's a
company in San Mateo that has excess computer capacity and is willing to lease some. I'd like authority from
the board of directors here to buy $20,000 worth of
computer time from that company."

"What's its name?" Lucas asked.

"Ringold Aviation," said Berger.

"Fine," said Lela, turning over on her stomach and
withdrawing from the conversation. "I vote for doing
it."

"It's unanimous," said Lucas dryly. "Let me see a
contract."

Lucas lay on his back on the couch in the living room.
Lela sat beside him, bent over him. They had awakened
and come out here from their bedroom, to look at the
ocean and the moonlight, and she had followed her
impulse and made love to him. He was satiated,
heavy-eyed, silent. She ran her tongue around the tip of
his penis, capturing the last drops of his semen that had
oozed out as his organ diminished and went limp, then
sucked hard on it, as if to draw out any more fluid that
remained.

Lela sat up. She drew a finger down his belly, over his navel, into his pubic hair. "You don't have to accept the money from my father," she said quietly.

"We need it," he said. "And I'm grateful for it. But I suppose you understand how I feel."

"Macho pride," she said. "I thought that was out of style."

He shrugged. "To me, Macho is the name of the sixth Marx brother."

Lela chuckled quietly. "You're the most macho man I know. In your way."

She rose from the couch and went to stand at the glass doors, looking out across the deck at the ocean. The reflection of the moon lay on the sea like a shimmering white road to Japan. No more than an hour was left of the night.

He sat up. "How can you say that?" he asked.

"The way you talk about your law firm, for example," she said. "You don't like hierarchy. You don't like to be anyone's subordinate. Not anyone's. You don't like the idea of starting at the bottom."

"I—"

"You call it the pissing contest."

Lucas laughed. "All right. What the hell?"

She slid back the glass door and stepped out into the night. It was cool, and they were naked, but she turned and beckoned, and he followed her to the railing at the edge of the deck. He put his arms around her and cupped her breasts in his hands.

"Just one thing I'd like to know about you, Doc," she said. "Is the transcriber your escape from a career that's soured on you, or do you want it for its own sake?"

"I want it because it'll be *mine*," he said firmly.

"What I figured," she said. "And all your talk about improving the quality of justice?"

"Nothing wrong with mixing motives," he said.

The next afternoon they ventured down to the cove. It was too cold for swimming, and they trooped back up and opened a bottle of champagne on the deck as they had done the afternoon before. All four were nude now. No one had said anything to Norma when she came out of the house in her white bikini, but when Dave tossed aside his pants and she was the only one covered, she pulled off the little bathing suit.

Norma turned out to have a wry sense of humor. She told how she had identified in the microbiology laboratory an unusual, perhaps new microorganism that, she said, was suspected of causing jock itch. "The one that causes syphilis is called a spirochete, you know," she said. "I've named this one the spiroagnew."

"Careful," laughed Dave Berger. "I'm not sure Lucas isn't a Republican."

"Why not, since I look like a Holiday Inn?"

Lela reached over and lifted his penis and scrotum in the palm of her hand. "You may *look* like a Holiday Inn, lover, but you're sure not *furnished* like one."

Norma giggled. "Dave's equipped like a *Ram*-ada Inn," she said.

"You can often judge a town by its water works," said Berger.

Lela was pouring more champagne into their glasses when the telephone rang in the kitchen. She went in and answered it and came back to say the call was for Dave Berger. "Why'd you have to leave word where you could be reached?" she asked.

Berger was in the kitchen for only a long moment.

He returned to the deck. "There's a telegram in my office," he said. He looked down at Lucas. "It's from Kansas City. I'm sorry, Lucas, but Catherine died this morning."

Lela came to their bedroom a few minutes later, as Lucas was dressing. "I'll come with you, Doc," she said. "Let me come with you. You'll need somebody."

He shook his head. "It was over, Lela. I . . . It's not going to be so bad for me. The only thing I might need help with is the only thing you couldn't help me with."

"Melanie," she said. "But I don't have to see anybody, Doc. I'll just go to a hotel and be there, and you can come when you feel like it. I mean, you shouldn't have to go to bed alone."

Lucas took her in his arms and held her close. "I'll come back to California as soon as I can," he said quietly.

1970

LUCAS PAULSON SHOOK the hand of the partner who had opened the double doors to admit him to the conference room, then turned his eyes to the seven lawyers sitting around the far end of the long table. The city was Houston, spread out in the relentless sun in the view from the conference-room windows. The firm was Broughton McNair Bright & Wetzel. The partners stared at him curiously, and the chairman pointed to a chair that had been drawn back from the table. Lucas sat down.

He was introduced, and he rose and spoke without notes. He spoke for ten minutes without interruption.

"Let's suppose," he said toward the end of his presentation, "you represent a utility asking for a rate increase. Your application is opposed, and the state utilities commission is holding a hearing. The hearing goes on for days, with lots of complex, contradictory testimony. How useful would it be to you to have, at the end of the day, for your overnight review, an accurate transcript of everything said during the day? Notice I am not saying a transcript *tomorrow* of what was said today, but a transcript *today* of what was said today. In fact, you could have at the lunch break a transcript of the morning session. I think you will agree that would be of tremendous value."

A thin, bald, elderly man who sat at the foot of the table had begun to shake his head. He put his cigarette aside. "I don't see how," he said. "What good would all that be?"

"Oh, for Christ's sake, Ned," grumbled another senior partner, a beefy man with steel-rimmed spectacles. "*Of course* it would be useful, if they can do it."

The first man picked up his cigarette and filled his mouth and lungs with smoke. "Don't see how," he muttered, letting smoke out with his words.

A third partner, a small man with a chain looped across his bulging vest, had been writing notes. "What would a service like this cost, Mr. Paulson?" he asked.

"I frankly don't know," said Lucas. "But whatever it turns out to cost, you deduct from it the cost of the stenographic services you use now, and I believe the new service will be economically feasible."

The smoking partner was, in fact, Ned Bright, whose name was included in the partnership name. He shook his head again. "You'd have to keep your stenographers at work, as a backup."

"No, I don't think so, sir," said Lucas. "Why would you need them?"

"You'd be putting a lot of faith in a technological gimmick. One day you'd finish a hearing and find out the thing hadn't been working all day and you didn't have any transcript."

"Anyway," said the man who was taking notes, "you don't have this thing in operation—or anywhere near it."

Lucas nodded. "A practical test is a year away."

The note-taker smiled. "Assuming you don't run out of money before the year is up. And that is why you are here. Right?"

"Exactly," said Lucas. "I am visiting major firms, so

far in Missouri, Oklahoma, and now Texas—asking them to invest in the preferred stock of Electroscript, Incorporated. Since it is the legal profession that will be the most immediate beneficiary of the service, we are asking the legal profession to supply the necessary capital."

"You are visiting other firms here in Houston?"

"Yes, sir. But you have the honor of being the first."

Some of the partners around the table laughed, and the one taking notes grinned and said, "We are honored. But tell me—how much have you raised so far?"

"Let me make a distinction," said Lucas. "I have one investor in California who is not a lawyer, and he has bought $25,000 worth of the stock. The law firms of Kansas City, St. Louis, Tulsa, and Oklahoma City have so far invested $82,000."

"So you have a little over $100,000. I take it, that's not much. I mean, I take it you will need . . . what? A million?"

"Yes. More than that. We are beginning to think we will need two million."

"Well, how did you come to choose Kansas City, St. Louis, Tulsa, Oklahoma City, and Houston?"

Lucas smiled. "On a most informal basis, I have to admit," he said. "I started in Kansas City because that is where I practice law. Then St. Louis because our firm could introduce me there. And then the question was, should I go to Chicago or New York—"

"Or refine your road show in the sticks before you risked the big time," interrupted Ned Bright.

"Well, I consider Houston the big time," said Lucas, nodding and letting a grin spread across his face.

The old man held his cigarette under his chin as he joined in the laughter. When the laughter died, he kept a sly little smile on his face, and he asked: "If our firm were to buy some of your stock, Mr. Paulson, how should we treat it on the books: as an investment or as a contribution for the good of the profession?"

"You buy it as an investment," said Lucas calmly. "However, you might choose to make a gift of it to, say, the Texas Bar Foundation, in which case you can take an immediate deduction for the charitable contribution."

The old man turned down the corners of his mouth and gave Lucas a mock bow. "Not a bad idea," he said.

The note-taker spoke. "My name, incidentally, Mr. Paulson, is Bob Tabor. I'm going to ask you a tough one. Just what chance do you think there is that this idea of yours will ever come to fruition? You're asking us to give you money for it. Are you, in fact, asking us to throw it away? What chance?"

"Mr. Tabor, all I can say is this. I've asked each firm that has invested to allow me to use its name. I'll be glad to tell you who has invested and how much. That will give you some idea, I hope, that other lawyers have judged our prospects of success reasonably good. Beyond that, I can point out that I have myself made a major investment, not in money terms but in terms of commitment, career commitment. Not that—"

"You're not practicing much law these days, are you?" asked the man wearing steel-rimmed glasses.

"No, I left my firm in May. Obviously, if I am doing what you see me doing, I wasn't carrying much of the load at Huggins, Dodd & Drake, so I separated from it."

"Are other firms donating their stock to foundations?" asked Tabor.

"About 20 percent," said Lucas.

Tabor nodded. "Well, in order to get this matter

before the management committee, I move that our firm buy a hundred shares of Electroscript, Incorporated."

Ned Bright shook his head. "Well . . . Ten thousand dollars." He drew a breath and sighed. "Okay, tell you what. I'll vote for your motion if you'll accept an amendment. I'd like to amend that we immediately donate the damned stock to the Texas Bar Foundation and take our tax deduction for the charitable contribution. That way it only costs us five thousand."

"Thank you, gentlemen. Thank you very much," said Lucas.

Dave Berger accompanied Lucas to the summer convention of the American Bar Association. They had been invited to make a presentation to the committee on law and technology, and together they had prepared a paper—a concise, factual report of the progress they had made toward developing a system that would listen to the testimony at a trial or hearing and instantly print a transcript of everything that was said.

The committee—twenty or so professors and young lawyers—sat on uncomfortable steel-and-vinyl chairs around a table covered with a holed and darned green cloth and set with two sweating pitchers of water, two trays of hotel water glasses, and half a dozen heavy glass ashtrays. Lucas was a member and so sat at the table. Dave sat behind him, on a chair against the wall.

The committee was called to order at two o'clock on Wednesday afternoon, half an hour past the scheduled time. The chairman, a professor of law from the University of Indiana, called for the reading of the minutes of the last meeting. Lucas would have risen to move the committee dispense with the reading of the minutes, but before he could rise, the secretary, an earnest young lawyer from Michigan, had begun. He read for twenty minutes.

"Mr. Chairman," said Lucas at the first opportunity. "I move that the minutes be received as read."

"Oh, no!" cried a professor from the University of Pennsylvania. "No. There is an error in the way my motion, that I made on the subject of the Harris project, was reported. I moved that the committee *authorize* the chairman to appoint a subcommittee to review *and evaluate* that project. The minutes read that I moved that such a subcommittee *be* appointed and that it only review, not necessarily evaluate, the project. I want to move a correction."

"In fact, Arthur," said another member, "you moved that the chairman be *directed* to appoint a subcommittee."

"No," said the man from Pennsylvania firmly. "Authorize."

"Anyway," said the chairman, "I did appoint—"

"So let the minutes show that you were authorized so to do," insisted the man from Pennsylvania. "Not directed."

"Well, the subcommittee's mandate, then—"

"I have a different problem," another member interrupted.

The committee on law and technology of the American Bar Association adjourned at six o'clock without reaching agreement on the final, official version of the minutes of its February meeting. It met again at half past nine on Thursday morning and resumed the debate. An hour and a half later the minutes of the last meeting were adopted, on a vote that left three members so annoyed that they spoke of withdrawing from the committee.

Finally, with less than an hour left before the committee was scheduled to break for lunch on Thursday, the chairman called for the reading of the first of several scheduled reports from people working on projects the subcommittee on program had judged likely to be of interest to the committee.

It was 4:15 before the chairman recognized Lucas Paulson to give a report on the electronic speech transcriber. Lucas introduced Professor David Berger of the University of California at Berkeley, and then read the report.

"Well!" said the professor from the University of Pennsylvania when Lucas had finished. "The Berkeley program. You *have* plunged ahead, haven't you? Didn't elect to wait until the Wertz group published their report. Don't you think it would have been wise to see what they came up with, before you rushed in headlong?"

"Professor Wertz and his group," said Lucas patiently, "have been studying the problem for—what?—two years. They may study it for two years more."

"And you can't wait?"

Lucas shrugged. "Why should we?"

The professor smiled. "Well," he answered with scorn he was at no effort to conceal, "you have, of course, formed a corporation and are going after the idea as a profit-making venture."

Lucas grinned. "A profit-*seeking* venture," he said.

"Mmm. Yes. I suppose there is a difference."

"Let me assure you there is."

The professor from the University of Pennsylvania smiled and shrugged and withdrew.

No one else had any questions or comments, and the chairman called for the next report.

The lawyer from Ohio, the one who had reported on

computer-assisted legal research in case law, invited Lucas and Dave to join him for a drink in the bar. They sat in a booth made of vinyl patterned to look like snakeskin and were served by a bare-legged girl with a tall, bouffant hairstyle and iridescent pink lipstick.

"Learn your lesson?" the Ohio man asked.

"I'll never attend another meeting of that goddamn committee," said Lucas.

The Ohio man laughed. "Then you won't hear what they're saying about you. Your program and mine have the same problem, so far as they are concerned. We've stopped talking and are going ahead and doing. Nothing spoils an academic's fun like the discovery that some of his ideas have been right and can actually be put into practice. That's worse than being proved wrong. You and I are a threat to their little mutual-admiration society."

"Congratulations to us," said Dave Berger.

"Don't underestimate them," said the man from Ohio. "Men who can spend a day and a half fussing over the minutes of their last meeting are capable of sustained pettiness. The problem is, as you go around the country looking for support for your project, a lot of people who should know better are going to ask you if it's been endorsed by the ABA committee on law and technology. You either make your peace with these characters or fight them."

"What are *you* doing?" Lucas asked.

The man from Ohio grinned. "Piss on 'em," he said.

The first week in December, Lucas flew to Cleveland —to meet with the principal law firms and to spend a weekend with Lela. It was his first visit to Cleveland. She had flown to Dallas and spent a weekend with him there when he was meeting the Dallas firms, and she had returned to San Francisco late in September to be with him as Dave Berger showed him what money and hard work had wrought: a new and improved version of the transcriber design, with the first heuristic element experimentally in place.

She met him at the airport. He hardly recognized her. Lela was wearing a mink jacket over a cream-white minidress; her legs were sheathed in nylon sparkling with some sort of glitter; and a silver-and-turquoise necklace hung in a heavy loop around her neck. Her hair was piled up and sprayed, and she wore pink lipstick and green eye shadow. In the parking lot, she led him to a silver-gray Mercedes.

"I've set up appointments for you," she said. "With five firms."

He nodded. "Where am I staying?" he asked.

"Lakefront Holiday Inn," she said with a smile. "I figured you wouldn't want the most expensive, and in this town a Holiday Inn is not much less than the best there is."

He found the city depressing. Soot-darkened snow was heaped along the streets, melting in an early winter thaw and filling every low place with black water. The Mercedes, which was already grimy, was repeatedly splashed with dirty slush and water as Lela drove through the downtown streets.

His room overlooked the gray waters of Lake Erie. He stood and looked out at a lake freighter easing its way past the breakwater. Lela tossed her mink on one of the beds and came to stand beside him.

"Squalid damn town," she said.

Lucas nodded. "I brought along a copy of the audit of Electroscript," he said.

"I don't care about that. I trust you."

"Well, you're an officer of the company."

The audit, based on the financial condition of the company as of October 31, showed that it had received $186,500 from the sale of preferred stock. It held due and payable subscriptions for another $22,300. It had $28,000 on hand in bank accounts. Lucas had spent a little more than $6,000 on travel and expenses such as long-distance telephone calls. Dave Berger had spent $700 for travel and about $400 for telephone calls. The only compensation paid by the company was $1,500 to Gabe Lincoln, the doctoral candidate in mathematics at Berkeley, for consulting fees and $900 to another Berkeley student for work in the computer center. Approximately $135,000 had been paid to Ringold Aviation, Incorporated, for computer services and about $15,000 to the University of California as compensation for use of its computer facility in the first days of the company. Electroscript owed Ringold $24,000.

Lela handed back the papers. "When're you going to take some compensation for yourself?" she asked.

He shrugged. "When I can."

They undressed, took a shower together, and stretched out naked on the bed. She was menstruating, she said, with painful cramps, but she would take care of him; and she did, with the maladroit enthusiasm that left him aching and sometimes, like this afternoon, half raw. It was odd to see Lela wipe lipstick from her mouth before she bent over him, and to feel stiffly lacquered hair on his belly. It was odd to see green eye shadow when she looked up at him, and it was odd to smell on her body the remnant of a scented oil that had survived their shower. It was odd later, when they dressed to go to dinner, to see her pull on her glittering pantyhose and to settle her cashmere minidress over

92

her long figure, and to restore her lipstick at the bathroom mirror.

The next morning she drove out to Case Western Reserve to teach two classes, and she dropped him off at the corner of Ninth and Euclid, for his appointments with Cleveland's chief law firms.

His first appointment was at the firm of Dwyer, Sandhurst & Emory. He was received, not in a partnership or committee meeting, but by one partner, George Jimson, in his office. Jimson was a loose-fleshed, late-middle-aged man. The shoulders of his rumpled brown suit were sprinkled with flakes of dandruff, his shirt bloused out in a generous roll at the waistband of his trousers, and his shiny maroon necktie was carelessly knotted on a frayed collar. Paint peeled from the ceiling of the little office, and the finish on Jimson's cheap old desk was cracked and scarred.

Jimson's telephone rang, and he took the call before he had even shaken Lucas's hand. He waved Lucas into a chair and engaged in a five-minute conversation that on his part consisted mostly of grunts and nods.

As he waited, Lucas looked around the shabby little office. Framed and hung on the wall—in the same frame with a letter of gratitude—was a white-on-black photocopy of a check for $1.75 billion, drawn on Manufacturers Hanover Trust and payable to the state of Ohio. It represented the proceeds of a bond issue for which the bond counsel had been George Jimson for Dwyer, Sandhurst & Emory. In a dusty glass case on the windowsill, there was a small and exquisitely detailed brass model of a steam locomotive, which had been presented to George Jimson by the Pennsylvania Railroad. Autographed pictures of governors and mayors hung about the walls in careless disarray—most of them tilting at crazy angles. Jimson, Lucas could see, was a bond lawyer. His specialty was guiding governments and corporations through the complexities of borrowing billions of dollars.

When he put down the phone, Jimson rose and shook Lucas's hand. "I was asked to meet with you because I'm the member of our firm who has dealt with the Ohio Bar automated-research program," he said. "They suppose I know something about computers." He smiled and shook his head. "Actually, though, I know a good deal about your project. I have a copy of the report you gave at the ABA meeting last summer. I've talked to some people about you." He glanced at his watch. "I have another appointment in ten minutes, so let me tell you pretty bluntly that I will not recommend to my firm that we buy any of your preferred stock. My objection is to the way you have your company organized. You're asking other people to put up money, but you're keeping control for yourself. In short, the lawyers who put money in Electroscript would be buying you a business."

"The project will benefit the profession enormously," said Lucas. "It doesn't seem unfair that the profession fund it."

"Here in Ohio," said Jimson, "we formed a not-for-profit corporation to own and operate the computerized-research project. The lawyers are putting up the money, but the profession will *own* what it has invested in. It will control it. You see the difference?"

"Of course. But—"

"What I would do if I were you, Mr. Paulson, is reorganize this whole thing. Form a not-for-profit corporation. Let the bar associations and the major firms choose a board of trustees of eminent lawyers. Then go to the firms all over the country with an issue of debentures. In other words, let the new non-profit

94

company borrow the money you need—and I would judge that's going to be five million or more. The profession will be much more willing to invest in a project it controls and, in effect, owns. With that kind of reorganization, my firm would be prepared to back you. So would the other Cleveland firms—and the New York firms. As it stands . . ." He shrugged.

Lucas shook his head uneasily. "Well, it's a lot to think about," he said quietly.

Jimson stood, ending the meeting. "The board of the new company would, of course, elect you president and give you a contract with a generous salary and benefits. I assume you would hire Professor Berger, and something equally generous could be worked out for him." He smiled and extended his hand. "I'm glad you came in. Let me know if you decide to reorganize."

Lucas returned to the Holiday Inn late in the afternoon. Lela was already there, lying nude on the bed and—to his surprise—smoking a cigarette.

"Sell any stock?" she asked.

He shook his head. "Not a share. A lot of talk had preceded me."

She sat up, frowning, and crushed her cigarette in the ashtray on the nightstand. "What's the problem?"

"They want to take over. That was the first thing I got this morning—form a not-for-profit corporation, surrender control to a board of trustees, take a salary."

"Become an employee?"

"Become an employee," he said. "Fit myself into a niche in the hierarchy—a notch above Dave Berger, who they said should work for me, and a notch below what Jimson called the 'eminent lawyers' who would be my bosses."

"For a salary."

"A *generous* salary, whatever that is."

She shook her head and sighed. "Which raises a question. What are you living on, Doc?" she asked.

He turned and looked out the window again. "My father made me counsel to his company—I mean, the automobile agency. I do some work for it, actually, and I'm picking up a few dollars. My old firm has referred a little work to me, small things it didn't want to take on. I—"

"You're living on peanuts," she interrupted.

He smiled. "When I can afford them."

"You can't go on this way."

"No, not very long."

"Neither can I," she said.

"You . . ."

"I can't stand this town! I can't stand the cold and wet and dirt and dark. I'm scared every time I walk on the street. I come back to the parking lot expecting my car to be stripped or gone. I open the door to my apartment expecting to find it ransacked—or a man waiting to attack me. The girl who shares the apartment with me was raped last year. She carries a gun! In her purse. I . . . Frankly, Lucas, I can't stand the *schwartzers!* They scare the hell out of me."

"What about your job?"

She sighed. "It's all right, I suppose. It's so different, though! Like everything else. I feel alien. Nothing's like—"

"California."

Her lips trembled. She nodded. "All right. Okay. That's fair." She lowered her head and sighed. "Can you imagine *me* . . . I thought I . . ." She sucked in her breath, closed her eyes tight, and sobbed.

Lucas put his hand on her shoulder. "You don't have to do it, after all," he said softly.

She looked up and with the back of her hand wiped

96

the tears from her eyes. "Doc? Do I hear you offering an alternative?" she whispered.

"You *have* alternatives."

She breathed deeply and regained her voice. "Let me suggest one," she said. "The chalet in Marin County. We can live there. You can bring your little girl. There are good schools there. It could be . . . Lucas, it could be so great!"

He shook his head. "I can't afford anything like that, Lela."

"You don't have to. Let me take care of everything until Electroscript is going and you have—"

"Lela." He stopped her. He patted her shoulder gently. "You're a good friend," he said. "You're a wonderful friend."

With an angry sweep of her hand she knocked the clock and ashtray off the nightstand, scattering butts and ashes across the carpet. "Fuck off, Lucas," she said bitterly.

6

May 1971

LUCAS ARRIVED IN San Francisco late in the afternoon of Sunday, May 16.

Dave Berger grabbed his bag. "Frankly, my friend, you don't look like you could carry it from here to the car."

"Just tired," said Lucas.

Berger was not convinced. Lucas slumped, slack and round-shouldered, when he sat down in the car, and his face sagged. He smelled of something he'd had to drink on the plane, probably Scotch, and his eyes seemed to focus only on the distance, seeing nothing in particular.

"I'm sorry I can't ask you to stay with me," said Berger. "I'm living with Norma. I mean, she'd be glad to have you, but we're just sharing an efficiency and sleep on a fold-out in the living room."

"That's okay," said Lucas wearily. "Frankly, if I stayed with you, I'd have to make an effort to be cordial. In a motel room, I can just flop."

"We'd planned on dinner," said Berger. "But . . ."

"If you don't mind, Dave. If I wake up before the coffee shop closes, I'll have a sandwich. . . . Otherwise, I may sleep through till breakfast. What's scheduled?"

"Look at the system in the morning. Tomorrow

afternoon, we are supposed to meet with Arthur Ringold."

"What's he want?"

"He wants to talk about the business, about money, I suspect."

"Couldn't be good news," sighed Lucas.

"We owe him about a hundred thousand dollars," said Berger. "But we have the cash to pay it, haven't we?"

Lucas nodded. "I deposited checks Thursday. Almost eighty thousand. We can pay Ringold. And there'll be a balance."

"I'd like to put Gabe Lincoln on a salary," said Berger. "Our first full-time employee. We can get him temporarily for fourteen thousand. If we don't, we'll lose him permanently. He has to take a job somewhere."

"All right."

Berger glanced at Lucas, whose eyes were now closed. "Maybe what we ought to do is pay *you* the fourteen. You've got to start taking compensation sometime."

"I'm managing," breathed Lucas.

"Yeah, I can see that."

Berger left Lucas in a small motel in San Mateo, not far from the Ringold computer center. Having seen that Lucas got a comfortable room, he stopped in the lobby and used the coin telephone to call Norma.

"Listen, there was a call on the recorder when I got home," she said. "Guess who's in town?"

"Who?"

"Lela. She left a number and wants you to call her."

"Do you think she knows Lucas is in town?" he asked. "Could you tell from her message?"

"Yes. She wants the four of us to have dinner."

"I think I had better see her alone, honey. I just put Lucas to bed. He's not up to having dinner with anybody."

"What's wrong?"

"He says he's just exhausted. I don't know. He looks bad. Did Lela leave a number?"

Lela was staying in a spare room in their old commune, where Gabe Lincoln still lived. "Weird, man," said Gabe when Berger saw him in the living room. "Sis has freaked."

She came downstairs, and Berger could see what Gabe meant. She was wearing ragged old jeans and a man's ribbed undershirt—the kind of clothes that had almost been a uniform with her two years ago—but her hair was piled high and sprayed, her eyelids were glittery green under brows plucked into thin arches. Her feet were tightly strapped into high-style Italian shoes. His thought was that she looked like a street hooker, but from the look on her face he judged she was far too vulnerable to hear even the most facetious suggestion of anything like that.

"Where's Doc?"

Berger shook his head. "Utterly exhausted and looking sick. I poured him into bed in a motel. I didn't find out until later that you were in town, and I judged it better not to wake him."

"Shit, McDonald. You his keeper now?"

Berger shrugged. "I'm telling you, Lela. Maybe tomorrow night."

"I won't be here tomorrow night. I promised to go back to Cleveland long enough to give and grade my final exams."

"So you get dinner with me. We'll talk."

She agreed to go with him to a Chinese restaurant

they had frequented in the past—not a very good one, actually, for San Francisco, but one where they were greeted and led by the broadly smiling manager to a corner booth. They sat in the light of paper lanterns, in the midst of much red and black lacquer, and Lela ordered a Mai Tai, which was served with a tiny parasol for a swizzle stick.

"What are you doing in San Francisco?" Berger asked.

"I came to California to cry on shoulders," she said. "Daddy's. Doctor Ledyard's. Ledyard is terribly disappointed in me, that I'm not staying on at Western Reserve."

"If you resign at Western Reserve, you may be resigning from academe entirely."

"I've already resigned, so don't lecture me." She gulped an icy swallow of the rum-laced fruit juice. "I'm coming home. My mother and father are pleased, anyway."

"What are you going to do with yourself?"

"Try to figure out who I am," she said. "I've gotta do that, Dave. I really don't know who I am."

"Why don't you look on your driver's license?" he asked curtly.

"You unsympathetic bastard."

"I'm bored with the cliché, Lela. I heard about the mink coat and the Mercedes. What's the idea? You trying to convert from flower child to Jewish-American princess?"

"I don't seem to work out very well as either," she said sadly.

"Post-university depression," he said, lifting his own Mai Tai and sipping the icy liquid that threatened to make his head ache. "It's an easy time for depression—your time of life, the times generally."

"The national malaise," she said. "Another cliché, McDonald."

"Seriously," he said. "It's a depressing goddamn time to be alive—I mean, in the reign of Richard Nixon and Spiro Agnew. The revolt of the pancake-eaters. We always knew they were still out there somewhere—I mean, all those Rotarians and Kiwanians and Civitans, all those Protestants and Catholics, hardware merchants, insurance salesmen, and house builders. There have always been an awful lot of them, and we had to know they'd someday turn away from the boob tube and take another look at what was happening to the world. We're all afraid, Lela. Hemingway said, when a man loses his optimism, it's time for him to die."

"You make dumb speeches, McDonald."

"Well, at least I know who I am, dear."

She snapped her finger at a nearby waiter and pointed at her empty glass.

"Tell me about Doc. Is he really sick, or is he putting me off?"

"Lela, I swear to you he doesn't know you're in town."

"How about if I went over to his motel later tonight and fucked him out of his mind. Would it make him feel better?"

"I'm not going to tell you not to," said Berger. "But I'm telling you: I've never seen him looking this bad. He's down, Lela. He's been traveling six days a week for the past four months. He's raised over a quarter of a million dollars, and he's exhausted."

"Needs his sleep, huh?"

Berger nodded. "That would be my judgment. If you decide to go, don't tell him your troubles or mine. Just fuck him out of his mind and let it go at that."

Lela shrugged. "Lucas can always find somebody to fuck him out of his mind. Some lucky girl."

Berger drew a deep breath. "Does he know you're in love with him?"

"Sure he does. But it isn't what he wants."

"Well, maybe you had better go over there and sleep with him."

She sighed. "Yeah. Maybe."

She didn't. When Berger went to the motel in San Mateo the next morning, Lucas said he'd had a good night's sleep. He was still pallid and tense and distracted, but he ate bacon and eggs and drank four cups of coffee and said he was ready to see what new marvels Dave and Gabe had programmed into the transcriber. Berger did not mention Lela until Lucas had finished his breakfast. Lucas heard that she had been in town, without comment. He said he was sorry she would not be there that evening.

They spent the morning in the computer center and then took Gabe Lincoln to lunch and put him on the payroll of Electroscript. In the middle of the afternoon, they kept their appointment with Arthur Ringold.

"To be utterly blunt with you, Mr. Paulson," said Ringold when they were settled in his office, "you look to me as though you are tired. Maybe it would be well if we postponed this discussion to another day."

"That's considerate of you, Mr. Ringold, but I'd at least like to know what you had in mind when you suggested this meeting."

"Oh, nothing that should be the source of apprehension," said Ringold. "I'm not about to demand you pay my bill or announce an increase in charges."

Arthur Ringold was a small, bald man who sat

behind a broad, glass-topped desk cluttered with files, mementoes, lighters, and packs of Pall Mall cigarettes. He peered up at Lucas from behind his thick, rimless eyeglasses with something of the air of Edmund Gwenn playing Santa Claus.

"I've brought a check for what we owe you," said Lucas.

"Seriously," said Ringold as he crushed a cigarette in the huge, butt-filled amber-glass ashtray that dominated the center of his desk, "I was not about to ask you for it. Actually, what I had in mind was to open a discussion with you on the possibility of your taking in a new partner."

"Uh . . . you?"

"My company."

"Well, I, uh . . . I try to be a good listener," said Lucas.

Ringold's brows rose high above his eyeglasses, and he pursed his lips. "I have been watching what you two have been doing in the computer center," he said. "I have two observations. The first is that you may have the beginnings of a highly successful, highly profitable business there. The second is that you are raising capital far too slowly. Indeed, you may never raise enough. I think you are going to find that the million dollars you are trying to raise will not be enough, that you are going to need two million, or five million, or maybe even ten million. You will never raise that kind of money from the law firms."

"The lawyers have been generous," interjected Berger. "I've been surprised at how much they've invested."

"A tribute to Mr. Paulson's abilities as a persuader," said Ringold as he snapped his lighter and lit another Pall Mall. "The problem is that the law firms are not in the business of accumulating and investing capital, and soon they are going to dry up on you. With the best will in the world, they simply don't have enough money to support the building of your business."

"Then . . . ?" asked Lucas.

"You remember what Willy Sutton said?" asked Ringold. "The bank robber? He said, if you want money, you go where the money is. To the banks."

"When we have an operating program, it will secure a loan," said Lucas.

Ringold shook his head. "If you had an operating program, you wouldn't *need* a loan. It's the old story."

"So you are suggesting a . . . merger?" asked Lucas.

"I propose," said Ringold, "that we explore the possibility. You know my company? Let me tell you a little about it."

"I know you have a fine, strong company," said Lucas.

"Started like you," said Ringold. "With an idea. During the war—I mean World War II—I was with Ferry Command. We delivered bombers to England by flying them over the North Atlantic. I was a navigator and in all modesty a damn good navigator, one of the best. But in those days you had to fly by the stars, and if you ran into clouds higher than your operational ceiling, you couldn't see the stars. I got lost at least ten times, and I hope I'll never be as terrified again. It was then that I saw the desperate need for far more sophisticated radio navigation equipment, and that was the business I went into when the war ended. Today we sell some 20 percent of the autopilot-coupled electronic gear that makes it possible for a 707 or 747 to fly a straight, predetermined course from Heathrow to Kennedy through the soup, without ever seeing either the ocean below or the sky above."

Berger prompted Ringold to tell a story about a westbound flight, carrying a delegation of Polish military officers to a conference with General Marshall in the winter of 1943; and Lucas studied the spartanly furnished office as Ringold somewhat reluctantly told of flying beyond the limited reach of radio beacons, of being driven off course by strong winds, and of almost running out of fuel before the high clouds cleared enough to let him make a star fix and direct the airplane toward Iceland. On Ringold's desk lay a big magnetic compass, obviously taken from a World War II–vintage airplane; and hanging on his wall was a heavy old altimeter that served as a superaccurate barometer. His walls were hung with very ordinary pictures of planes that carried Ringold navigation equipment—Boeing and Douglas airliners, Lear jets, and an assortment of military and naval aircraft. His one autographed picture was of Juan Trippe.

"There are at least two possibilities we might explore," said Ringold, deftly redirecting the conversation. "One is that you issue more voting stock in Electroscript and sell it to Ringold Aviation. Ringold will borrow on its established credit to buy the Electroscript stock. The other way would be to merge Electroscript into Ringold Aviation. You would take Ringold Aviation stock for your Electroscript stock. Once again, Ringold Aviation would borrow the several millions you will need to make the transcriber a viable commercial venture."

Lucas nodded. "I'll speak frankly," he said. "I'm reluctant to surrender control."

Ringold smiled benignly. "So was I. So is anybody. I'm still the largest single stockholder in Ringold Aviation, but if the other stockholders ganged up on me, they could take the company away from me. It's the price of capital, Mr. Paulson. Or the price of bigness. None of us can raise enough all by ourselves to make a company big enough to function in a national market."

Lucas pressed the fingertips of both hands to his eyes. "If you would like to make a specific proposal, in some detail, certainly we would have to give it serious consideration," he said. "We'll need time, of course."

Ringold's lids dropped across his eyes for a moment, and he nodded. The meeting was ended.

When Lucas returned to his motel room, the red message light was blinking on the telephone. The clerk told him there was an envelope for him at the desk, something that had been dropped off during the morning. Berger had suggested they simply have dinner there in the motel, and when Lucas went down to join him he picked up the big manila envelope at the desk. They found the brightly lighted dining room noisy with "family" trade—shrieking children, shrilling matrons—and chose to spend the ten-dollar cover charge to enter the "stag" bar.

"One thing Arthur Ringold didn't mention," said Berger as soon as Lucas sat down and before he could open the envelope, "is that he has fended off a dozen raids by bigger companies that would like to acquire Ringold Aviation. He's a shrewd old bastard, and fiercely independent. What ya got?"

Lucas glanced around. "Nothing, I hope, that takes a lot of light to read," he said. The stag bar was one of those places that motel chains decorate in heavy walnut and shades of red—dark except for flickering candles in red glasses on the tables. "Got a flashlight?"

He tore open the envelope, frowned for a moment over the contents, and handed it all to Berger. The two sheets of paper were two stock certificates, both endorsed to Lucas—one representing Lela's shares in the common stock of Electroscript, the stock she had bought for the one hundred dollars she had contributed to help organize the corporation, the other representing her father's 250 shares of preferred stock. There was no note, just the two certificates.

"I guess I don't understand," said Lucas grimly. "Should I?"

Berger nodded. "I think you should. I think you do."

"I—"

"Y'all like somethin' from the bar?"

Their conversation was interrupted by their waitress, an exceptionally tall girl with mousy blonde hair piled high and sprayed, wearing a tight red satin corselet that pushed her white, blue-veined breasts up and out for display, pinching forward her pink nipples that were almost as big around as coffee cups. Her long, shapely legs were accented by the tiny red skirt and fluffy starched white petticoat that stood out from her hips, by high-heeled black shoes, and by fine-mesh black net stockings.

"Uh . . . Scotch on the rocks," said Lucas. "Make it a double."

"Mizz-ur-uh, I bet! I'd bet anything in the world!" she exclaimed.

"KC," said Lucas glumly.

"Jefferson," she said happily. "Welcome to California."

Lucas nodded and tried to smile. Berger ordered a drink.

"I've got to work on that," said Lucas as he watched the girl twitch away toward the bar.

"Her?" said Berger. "I'm sure it could be arranged."

"No. The accent. It bothers me when people can locate me like that from the way I talk." He sighed.

"She couldn't have done it if I weren't tired. I can subdue it when I think about it. Anyway . . . Lela."

"We don't have to talk about it."

"You slept with her, too, didn't you?" Lucas asked. His eyes fastened hard on Berger's face, not accusingly, but demanding an answer. "I mean, even after I was." He shrugged. "Why not, after all? I only saw her every two or three months. Sometimes not that often."

"You didn't do anything wrong," said Berger.

"I thought I was, at first. I'm an old-fashioned guy, some ways. I thought I was taking advantage of her—I mean, to do what I did with her, without any intention of . . . of any other kind of involvement. She'd have laughed at me if she'd known I felt that way. Wouldn't she? Wouldn't she have, Dave?"

Berger nodded. "Absolutely. At first."

"Child of the sexual revolution," said Lucas with irony. "Wasn't she?"

"I suppose she thought so," said Berger. "That and half a dozen other kinds of revolution."

The cocktail waitress returned. "Say, is the old Stockyard Inn still open?" she asked Lucas. He nodded, and she went on, "I love San Francisco, but I miss Missouri." She stood so near to him that her petticoat brushed his shoulder, and he couldn't keep his eyes off the extraordinary display of her breasts. "Anything else? You let me know if you want anything else."

Once again Lucas watched the girl walk away. "I don't know what to do about this," he said, putting a finger on the stock certificates. "That's a $25,000 gift. An expensive gesture."

"Let her make it," said Berger firmly. "Don't take that away from her."

"You mean, being able to splash money around is all she's got left of her self-worth?"

"Something like that."

"Jesus," said Lucas. He lifted his glass and drank thirstily of the Scotch.

"Let's talk about Arthur Ringold," said Berger.

They did, for half an hour. Lucas called for a second double Scotch, and they returned to a subject they had discussed in the morning and over lunch: the cost of leasing their own disk drives, since they were overburdening the memory capacity of the Ringold Aviation computer center. It was plain that the original business plan, the one they had worked out on Lela's mattress, had grossly underestimated the cost of making the transcriber operational. Lucas had raised more than half a million dollars now, but the demands of the project grew faster than he could meet them; and already they were deferring work that needed to be done until more money came in. Lucas had not yet visited the law firms on the Eastern Seaboard—New York, Boston, Philadelphia, Washington—and he had been telling himself for a long time that when he ventured there he would come back with the balance of the million dollars they had supposed would be all they needed.

"Demonstration equipment . . ." Lucas mused. "Communications. I don't want to go into New York without the ability to set up a demonstration."

"You could fly a dozen New York lawyers here for a demonstration for half what it's going to cost to set up a demonstration in New York."

"Yeah, but not nearly so impressive. Anyway, it's a bullet we've got to bite sooner or later. We haven't faced the problems of communication between the courtroom and the computer center. We can't put that off forever."

A waiter came to their table and asked if they were

ready to order. They ordered steaks. The waitress came with Lucas's third drink, and he told her to bring them a liter of red wine to go with their dinner. He sipped quickly and heavily from the third Scotch. It began to take effect.

"A million dollars . . ." Lucas sighed. "We're going to raise a million dollars. Who would have thought it possible? The KC firms have come around for a second time, more than tripled their original investment. And . . . the goddamn million isn't going to make it."

"What happens to all that preferred stock if Electroscript is merged into Ringold?" Berger asked.

"Damned good question."

With the wine, the waitress brought a plate of celery, carrot sticks, radishes, cherry tomatoes, and olives from the salad bar. "One Miss-ur'n to another," she said to Lucas, brushing his shoulder with her hip.

Lucas gulped down his Scotch and poured himself a glass of red wine, overlooking Berger's concerned frown. "It's like that fat prick in Cleveland wanted," said Lucas. "Control. He who pays the piper calls the tune. Our law firms have paid the piper and haven't tried to call the tune."

"But Arthur Ringold is right," said Berger. "They don't have enough money."

Lucas nodded and sighed. "Yeah, I'm afraid so." He flexed his shoulders, and his eyes wandered. "Y' know, I . . . I mean, what could I do about Lela? Would *you* marry her, Dave? She wanted me to bring Melanie to California, and we'd all live together out there in her father's chalet." He stopped and shook his head.

"No, you couldn't do that," said Berger.

Lucas drank half his glass of wine. "I was stupid enough once," he said. "I wouldn't want to be twenty years old again." He shook his head. "But it would be nice to be that stupid again, to have all the confidence, all the *arrogance,* that goes with stupidity. That's a luxury. You know, that's what people really mean when they say they wish they had their youth back. They want to be as dumb as they used to be, and as optimistic."

Berger poured himself a glass of the wine. "Sure," he said.

"Show you somethin'," said Lucas. He hauled his billfold from his hip pocket, flipped through the compartments inside, and handed Berger a limp and ragged little photograph. "Catherine," he said.

The sleek plump girl in the photograph was nude, standing at what looked like a kitchen sink, opening a bottle of beer with a church-key opener. Obviously surprised by the camera, she looked as if she were howling with laughter. When Berger had looked at the picture for a moment, Lucas reached for it. He stared at it for a moment before he returned it to his billfold.

"We were so goddamn young," Lucas whispered hoarsely, unable to find his voice. "We used to go bowling, and she drank so much beer at the bowling alley that she gained ten pounds. We used to laugh. God, how we laughed! I wish I could forget everything about her but the way we laughed. She forgot how."

Lucas ate little. The rare steaks were crusted hard by the flaring yellow flame on the grill behind the counter, and he said he didn't like them that way. He nibbled at his French fries and chewed morosely on two or three bites of meat, and he sipped more wine. Conversation stopped. Lucas handed Berger two twenty-dollar bills finally and asked him to pay the check and take care of the tip.

"Gentleman sick?" the Missouri cocktail waitress

asked, genuinely concerned, as Berger led Lucas out of the restaurant.

"Tired," said Berger. It was a euphemism for drunk.

But that was not what was the matter. In his bathroom, Lucas vomited repeatedly and in the intervals lay across his bed, only half conscious and sweating. Berger was reluctant to call a doctor, for fear the diagnosis would be only that the gentleman was ingloriously drunk. He remembered that Norma had a close friend who was a nurse at Kennedy Memorial Hospital, and he called Norma and asked her to bring the nurse to the motel. In half an hour the two women arrived, and the nurse picked up the telephone and called the emergency squad.

For two days it was uncertain whether or not Lucas would live. He was suffering from acute pancreatitis, and when his father and mother arrived from Kansas City they found him in an intensive-care unit, attached to tubes, slipping in and out of a coma, unable to recognize them. After two days he began slowly to recover, and the doctors diagnosed the cause of his pancreatitis as a duodenal ulcer. He remained in the hospital for three weeks, after which his father took him home to Kansas City.

August–December 1971

THE LUCAS PAULSON who returned to San Francisco on
Monday, August 2, 1971, was a changed man. He was
thin, yet looked fit and healthy: deeply tanned, erect,
with a brisk, purposeful stride. The gray hair that had
silvered his temples had spread all across his head now,
adding shining highlights to the dark hair that was
gradually diminishing. He wore a summer-weight dark
blue jacket, gray slacks, and black loafers.

He had spent the summer in Kansas City, living with
his parents, relaxing, recovering. His doctors had insisted he should spend at least a month just lying in the
sun, swimming maybe; he could even play a little tennis
if he did not throw himself into it with too much
commitment; but he was not to travel, and he was not
to spend his time on the telephone, trying to raise
money. He had been a dutiful patient, constantly
prompted by his mother and father and by the
D'Annunzios.

Dave Berger had come to Kansas City in June and
had insisted that Lucas pay himself ten thousand dollars
out of the dwindling treasury of Electroscript, Incorporated. Reluctantly, Lucas had taken five thousand. It
had been more than enough to tide him over, even
enough to buy him some new clothes to fit his trimmer,
more muscular figure.

114

Melanie was eight now. For the first time, she had cried at the airport when he left for San Francisco. He had spent more time with her that summer than he had been able to spend with her since she was an infant, and she had learned to know her father. He felt like a parent again, and it had been difficult to leave her.

Electroscript had one full-time employee: Gabe Lincoln, who ambled about the computer center in his jeans and T-shirts, still bearded, still sometimes a little vacant from the grass he smoked, but wearing shoes and socks as a concession to the sober-sided technicians of the computer center. Dave Berger worked many hours on the transcriber but took no compensation. He was still a full-time member of the Berkeley faculty. During the summer the two of them had solved some thorny problems in the heuristic facility of the transcriber, but they were reaching a point where a new infusion of funds would be necessary if the project were not to stall. Lucas listened to them tell this during the afternoon of his arrival.

The next morning, August 3, Lucas and Berger met with Arthur Ringold.

Ringold's eyes sometimes all but disappeared behind the stream of smoke rising from the cigarettes that he often held in his mouth, letting them wobble as he talked. "To be altogether frank with you, gentlemen," he said a few minutes into their meeting, "I suspect I have you by the short hairs. You've just about exhausted your capital." He stopped and let a blob of smoke roll from between his lips. "I want to get that on the table. I want it out there because I hope you will believe I've not taken advantage of it in the proposal I've made to you."

"I don't think you've taken any unfair advantage,

Mr. Ringold," said Lucas quietly. "There are some things in your proposal that I hope we can change, but it certainly constitutes a good basis to open negotiations. So let *me* put something on the table. It is true, of course, that Electroscript is running out of money. But I'm sure you understand that what you are offering to buy is not just a bankrupt little company. It—"

"It certainly is not bankrupt," Ringold interrupted. "The system design, incomplete as it is, is a valuable property."

"No, it's not. It's worthless," said Lucas bluntly.

A wide smile came over Ringold's face, and he reached across his desk and crushed the butt of his cigarette in his big ashtray. "I think I know what you're about to tell me," he said. "But go on."

"The system design, the programming work that's been done," said Lucas gravely, "is brilliant if I do say so: a tribute to Dave Berger here and to Gabe Lincoln. But it can be duplicated. What they've done, someone else can do, given time and money. What Electroscript is worth is the loyalty of those two men. Without them, there is no Electroscript."

"Without *three* men," said Berger.

"Yes, don't omit yourself," said Ringold.

"All right," Lucas agreed. "Electroscript is brains. That's all it is, plus the reputation I've built for it among the lawyers. Maybe reputation isn't the right word. Maybe I should say anticipation."

"Good will, the accountants call it," said Arthur Ringold. "I quite agree with you, Mr. Paulson. What you have for assets is personnel and good will. I understood that when I made my offer."

The offer, which Ringold had sent to Lucas in Kansas City in mid-July, was that Electroscript was to become a wholly owned subsidiary of Ringold Aviation, which would change its name to Ringold Corporation since it would be entering a non-aviation-related field. Lucas Paulson, David Berger, and Lela Reese (Arthur Ringold not knowing that Lela had given her shares to Lucas) were to exchange their voting stock in Electroscript for shares of Ringold Corporation, on the basis of 3.5 shares of Ringold for each share of Electroscript. Ringold was traded only over-the-counter, and the last quotation was $119.50.

Lucas and Berger had discussed the offer the evening before. Lucas would receive fourteen hundred shares of Ringold for his four hundred shares of Electroscript. Berger would receive three hundred fifty shares of Ringold for his one hundred shares of Electroscript. Arthur Ringold was, in effect, offering them roughly $208,000 for Electroscript—$166,000 to Lucas and $42,000 to Berger. The preferred stock purchased by the law firms would be repurchased for what they had paid for it—one hundred dollars a share.

Another element of the proposal was that Lucas was to be the president of the Electroscript Division of Ringold Corporation, with a contract guaranteeing him five years' employment at a salary not less than $75,000 per year. Other benefits, plus a salary or consulting contract for Berger, could be negotiated.

All this was in writing, in a long letter from Arthur Ringold to Lucas, which had been sent to Kansas City two weeks ago. Lucas had the letter before him. Berger frowned over his copy. Ringold lit another cigarette as he watched the two scan the offer once more.

"I was thinking in somewhat different terms," said Lucas to Ringold. "I've been thinking about the subject all summer, as you might imagine."

"You want to make a counteroffer?" asked Ringold.

"Suppose," said Lucas, "Electroscript were to continue to exist as a corporation, rather than be merged and go out of existence. Suppose the stockholders and directors of Electroscript were to issue additional shares of the common stock and Ringold Corporation were to buy them. I'm reconciled to the idea that I have to give up control of Electroscript, so suppose the number of shares purchased by Ringold Corporation clearly gives Ringold control. On the other hand, I'd rather own a big minority interest in Electroscript than a small minority interest in Ringold Corporation."

"In other words," said Arthur Ringold, "you don't want to be diluted."

"I don't want to work my tail off to see if I can increase the profits of Ringold Corporation by two percent—or the value of my Ringold stock by one percent," said Lucas. "I'd rather work my tail off to see if I can increase the profits of Electroscript by 40 percent—and the value of my Electroscript stock accordingly."

Ringold leaned back in his chair and contemplated the burning tip of his cigarette. "You're talking about giving up about $126,000," he said.

"About $166,000," said Lucas. "I own the Lela Reese shares."

"You're willing to give that up to hold your equity?"

"I've got more than that invested in the transcriber," said Lucas. "In time and effort, lost opportunities, career . . ."

Ringold chuckled, the smoke bubbling out of his mouth. "I'm not surprised. We can turn the negotiation to something along those lines, I think."

They talked all day Tuesday and Wednesday and all Thursday morning—finally reaching the basic terms of an agreement that, over the next eight weeks, was

118

reviewed by counsel, reduced to a long written contract, and put into effect.

Under the agreement, Electroscript, Incorporated continued to exist. Electroscript issued another five hundred shares, making an even thousand. Ringold Aviation purchased six hundred—the five hundred new shares plus Berger's one hundred. With the cash Berger received for his one hundred shares, he bought two hundred shares of Lucas's stock, so that each of them now would own an equal amount of the voting stock, two hundred shares apiece. Arthur Ringold and Ringold Aviation signed a contract agreeing to borrow and invest the necessary capital to continue the development of the speech transcriber and to market it nationwide—at least five million dollars.

Arthur Ringold was elected chairman of the board of directors of Electroscript. He nominated and elected three other members. Lucas and Berger were also members. Lucas Paulson was elected president and chief operating officer of Electroscript. His employment contract guaranteed him a base salary of $75,000 per year, plus health and retirement benefits and a profit-sharing program. David Berger chose not to resign his faculty position to take employment with Electroscript, so he was given a long-term consulting contract with a guarantee of minimum annual fees of $25,000.

Repurchase of the preferred stock that had been purchased by so many law firms was a sticky point. Much of it was in the hands of bar foundations. Lucas argued that the early investors in the transcriber were entitled to something better than repurchase for their original purchase price. Ultimately, Arthur Ringold agreed to offer the preferred shareholders $110 per share. Almost all the shares came back at that price, leaving Electroscript with only a few preferred shares outstanding. Those who had them were entitled to a preference when and if Electroscript began to pay dividends.

Lucas wrote a letter to Jacob Riis, offering to reassign to him the 250 shares he had given to Lucas through Lela. Jacob Riis returned a polite but cool letter, saying he had followed his daughter's wishes with regard to the shares and would not accept their return. Lucas sold them to Electroscript on the same terms as those received by the other holders of preferred shares. It netted him $27,500. He held out $2,500 for a vacation trip for him and Melanie and put $25,000 in a trust for her education.

Lucas felt he could not yet take custody of Melanie. His duties under the new arrangements involved constant travel; besides, she was comfortable living with her grandparents, secure in their love. He talked to John and Mary D'Annunzio, and they urged him to let the little girl stay with them, at least for another year or so. He talked to Melanie, and she said she wanted her daddy to come live with grandpa and grandma. The last two weeks in August, while the lawyers were nitpicking the Ringold-Electroscript agreement, he took her to Pompano Beach, to taste saltwater for the first time and to splash in the great, rolling breakers. He took her to see the porpoises play at the Seaquarium and to see the alligators lying in the swamp water of the Everglades. When he took her home he promised they would go to Florida again during her school's Christmas vacation, and he made the reservations with a travel agency before he returned to California.

He drove his car—a Chevrolet from his father's agency—to San Francisco, and he rented a furnished apartment in San Mateo. Arthur Ringold gave him an office in the Ringold Aviation building. By the first of November, Lucas was a settled resident of California.

Wednesday, December 8. Lucas's telephone rang about eleven o'clock. It was Gabe Lincoln, calling from the Ringold-Electroscript computer center. "Hey, man. You better come over here. We got a little problem."

Lucas left his office and walked across the parking lot to the low brick building that housed the computers. Gabe Lincoln was standing in the door to the computer room, confronted by three obviously angry men.

"Here's the president of the company," Lincoln said as Lucas walked up behind them. "You can talk to him."

"Problem?" asked Lucas calmly.

"*Yes*, there's a problem," snapped William Drexel, turning to Lucas. Drexel was corporate comptroller of Ringold Corporation: a ruddy-faced former FBI agent with the broad shoulders of the athlete he had once been and the bristly crew cut with which he advertised his political philosophy. "This man—"

"Won't do a show-and-tell on the transcriber," interrupted Gabe Lincoln.

"These men," said Drexel through clenched teeth and white lips, "are from First Pacific Bank."

"Not so," said Gabe Lincoln.

"Mr. . . . uh, Paulson," said one of the other men. "I am Douglas Rupert, senior vice president, First Pacific." He was a tall, long-faced, balding man. "Before the bank can make the kind of loan your company

121

is asking for, we have to know a great deal more about this computer program than is revealed in the loan application. I've brought Mr. James Lipton, a computer consultant from the firm of Drumm, Lipton & Associates. Mr. Lipton will examine your system design and advise the bank."

Lipton nodded. He was a dark, solid, youngish man, wearing an IBM business suit and shoes and still facing Gabe Lincoln with an aggressive scowl. He turned to Lucas. "I have quite a few questions," he said.

"I imagine you do," said Lucas. "You understand, of course, that we're not going to answer them."

"Just what's *that* supposed to mean?" demanded Drexel.

Lucas smiled at him. "We're not giving away the business, that's all. We're not giving Drumm, Lipton, or any other consultants a crash course in heuristic speech transcribers." He spoke to Lipton. "It's a pretty straightforward design. You can probably guess the basics. But we've invested a lot of time and money in identifying the problems and solving most of them, and I'm not going to tell you what those problems are or how we solve them. Nothing personal, of course."

"That may make it impossible for our bank to make the loan," said Rupert bluntly.

"We're not pledging the system design as security for the loan," said Lucas. "We're borrowing on the credit of Ringold Corporation. If your bank doesn't want to make the loan on that basis . . ." He shrugged. "So be it."

"No bank," said Rupert grimly, "is going to lend you a million dollars without a thorough examination of the computer system."

"No other bank," Lucas responded bluntly, "is going to bring its pet consulting firm around and try to arrange for it a free education in a highly confidential new system design."

"Are you accusing us of—"

"You bet I am. What's more, I give you about two minutes to get off the premises, before I call one of the guards and have you escorted off."

"This is outrageous!" cried Rupert.

"I think so," said Lucas.

Rupert glared at Drexel, whose face had turned bright pink. "You may regard the loan application as denied," he said.

As the banker and the consultant stalked out of the building, Gabe Lincoln began to laugh. "Crazy, man, crazy," he said.

Drexel shot an angry glance at Lincoln, then turned to Lucas. "I have my very grave doubts you understand what you've done," he growled.

"I'll understand better after I speak with the president of First Pacific Bank," said Lucas.

"What are you going to do, call and apologize?"

"Why? Because one of his vice presidents has a cozy relationship with a consulting outfit and tried to worm it in here for a little industrial espionage? My question is, does the president know it?"

"You have a vivid imagination, Paulson."

"Good for me," said Lucas. "And let's get something else straight. Hereafter, if you have any questions about the operations of Electroscript or want to bring visitors here to see it, you come to me. Don't come in here and make demands on people who work for me."

"I am the comptroller of the parent corporation," said Drexel. "I will ask any questions I choose of anyone I choose."

"My staff will have standing orders not to talk to you," said Lucas. "On the ground that you are a potential leak. You were trying to give away the store this morning. When you talk to Art Ringold, be sure you tell him that part of the story."

Lucas returned to Kansas City for Christmas; and, as he had promised Melanie and arranged, he flew with her to Pompano Beach the day after Christmas. It was during that week that she asked him if she could leave the parochial school after this year and go to the public school for her fourth-grade year. When they returned to Kansas City he discussed her request with her D'Annunzio grandparents. They showed him a letter from Sister Teresa Immaculata, Melanie's teacher.

"Melanie is an exceptionally bright child," it read. "She has completely recovered from the loss of her mother and seems emotionally stable. I must suggest, however, that her independence of mind and spirit are troubling. She is the most inquisitive child I have ever encountered and the most determined to follow her own lines of inquiry, no matter where they may lead. She needs careful and constant guidance, lest independence develop into rebelliousness."

Although Melanie's grandmother was troubled by the decision, her grandfather agreed with Lucas that Melanie should be enrolled in a public school, not next September but immediately. Lucas stayed over in Kansas City for a week, until Melanie was settled in her new school. She left the parochial school as a third-grade student, but on the basis of her scores on a set of admission tests, she was received in the fourth grade in the public school. She took that as a triumph, and when he left her she was beaming with happy pride.

Lucas arrived back in San Francisco on Saturday, January 8, 1972. He telephoned Dave Berger, and

Dave and Norma asked him to come to their apartment for drinks, then to go out to dinner that evening. He went. He wasn't drinking anything at the time but an occasional beer or a glass of white wine, and that night for the first time since his pancreatitis attack he accepted a Scotch and soda. They were settled in to talk when the telephone rang.

Dave went to the bedroom to answer, and after a couple of minutes he returned and dropped heavily onto the couch beside Norma. His shoulders were round and slack, and he glanced first at Norma, then at Lucas, shaking his head.

"What is it, Dave? What's wrong?"

Berger drew a deep breath. "Lela . . ." he said. "That was the police, Marin County. They want me to come out there. I . . . They wouldn't say, but I think she's dying. They—"

"I'll go with you," said Lucas firmly.

It took an hour to drive to the hospital. By the time they arrived, Lela was dead. They sat down in a small conference room with a police detective, under a bank of glaring, blinking fluorescent tubes. The room was filled with a blue haze from the detective's cigarette smoke.

"I called you, Professor, because we found your name and number in the little telephone pad in the house. And Mr. Paulson . . . ?"

"He's a close friend," said Berger. "We are—were—both her . . . closest friends."

"You haven't even told us what happened to her," said Lucas.

"OD," said the detective. "Heroin. But maybe a suicide. She was on the beach, in a little cove under that big house her family has. The stuff was there, and the syringe. It looked like maybe she'd sat down on the beach and shot the stuff, like maybe she thought the tide would come up and get her. Anyway, some guys in a boat going by, they saw her. We were able to get her to the hospital, but . . . Do either of you have any idea where she was getting the stuff?"

"What do you mean, 'getting' it?" Lucas asked. "Are you saying she was a user?"

The detective nodded. "Tracks on her arms. Yes, sir, she had a real habit. Are you guys telling me you haven't seen her for a long time?"

"Yeah," Lucas muttered. "Some good friends she had, huh? Jesus Christ! Lela!"

8

1972

THE TRANSCRIBER WAS worthless, as Lucas repeatedly pointed out, until it was attached to a communications system. Without communications capacity, the transcriber could listen only to voices spoken in the computer center, could display and print a transcript only at the length of a wire attached directly to the computer. Neither Dave Berger nor Gabe Lincoln was an expert in computer communications, so, in the spring of 1972, Lucas stole a man from IBM. Martin Kent joined the staff of Electroscript, with responsibility for making the transcriber listen and talk coast to coast. By August, he was ready with an initial demonstration.

On Thursday, August 24, a CCI terminal was set up in a motel room in Oakland, roughly eighteen miles from the computer center in San Mateo, and a small group was invited to see the transcriber operate in something approaching a realistic environment. Lucas was there, with Dave Berger and Martin Kent. Arthur Ringold was there, with two other directors of Electroscript. John Paisley, president of First Pacific Bank, was there. The men gathered in the sitting room of the tenth-floor suite and drank coffee and munched Danish as Kent ran through some last-minute tests with Gabe Lincoln, who remained in the computer center, troubleshooting at that end.

The CCI terminal consisted of a small Sony color television set, a steel box of electronics under the table, a keyboard, and a communications modem. As the group watched curiously, the screen filled with characters and Kent sat with the telephone pinned between his cheek and shoulder as he talked with Gabe Lincoln. Twenty minutes after the hour when the demonstration had been scheduled to begin, Kent turned to Lucas, nodded, and rose from the chair. He stood aside and continued talking quietly on the telephone as Lucas sat down at the terminal.

"Gentlemen," said Lucas, "I'd like to be as brief as possible, so that we can go directly to the demonstration. I do have to say, however, that what we are doing here is communicating across the Bay to San Mateo by microwave, not by telephone. For the moment, we and the telephone company continue to work on some difficult problems. One of our alternatives is, of course, microwave transmission. We have a dish on the roof of the motel and one on the roof of the Ringold Corporation building in San Mateo. The computer and the terminal have been communicating accurately for the past few minutes. The reason we've been delayed was for some final adjustments and accuracy checks. Martin is also talking to the computer center by telephone—that is, talking to another human being in the center. For that purpose, the telephone seems to work just fine."

He got the appreciative little murmur of laughter he had hoped would serve to lighten the atmosphere of the meeting just a bit.

"All right. I will speak into the microphone here, and the system should print what I say on the terminal screen. Okay. Good morning, Electroscript."

The screen was blue and blank. Two seconds after

Lucas spoke, a line of white letters appeared across the top:

GOOD MORNING ELECTROSCRIPT

"Are you ready to listen to some speech?"

ARE YOU READY TO LISTEN TO SOME SPEECH

"This is Mr. John Paisley, president of First Pacific Bank. He will talk to you."

THIS IS MISTER JOHN PASELY PRESIDENT OF FIRST PACIFIC BANK. HE WILL TALK TO YOU.

"Let me point out two things, gentlemen, before I hand over the microphone. First, notice that the transcriber did put a period at the end of my first sentence. That is because I paused there. Otherwise, the operator would have to insert the period, or it would have to be inserted by the reporter's office. Let me show you, though, how we correct the spelling of the name."

Lucas turned to the screen, used the keys to bring the cursor to the name, and typed the correct spelling. "All right, sir. Would you begin by introducing yourself to the computer?"

The small, squat banker took the microphone. "I am John Paisley," he said self-consciously.

I AM JOHN PAISLEY

"Notice," said Lucas. "It has learned to spell the name."

"Damn good!" exclaimed Paisley.

DAM GOOD

Paisley laughed.

XXX XXX XXXXX XXX XXXX

"All right," said Lucas. "It is telling us it doesn't understand. You laughed into the microphone. The computer heard the sound but doesn't recognize the sound of laughter as words."

"It's marvelous," said Paisley. "When you going to teach it to laugh, Lucas?"

ITS MARVELUS WHEN YOU GOING TO TEACH IT TO LAF
LUCAS

"We still have a few problems, as you can see," said
Lucas.

"I'd judge you are getting them under control," said
Paisley.

I'D JUDGE %$$%&&***%/\%$£ CUN&%$%$%£

"Microwave interference," said Kent immediately.
"He's got it on the screen in the center. I mean, Gabe's
got the words over there. Something, uh, in the trans-
mission back here."

Ten months later, on June 6, 1973, they performed a
similar demonstration in a room in the London Hilton.
Communication was through ordinary voice-grade tele-
phone circuits, running through wires to the Post Office
Tower in central London, from there to a satellite, then
down to a receiving station in the States, and finally by
AT&T microwave and wires to the computer center in
San Mateo.

The London demonstration was a dramatic success
for Electroscript, better than anything they had been
able to achieve so far in the United States. In the
morning a small group of judges, barristers, and solici-
tors were reservedly appreciative. Of the news media
representatives invited, only two appeared, one from
The Times, a tweedy old fellow to whom computer
technology was mysterious and threatening, but also
one from *Financial Times,* young and knowledgeable
and crisply skeptical. Late in the morning they received
a call from Buckingham Palace, saying that His Royal
Highness Prince Philip, Duke of Edinburgh, on whose
behalf the palace had earlier sent regrets that he would
be unable to attend a demonstration of a heuristic

speech transcriber, had found a break in his appointments schedule and would like to see the transcriber at two o'clock. He appeared promptly at two, followed by Her Majesty's minister of transportation and communication. By 2:15 the suite was crowded with reporters, including Americans from UPI and the AP.

"Can you teach it to spell 'labour,' 'colour,' and so forth, in the English manner, or does it always write American?" Prince Philip asked. He had spoken into the microphone Lucas held up, and the transcriber printed:

CAN YOU TEACH IT TO SAY LABOUR COLOUR AND SO FORTH IN THE ENGLISH MANNER OR DOES IT ALWAYS SPEAK AMERICAN.

As the prince laughed, Lucas explained that they had programmed in many English spellings in preparation for the London demonstration.

"Anyway, it doesn't punctuate very well yet, does it?" the prince observed.

"Lots of problems remain to be solved," said Lucas.

"I hope you don't require as many years to teach it punctuation as my teachers required to teach it to me," said the prince.

"We are optimistic," said Lucas.

"Actually, I should say you've achieved nothing much short of a miracle in teaching it to cope with varying accents, English and American," said the prince. "It seems to understand me better than American reporters do."

"Teaching it to understand you is simple compared to teaching it to understand a Texan, say, or a Brooklyn cabbie," said Lucas. "I have a staff of twenty working on English-language accents."

"They have work yet to do," laughed Prince Philip,

pointing at the screen. The system had continued to transcribe the conversation, and it had transcribed Lucas's word "accent" correctly but the prince's pronunciation of the same word as "aksunt."

They were operating a printer in one of the bedrooms of the suite and so were able to present the prince with a souvenir transcript of his entire conversation with Lucas Paulson, some fifteen minutes of talk that had rolled across the screen and disappeared but had been dumped in the printer's buffer and printed at a slower speed.

After the prince left, the reporters crowded around the terminal, and the demonstrations and interviews continued all afternoon. Most of the American lay public learned of Electroscript for the first time from a two-minute network story on the evening news, transmitted by satellite from London.

On Thursday, June 28, 1973, the board of directors of Ringold Corporation met in a conference room in its headquarters building in San Mateo. Lucas Paulson and David Berger were summoned to report on the progress of Electroscript. Lucas took ten minutes to report their London triumph.

"In short, we were in communication between London and San Mateo for six hours and forty-five minutes, and during all that time we took only three interruptions: one of two minutes, the other two of less than half a minute. I need hardly tell you that reliability is essential, and the kind of reliability we achieved in communication to and from London approaches that total reliability we have to achieve to make the transcriber commercially feasible."

"You achieved it principally by redundancy, as I

understand it," said Robert Morgan, one of the directors. "In other words, you kept *two* transatlantic telephone circuits alive for six hours and forty-five minutes."

"Yes," said Lucas. "The interruptions were in the equipment here in San Mateo. If we'd had redundancy here, we'd have experienced no interruptions at all."

"Are we to understand then that each Electroscript installation is going to require double communications lines and double equipment?"

Lucas nodded. "For the foreseeable future, yes."

"And similarly, everything in the computer center will have to have a backup?"

"Every reliable system has redundancy," said Lucas.

"Which doubles the cost, I suppose," said Morgan, nodding glumly.

"Not exactly," said Lucas. "But . . . as a point of departure for a discussion, I'll accept that."

Morgan was a thin man of less than medium height, with a weathered, mobile face. He spoke slowly with a Midwestern twang. "Point is," he said now, "you've run through the five million dollars this company promised you, you're talking about another five, and you don't have a commercially feasible system yet. How many more dollars, Mr. Paulson?"

"I believe you will agree we've made a tremendous amount of progress in the past two years," said Lucas.

"Oh, I have no doubt," said Morgan. "The transcriber's an impressive machine. But it's no good for anything yet."

"Put it this way, Mr. Morgan," Dave Berger intervened. "Suppose we were building an automobile. Everything's fine: a great engine, a fine transmission, air conditioning, comfortable seats, a wonderful radio

133

. . . but we haven't quite succeeded in finding the right wheels for it. It's no good for anything, but the work done has by no means been wasted."

"My question," said Morgan emphatically, "is how long it's going to take to find those wheels and how much you think it's going to cost."

"I would like," said Lucas, "to have a pilot project going within the next six months. Roughly estimated, we will need another two million dollars or so to keep the organization going and finish the developmental work necessary to support a pilot project. The project itself will cost two or three hundred thousand dollars at least."

"What *is* this pilot project?" asked Morgan.

"To a degree this is confidential," said Lucas. "I have discussed with the senior litigation partner in a major Chicago law firm the idea of using the Electroscript system to transcribe the depositions they will be taking later this year in a very important antitrust case. It's an attractive proposition because the depositions will be taken in San Francisco. If opposing counsel will agree—"

"What will they pay for the service?" asked Morgan.

"Nothing in cash," said Lucas. "Since they can't yet be absolutely sure the system will work, they'll back it up with their usual stenographic service. That means it will cost them just as much as ever to produce the record. But they will allow us to use their name. If we can go out afterward and say this firm used Electroscript successfully, if we can advertise that our system transcribed an important deposition in a big case . . . Well, it will put us in the business."

"How long will this project continue?"

"Eight weeks or so. The system will have to run

optimally for eight weeks, without breakdowns or grinches."

"And after that we can start selling it?" Morgan asked. "Start earning revenue?"

Lucas nodded. "Assuming the pilot project is successful."

Morgan pursed his lips and nodded skeptically. He turned to Arthur Ringold, who was just crushing a cigarette in an oversized glass ashtray. "Are you satisfied with this, Art?"

Ringold nodded. "I never believed we'd bring it in for five million—as I told you two years ago."

"Will the bank go along with another five million?"

Ringold shook his head. "Not First Pacific. We've reached our limit with them. I've spoken to United California. They'll lend us what we need."

"On the credit of the Ringold Corporation, I suppose," said Morgan.

Ringold nodded as he tapped another Pall Mall from his package. "Betting the company," he said.

"Uhmm," said Morgan, nodding, frowning, again pursing his lips. "Awright. More borrowing will require specific authority from the board, so we'll be taking more looks at this. Meantime, Mr. Paulson, I have some other questions."

"Certainly," said Lucas.

"Question is, do you think you're running Electroscript as economically as possible? I mean, considering the fact that it runs entirely on borrowed money, not on anything it earns, don't you think it behooves you to save money when you can?"

Lucas nodded. "Absolutely."

"I'm looking at a list of the hotels where you stay when you travel," said Morgan. "Warwick in Houston.

135

Waldorf in New York. Pontchartrain in Detroit. Hyatt Regency in Chicago. Barclay in Philadelphia. And so on—all first-class, expensive hotels. Mr. Drexel supplied this list from your expense-account statements. You stay at the best, don't you?"

"Bob," interrupted Arthur Ringold. "I don't think we should go into this kind of stuff. Lucas is the president of a subsidiary company, not a salesman. I don't think we need to nit-pick his expense accounts."

"I'm willing," said Lucas thinly.

"I'm not," said Ringold abruptly.

"All right," said Morgan. "When you went to England, Mr. Paulson, you took along a young woman named Jocelyn Merritt. Right? Who's she, and why did she travel to England at the expense of the company?"

"She did more than travel at the expense of Electroscript, Mr. Morgan," said Lucas. "We also paid her a fee of four hundred dollars a day for the twelve days she was in England. Mrs. Merritt is a highly qualified consultant in the field of corporate public relations, and she's done some important work for us. She arrived in London a week before I did. By the time I got there, she had done extensive work, setting up the meetings at the Hilton, issuing invitations, getting out news releases, initiating the contact with Buckingham Palace that ultimately resulted in our getting the Duke of Edinburgh to our suite. . . . And she did follow-up. I—"

"That was an expensive trip, wasn't it?"

"Very expensive. It was Mrs. Merritt's idea, as a matter of fact. We had had little success in getting media attention for Electroscript until she came up with the idea of doing a demonstration as far away as England, showing the system transmitting and receiving over thousands of miles. We'd held a New York press conference and got almost nothing out of it. London . . . Well, I need hardly tell you."

"A publicity stunt."

"It has produced hundreds of inquiries from firms and companies wanting to know when they can use Electroscript. Someday some of those will turn into contracts."

"You and Mrs. Merritt are pretty good friends, too, aren't you?"

"Yes, quite good friends."

"So I've heard," said Morgan dryly.

Lucas repeated the conversation to her that evening over dinner at Chez Panisse in Berkeley. Jocelyn lifted her eyebrows slightly, sipped Dom Pérignon, and changed the subject.

She was not likely to care. Electroscript was only one of her clients and not her best one. At thirty-one, she was an acknowledged wizard in her business, one of the most effective public-relations counselors in the country. She stressed that Merritt & Associates was a firm of consultants, advisors in the field of corporate public relations, and emphatically not a gaggle of flamboyant flacks. She did not mount campaigns. She did not play tricks to gain media attention for her clients. She did not do hype. She taught businessmen how to win the respect of the news media and to nurse their own messages, not reporters' condensations with comment, into print or onto the air.

The demonstration in London had—as Lucas had said—been her idea. It had been her idea to send the invitation to the palace; and she had, through calls and correspondence, learned exactly how to do it. The invitation had been correctly worded and in perfect form, so that when it reached the palace staff it had been considered, not just disposed of with a form rejection. She had sent other invitations to the inns of court and still others to the ministries. When word came late in the morning that the Duke of Edinburgh would appear, she made discreet calls to a few acquaintances at the papers and at the BBC. After the meetings, she composed and sent the proper letters of appreciation. Finally, she prepared a folder, containing a small brochure on Electroscript, selected clippings from British and American newspapers and magazines, and a color photograph of Prince Philip laughing with Lucas Paulson.

Jocelyn was as tall as Lucas. She was boyishly slender. She wore her dark brown hair clipped very short around her head; her dark blue eyes lay beneath arched brows and lazy lids. Her skin was flawless, and the bones of her cheeks and jaw firmly outlined the classic shape of her long face. She was the kind of woman who was never overlooked and not soon forgotten by anyone who saw her. She knew it, accepted the admiration she received, and took full advantage.

"Do you want to read Swanberg on Luce?" she asked.

"Have you finished it?"

"Not quite, but I will later this evening—that is . . . I will if you go home," she said, showing so faint a trace of a smile that he would not have detected it if he had not been experienced with her.

"That depends on your sense of values," he said. "What's more important? Book or—"

"Cock," she said, finishing his sentence. She spoke the word quietly, without a smile, arching one eyebrow slightly as she glanced up from her champagne.

"Well, which is? Which is more important?"

She settled a cool gaze on him. "Are you capable of a memorable performance?"

Lucas smiled. "Huh-uh. No."

"Well, then . . ."

"Of course," he said with a shrug, "if *you* are capable of a memorable performance, you might inspire one from me."

"Rationalization," she said blandly.

They ate the inspired cuisine of Alice Waters—this evening the main course was veal with mushrooms in a light, mysterious sauce, served with selected fresh California vegetables *au dent*. Chez Panisse was Jocelyn's find; it had been open only one year, and few people had as yet discovered that one of the finest restaurants in America was to be found in Berkeley. Her specialty was knowing things like this; and she had made it another specialty to educate Lucas.

For the moment, neither of them was seeing anyone else, though neither had made any promises. She had encouraged him to buy a condominium near her own, in Sausalito, where from their small balconies they had a view of the Bay. When he left her bed, he could walk the short distance to his own condominium.

She never visited his bedroom. She invited him to hers: an airy room crowded with flowering plants growing in pots and tubs, the white walls decorated with bright abstract prints, two of them, on close examination, boldly erotic. Her sheets were invariably smooth, cool, and lightly scented. She liked the room fully lighted when they went to bed.

Jocelyn did not like romping, sweaty sex. What she liked was for him to lie on his back on her bed, and she would straddle his thighs, lowering herself until his erect phallus was thrust deep inside her. Then, sitting

139

high and solemn, with hardly any movement except rhythmic contractions of her internal muscles, squeezing him and releasing again and again at a studied pace, she would bring herself to repeated climaxes. His single orgasm, when at last it came, was invariably long and complete, draining him.

Their sex was quiet and prolonged. Always she wore on her naked body whatever jewelry she had worn during the day, dusted herself with subtly perfumed talcum powder, and freshened her dark makeup if necessary. Though she always uncovered her small breasts, often she kept her skirt on, or a half slip, spreading a canopy of bright silk over her thighs and his. Usually there was quiet music on her stereo, and chilled wine or champagne at hand for sipping. Almost always they talked quietly until she approached a peak where her face flushed and she closed her eyes and her words stopped. Finally, when he would have liked to go to sleep in her bed, she would gently usher him to the door. She let him wonder how she looked when she awoke mornings.

"Surprise," he said quietly when she lifted her white slip that night.

"What you wanted," she said.

He had suggested she shave off her pubic hair. From the tiny wisp that had afforded an odd little accent to her lower belly to the other wisps that grew on her inner thighs, she had removed all her hair and was smooth and talcumed. It was strange: Jocelyn was a little shy about this, and she lowered her slip over her hips as soon as she could.

Lucas reached up and pushed it back. He was fascinated by the way her body conformed itself to the shape of his penis. He had not fully realized before how similarly a woman's oral and vaginal lips constricted on an entering male organ.

Smiling at him with that mysterious, faintly superior smile she often affected during sex, Jocelyn closed her eyes and sighed.

"Hey," he said suddenly.

She opened her eyes. "Hmmm?"

"I want to do it the other way."

"What other way?"

"You on your back."

"It's not as good. Be grateful for what you've got."

"Even so . . ."

"Seriously?" she asked, opening her eyes wide.

"Have you ever done it?"

"Of course I have," she said. "I—"

"Then?"

"But *why*, Lucas? This is supposed to be the . . . the *supreme* erotic experience of them all."

He smiled. "It's cold," he said. "I want to feel your warmth."

She lifted her chin high. "What if I'm not particularly warm?"

"You're warm," he said.

She was. When they were finished, she snuggled up to him and told him it had been good. Then they went to sleep together.

9

CHRISTMAS WAS ON Tuesday. Lucas flew to Kansas City on the preceding Thursday. On Christmas day he opened presents with Melanie at her D'Annunzio grandparents' house, took her to Christmas dinner with her Paulson grandparents, and packed her suitcase on Christmas night, since she was flying back to San Francisco with him the next morning.

She loved his apartment in Sausalito. She loved the view of the Bay. Melanie was ten years old now and had developed—perhaps from the teaching of her D'Annunzio grandmother—what he supposed was a womanly concern for her father's living arrangements. He was unable to discourage her from running the vacuum cleaner and sorting and restacking his dishes and pans. She had grown into a beautiful, graceful child, but one who was maturing too quickly, he thought. To his surprise, she liked Jocelyn; she saw a style in her that she had never before seen in a woman; and she was ingenuous in her admiration and curiosity.

"My mother died," she told Jocelyn. "Of course, my mother and father were divorced before that. Did your husband die? Or are you just divorced?"

"Just divorced," said Jocelyn.

"Do you have any children?"

"No. No children."

142

A flicker of understanding passed across both their faces, and Lucas, who had been about to interrupt the questions, held back and let them talk.

"Maybe I shouldn't ask so many questions," said Melanie.

"I'm glad you ask questions," said Jocelyn. "If you ask any I don't want to answer, I just won't answer."

"My grandmothers," said Melanie soberly, "say I ask too many questions." She frowned and tipped her head. "That's because they try to keep me from finding things out." She shook her head and added, "It doesn't work."

On New Year's Eve they were invited to a dinner party at the Ringolds'. Lucas had declined, since his daughter would be with him; but Mrs. Ringold had called him before he went to Kansas City, to insist that Melanie was more than welcome and would not be the only child there. The invitation was so emphatic that he felt he could not refuse, so the three of them went together: Lucas, Jocelyn, and Melanie.

The Ringold home was a great old Victorian mansion with a wide, shady porch that circled three sides, gables, and corner towers with conical slate roofs. Inside it was all dark red draperies, Oriental rugs, buff-and-pink wallpaper, heavy plush furniture, and dark oak—and a hundred people milling through all the rooms, jostling the dozen young waiters and waitresses carrying trays of drinks and food.

"I thought it was a sit-down dinner," Lucas muttered to Jocelyn. "Christ!"

Jocelyn eyed the throng with cool insouciance. "We'll enjoy it, I'm sure," she said.

The men wore dinner jackets, the women cocktail dresses. Jocelyn wore red, green, and violet taffeta. Her shoulders were bare, and a necklace of white gold

143

and diamonds lay around her throat. Melanie was pretty in a little-girl's white frock. Melanie secretly wished that she wore colors as beautiful as Jocelyn's instead of what she thought of as her communion dress.

"Ah, good evening, Lucas," said Arthur Ringold. He was a bit unsteady and looked faintly ludicrous in his dinner jacket, with gray cigarette ash streaking one of his satin lapels. "And Mrs. Merritt, so nice to see you. And . . . Melanie!"

"It's a wonderful big party, Arthur," said Lucas. "I didn't realize."

"We do it on New Year's, about every other year. This time in honor of my wife's brother, here from New York. I'd like you to meet someone, by the way. Have you had a drink? Uh, Susie! Is that champagne? Two, please. And for the little girl . . . ginger ale, dear?"

Melanie had stepped back a pace, in real fear of the lit cigarette with which he gestured.

"Uh, yes," Arthur went on. "I want you to meet someone. I . . . right here! Ah, General!"

A man with a studied military bearing turned slowly and looked down at Arthur Ringold. His hair was gray, his eyes cold blue, his skin tanned. He was a handsome man, and he looked past Arthur Ringold and settled an appreciative gaze on Jocelyn.

"Uh, Mrs. Jocelyn Merritt, Lucas Paulson, and his daughter Melanie," bubbled Arthur. "Let me introduce General Matthew Fraser. General Fraser is a vice president of United Northeastern Industries."

General Fraser bowed to Jocelyn, lifted her hand to his lips, and murmured that he was pleased to meet her. He smiled down at Melanie without a word. "Paulson, you say?" he said to Lucas. "Electroscript, hmm? I've heard a great deal about you. Good to meet you."

"We've met before," said Lucas coldly.

"I don't believe so," said General Fraser firmly. He nodded. "If you'll excuse me. My wife . . ." He turned and walked away.

"I think you've just been put down," said Jocelyn quietly to Lucas.

"Probably he doesn't remember me," said Lucas grimly. "He's the chicken-shit colonel who damn near got me killed in Vietnam."

"How'd he do that?" asked Arthur.

Lucas glanced down at Melanie, who, distracted, was not listening. "By being an incompetent ass," said Lucas.

"Retired major general," said Jocelyn. "Vice president UNI." She nodded. "Subject of a profile in *Fortune* a few months ago. Are you curious as to why he's here?"

Lucas shook his head.

"You had better be. UNI is aggressively acquiring technology. Ringold could be a target. Electroscript could be."

Lucas shook his head again. Arthur smiled and shrugged and walked away.

"It's going to strain Ringold to borrow more than another ten million, and you're going to need more than that," Jocelyn went on.

"No. No, not that much. Anyway—"

"You haven't even looked at marketing costs yet," she said.

"I have nothing ready to sell."

"Precisely. Ten more million. Twenty more million . . . You're going to outgrow Ringold. That could be why the general is here. I'd want to know, if I were you."

Lucas looked across the room where General Fraser was talking gravely to one of Ringold's vice presidents. "New Year's Eve," he said to Jocelyn. "I suppose I should wonder what's so important as to bring him out here on New Year's Eve."

The general gave him another opportunity for conversation half an hour later, when he sought out Jocelyn, favored her with a short but courtly bow, and told her that she was the most beautiful woman at the party.

"If I had not been brought here by the most handsome man, General, I would reciprocate the compliment," she said.

General Fraser looked around. "Where's the little girl?" he asked.

"Upstairs watching television and sharing a tea party with another little girl her age," said Lucas. "We're going to take her home shortly."

"My own daughter is seven," said the general. "She was born in Japan."

"Melanie was born while I was in Vietnam," said Lucas—his final attempt at prompting General Fraser to remember.

"I was in Korea when my son was born," said the general. "That is, my son by my first wife. He'll graduate from the Point next spring." He smiled. "There are thirteen years between my two children." His expression darkened as he seemed to detect that Jocelyn had withdrawn from a conversation she did not find stimulating and was looking past him. "Anyway . . . I understand you are responsible for the London show that won so much attention for Electroscript, Mrs. Merritt."

"It was the product that won attention," said Jocelyn smoothly. "I did some public-relations work."

"I'd like to see a demonstration," said the general to Lucas.

"It can be arranged. Will you be in San Francisco long?"

"No. I'm flying back to New York tomorrow evening. Will you be showing the service in New York?"

"I'd like to. We have no plans."

"I suggested to Art Ringold," said the general, "that you bring your system to the Tech Serv show—the annual trade show of the National Technological Services Association. I hope I'll see you there."

The show was held in June at the New York Hilton. In spite of every objection that Lucas could raise—that it was a waste of time and money, that potential customers for Electroscript would not be there, that they would wind up just showing their system to industry spies—Arthur Ringold insisted it was important to take Electroscript to the New York show, and he pushed at Lucas the money for a booth on the trade-show floor and a suite for VIP shows. He insisted, too, on making the non-technological arrangements through a New York trade-show management company.

The show opened on June 19. The booth, a plywood construction painted with an attention-getting geometric pattern in red, yellow, and orange, occupied a central site in the convention hall and was big enough for two Electroscript terminals—though the computer was still only capable of talking with one. The Sony television sets Electroscript used as monitor screens had been supplemented with twenty-seven-inch Magnavox sets, placed on high pedestals, so that the transcripts flowing down the tubes could be read from ten feet away. Pretty young models in red, yellow, and orange corselets and black stockings passed out

147

Electroscript brochures through the hall. Two other smiling girls stood just before the booth, and invited everyone to come in and see "speech transcribed by computer."

Another terminal was set up in the Electroscript suite. In one of the bedrooms a company command post, with telephone lines to the booth as well as to California, had been installed. As the show opened, Dave Berger and Martin Kent manned two telephones, hissing orders, growling complaints.

Arthur Ringold stood by the bedroom door, pale and grim, sucking on a cigarette. He turned to Lucas, who was at the terminal, which was for now slaved to the one that was alive in the booth, so they could see how the show was going.

"Lucas," whispered Ringold hoarsely. "If we look like a bunch of incompetent idiots here, we're out of business. You understand that?"

"Well, let the boys do what they have to do," said Lucas. "Leave them alone."

"If it isn't working two minutes before the doors open downstairs, then when's it going to work?" Ringold demanded.

Lucas looked up into his face. Arthur Ringold was not angry; he was frightened.

Dave Berger appeared in the bedroom door and tossed his chin to summon Lucas. "There's a problem in the active terminal downstairs," he said.

"Well, shift to the backup."

"Can't. The son of a bitch has a bad board in it. One's on its way from Los Angeles, but it won't be here before five this afternoon."

"That means this one goes down," said Lucas.

Berger nodded. "It has to be unhooked. I have to

have a union electrician do that. I have to be escorted down by hotel security. I—"

"Fuck all that," said Lucas. "Move it."

Berger nodded. "Wish me luck," he whispered.

Lucas hurried to the elevator and went down to the convention floor. Since no one had told the Electroscript girls to hold off, the first registrants were wandering into the exhibit area.

"What's the matter with it?" Lucas asked a young man and young woman huddled over the terminal.

The young man looked up. "Overheating, Mr. Paulson," he said. "It'll work five minutes and then—"

"Well, *why* is it overheating?" Lucas demanded.

The young man—his name was Winkel, Lucas recalled—knelt by the controller box under the table: a steel box filled with all the electronic components of the terminal. The box was open at the top and back and was turned around, and Winkel pointed to the cooling fan. Lucas knelt beside him and peered into the box.

"Blade got broken in the move from California," he said. He pointed to a small plastic fan blade mounted on the thin shaft of a little electric motor. "Just broken enough that it's loose on the shaft. The motor runs, the blade turns a little, but it's not tight on the shaft, so it won't turn fast and blow air over the rectifier."

"Pull the blade off the other one," said Lucas, pointing at the terminal disabled by a bad board.

Winkel shook his head. "I'd have done that half an hour ago," he said. "But they're bonded to the shaft— that is, glued. It'd break pulling off. It'd be loose just like this one."

"Switch the whole unit," said Lucas. "Motor and all."

"Have to cut rivets," said Winkel. "I've sent out for

149

a little hacksaw and for bolts to replace the rivets. . . ." He glanced at his watch. "Half an hour maybe. Forty-five minutes. Maybe the one from upstairs will be here faster."

Lucas glanced around. Two curious men were staring at their huddle. Arthur Ringold came up behind them and tried weakly to engage them in conversation.

Lucas sighed.

"During the tests," said Winkel thinly, "we never had to run them more than five minutes. We discovered the faulty board in the other one—"

"Son of a bitch," Lucas muttered. He stood. "Uh . . ." He stepped to the front of the booth. "Miss!" He called to one of the models working before the booth. She turned. "Is that gum you're chewing?"

"Nobody said not to," said the blonde girl defensively.

"Nobody's telling you not to," said Lucas. "C'mere a minute. Look. See the little fan blade? It's not tight on the shaft, so it won't run and blow air."

"Uh-huh," she said, interested.

"Well," said Lucas. "You get down there and push your chewing gum onto the shaft and the blade. Maybe that'll stick it enough so it'll run right. If it does, that'll make you a heroine."

The girl laughed. She knelt beside the controller box and pressed the sticky pink gum all around the shaft and the blade. Lucas pointed to the power switch, and Winkel turned it on. The little fan began to whir, blowing a steady stream of cooling air across the rectifier and transformers. Lucas handed the girl a ten-dollar bill and told her to buy herself some more gum. Then he picked up the telephone to the suite and told Berger not to move the terminal.

"Uh, Lucas," said Arthur Ringold. "This is Mr. Morgenthau."

Lucas picked up the microphone by the terminal. "Good morning, Mr. Morgenthau," he said. "Speak into this. Say hello to Electroscript and tell it your name."

"Hello, Electroscript," said the pink-faced, white-haired man. "My name is William Morgenthau."

HELLO ELECTROSCRIPT. MY NAME IS WILLIAM MORGAN THAW.

At five on Thursday afternoon, the Electroscript suite was closed for a private demonstration. General Matthew Fraser and a group of other executives from United Northeastern Industries, Incorporated wanted to see what Electroscript could do.

They were twenty minutes late, and Arthur Ringold was glad of it; he insisted the technicians use the time to run repeated checks of the system, even though it had run close to flawlessly since Wednesday morning. Lucas was almost comfortable in his renewed confidence. Ringold had hired one of the models from the convention floor to come to the suite in her revealing orange corselet and serve drinks, and Lucas accepted a glass of champagne.

At 5:20, Fraser and his associates arrived, without a word of apology or explanation. The general pulled a chair closer to the terminal and asked for the microphone.

"This thing on?"

THIS THING ON

"No punctuation?"

NO PUNCTUATION

"I'll be damned."

I'LL BE DAMMED

"Ah. No profanity. How 'bout French? Can it understand hors d'oeuvres?"

AH NO PROFANITY. HOW BOUT FRENCH. CAN IT UNDERSTAND OR XXX

Dave Berger stepped between the general and the terminal and tapped the keys for a moment. "Ask it about hors d'oeuvres again," he said.

General Fraser's chin had risen, and his face clouded slightly, but he spoke into the microphone. "Hors d'oeuvres."

HORS D'OEUVRES

"Jim," said the general. "Want to try it?"

JIM. WANT TO TRY IT.

James Cahill, who had a martini in one hand, accepted the microphone in his other. "My name is James Cahill," he said.

MY NAME IS JAMES KAYHILL

"No," said Cahill as Berger reached for the keyboard. "We understand you can tell it to spell a word or name correctly. I mean, suppose my name were Katz, though. How would you teach it to distinguish between the name Katz and the plural form of the word "cat"?"

"All right," said Berger. "Talk to it, using the name and the word."

Cahill looked over his glasses and grinned. "All right. My name is James Katz. I own four cats."

MY NAME IS JAMES CATS. I OWN FOUR CATS.

"Okay," said Berger, again reaching to the keys. "One way we can fix that is . . . Okay. Say something similar."

"James Katz likes cats," said Cahill.

JAMES KATZ LIKES CATS.

"Simple word association," said Berger. "I told it to

hear 'Katz,' not 'cats,' when the preceding word was 'James.' Of course, we could teach it similarly if the word were 'mister,' or 'Jim,' and so on."

"Time consuming," said General Fraser, "when you have to tap in the instructions on the keyboard every time."

"Right," said Lucas. "In a future version we'll use a light pen."

Cahill nodded. "Show it alternatives and pick one with the light pen, I suppose."

"Exactly," said Berger.

"So," said Cahill. "What have you done about the problem of two or more people talking at once?"

"Let's set up a demonstration of that," interjected Berger. "We have two mikes. It could be five or six. If you'll give us a moment on the keyboard, we'll identify General Fraser as microphone 1 and Mr. Cahill as microphone 2. Then . . ."

Berger tapped some keys, then handed the microphones to the two men.

"We're both supposed to talk at once?" asked General Fraser.

GENERAL FRASER: WE'RE BOTH SUPPOSED TO TALK AT ONCE

"That's what the man said," laughed Cahill.

MR. CAHILL: THAT'S WHAT THE MAN SAID

"If he said that, that's what we'll do," said the general; and simultaneously Cahill said, "Which should provide a good test."

GENERAL FRASER: IF HE SAID THAT THAT'S WHAT WE'LL DO

MR. CAHILL: WHICH SHOULD PROVIDE A GOOD TEST

"Jesus Christ!" said General Fraser.

GENERAL FRASER: JESUS CHRIST

The general handed the microphone to Berger. "Damned impressive," he said. "When you going on the market?"

Lucas stepped in and leaned against the table where the keyboard and monitor sat. "Immediately," he said. "Even if we have to patch it together with chewing gum."

_____ **10**

Summer 1974

TENSE AND ANGRY, Lucas whipped his Porsche into his parking space in the Ringold Corporation lot and stalked toward the entrance to the main building. He had slept only four hours in his room at the Hyatt Regency in Houston the night before and had taken a cab to the airport to catch the earliest flight for San Francisco. It was July 25. It had been steamy and hot in Houston, and it was no better here. The temperamental Porsche engine did not like this kind of weather and had bucked and missed at almost every gear change— contributing another annoyance to a series that had piled up over the past twelve hours.

He had returned from dinner the previous night to find the red message light blinking on his hotel-room telephone. The message at the desk was to call Professor David Berger as soon as possible.

"You had better get back here, Lucas. We've got a big problem."

"What big problem?"

"United Northeastern Industries is offering to buy Electroscript. I got an offer for my stock, delivered by telegram this afternoon. Presumably you have one waiting. What's more to the point, Ringold has one, and I think he wants to sell."

"Have you talked to Art?"

155

"Yes. He wants to meet with you and me as early as possible tomorrow morning. I've already checked the airlines. You can't get a flight out of there until about 6:30 A.M., but I suggest you be on it."

"United Northeastern . . . Meaning Fraser."

"Meaning Fraser."

"I was coming home with good news," Lucas said to Arthur Ringold. "The Texas Public Service Commission has accepted the proposal from Broughton McNair Bright & Wetzel. That big rate hearing will be transcribed on Electroscript. No shorthand reporters. No Stenotype. Just Electroscript. A quarter of a million dollars revenue, at least."

Arthur Ringold ran his hand across the top of his bald, liver-spotted head. "I, uh, restricted this meeting to the three of us," he said. "And . . . uh, ordered the coffee and Danish. I knew you had to leave Houston before breakfast."

"I ate on the plane," said Lucas.

Ringold reached across his desk to crush a butt in his huge amber-glass ashtray. "We've reached no decision," he said.

"Art . . ." Lucas sighed. "You'd like to bail out, wouldn't you? It's turned out to be too big, too much money."

"Three years ago," said Ringold thoughtfully, "we talked about five million dollars. You were trying to raise one million, and I told you you'd need five million and probably more. Well, it's approaching twelve million now. It's approaching twelve million, and we're still a long way from being commercially feasible."

"The Texas contract will prove we're commercially feasible," said Lucas.

The White Knight

"Dave," said Ringold. "Is it going to work? Can you really say it's ready?"

"It'll work," said Berger. "It will make the transcript in this Texas hearing."

Ringold nodded. "Suppose it does. Suppose we receive a check for a quarter of a million. It's going to cost more than that to run it."

"No," said Lucas.

"Yes," said Ringold. He ran his fingers under his thick, rimless glasses and rubbed his eyes wearily. "The hearing will go on for what? Two weeks? Let's suppose, optimally, we spend no more than two weeks moving in equipment, testing, getting everything ready. A month. For a month, Electroscript is committed to doing this job, demonstrating its commercial feasibility. Boys, we're spending money at a rate exceeding a quarter of a million a month. We're paying almost $50,000 a month in interest on the money we've borrowed. Payroll $110,000 . . . equipment   leases . . . telephone . . ." He shrugged.

"Your stockholders—"

"Not the problem," Ringold interrupted. "The problem is, we're running out of credit. That is, we're running out of what Ringold Corporation can afford to devote to Electroscript."

"Shortly," said Berger, "Electroscript should have credit of its own."

"Secured with what?" Ringold asked. "Accounts receivable?"

"Yes or no, Art," said Lucas. "Are you going to sell?"

"What's the difference?" Ringold asked. He shook out a Pall Mall and frowned over it as he lit it. "The offer is conditioned on sale of 75 percent, and Ringold

157

Corporation only has 60 percent. The question is, will *you* sell?"

There were one thousand shares in Electroscript: six hundred owned by Ringold Corporation and two hundred apiece by Lucas Paulson and David Berger. United Northeastern Industries offered $3,000 a share for 75 percent of the stock, conditioned on its acquiring that much. Under its proposal, Ringold Corporation would receive $1.35 million in cash and would remain a 15-percent owner in Electroscript. Paulson and Berger would receive $450,000 apiece, and each would remain a 5-percent owner. UNI would assume and refinance the Electroscript debt. Paulson was offered a vice-presidency of Electroscript, with a salary of $100,000 a year, guaranteed for five years. Berger's consulting contract would be continued for five years, with a minimum fee guaranteed, depending on how much time he committed to the company.

"I suppose," said Arthur Ringold, "I can talk my board into backing another two or three million in loans, bringing us up to fifteen million. Can you promise me Electroscript can be made self-supporting for that much?"

"No," said Lucas bluntly.

"Well, now . . ." said Berger, shaking his head. "I don't know. I . . . Three million?"

"What's the biggest problem right now?" asked Ringold.

It was a rhetorical question. They all knew. The biggest problem was that the system could only support one terminal—or maybe two at best, with some patching and compromise. To be commercially feasible, it had to support five lines, ten, or more. They were working on the problem. They knew the dimensions of

158

the solution. It would require extensive new program ming, plus the leasing of extensive new equipment. Lucas could not promise the system could be made commercially feasible for the investment of another three million dollars.

Ringold shrugged. "So what are our options?" he asked.

Lucas sighed loudly and drove one fist into the palm of his other hand. "Fraser . . ." he muttered. "Is there no alternative? Doesn't anybody else want to buy in?"

"IBM," suggested Berger. "RCA. NCR. A computer manufacturer."

Lucas shook his head. "Something like this creates a big problem for them. If they get into the business of selling computer *services,* as well as computer hardware, they are, in effect, going into competition with their own customers. That has antitrust implications, to start with, and it has bad business implications besides."

"What've you got against General Fraser?" asked Ringold.

"I worked for him once before, for a short time," said Lucas. "He doesn't remember, but *I* do, very well; and I don't like the idea of working for him again."

"In the army?"

"Yes, but since he doesn't remember, I don't want to remind him. Let's just leave it alone."

"Gentlemen," said Arthur Ringold, rolling thick white smoke off his tongue. "I am willing to explore alternatives, if anyone has any."

"What kind of security can we get for our employees?" Lucas asked.

Ringold tapped the letter containing the offer. "I

159

suppose this is negotiable. But do you authorize me to respond to the offer in a way that opens negotiations?"

Lucas nodded grimly. Berger shrugged.

On August 10, 1974, at a meeting held in the Rockefeller Center offices of United Northeastern Industries, UNI bought 75 percent of the common stock of Electroscript, Incorporated; and the documents were signed to effect the remaining elements of the acquisition agreement. A stockholders' meeting was held immediately. Arthur Ringold, but not Lucas Paulson or David Berger, was elected to the new board of directors. Then the board met. It elected General Matthew Fraser president, James Cahill senior vice president, Lucas Paulson vice president for product development . . . and so on: five vice presidents, a secretary, and a treasurer.

Cahill stopped Lucas on his way out of the meeting room. "Tell me about the contract with the Houston law firm and the State of Texas," he said.

Lucas glanced at the dozen or so men still around the meeting table, gathering up their papers and stuffing their briefcases: dark-suited, thoughtful, stiff. "Uh . . ." he said to Cahill. "It's a demonstration of the commercial feasibility of Electroscript. We'll take the transcript of a hearing. It will last maybe two weeks. Assuming we're 100 percent successful—and I think we can assume that—we'll have a new reputation."

"How firm is the commitment?" Cahill asked.

"What do you mean, how firm?"

"Is there a signed contract?"

Lucas shook his head. "A handshake."

Cahill nodded, his nervous smile spreading over his

bespectacled face. "Good," he said. "Matt wants you to get us out of it."

"Out of it? Meaning . . . ?"

"Meaning Matt wants you to get us out of it," said Cahill, his smile having now spread into an almost maniacal grin. "We have plans to improve the system in important ways, and Matt doesn't want to risk a premature showing."

"We have a commitment," said Lucas. "It's not in writing, actually, but . . ."

Cahill shrugged and turned up his hands. "Matt wants out of it," he said with an air of finality.

They assembled for dinner that evening, at Lutèce. General Fraser presided at the head of a table for eight, dominating the conversation, conferring privately with the waiter and sommelier, firmly suggesting what people should order, twice sending back dishes brought to others.

Lucas sat to the left of General Fraser, Arthur Ringold to his right. Cahill sat at the far end of the table. Officers of UNI filled the remaining seats.

"I understand you appreciate good wines," said General Fraser to Lucas early in the meal.

"I'm learning," said Lucas. "Trying to, anyway."

"You and I and Arthur are sharing this," said the general, touching the bottle of vintage wine before him. "Château Latour 1944. It should be exceptional."

"I'll acknowledge I've never had anything like it," said Lucas.

The general smiled. "Few have," he said.

A little later, Lucas raised the subject of the Texas hearing. General Fraser dismissed it quickly: "You stuck your neck out to get that contract," he said. "I appreciate that. But I want out of it. In six months we're going to have an improved system. That's the one I want to show the world, not the pre-prototype you have now."

"It puts me in an awkward position," said Lucas.

"That's what I'm paying you a hundred thousand a year for."

Lucas cocked his head and nodded. "I wondered," he said.

At the far end of the table, Berger talked with Cahill. He found him surprisingly knowledgeable. It was evident that Cahill, not General Fraser, knew about computers and had been talking with consultants who had looked at Electroscript and evaluated its strengths and weaknesses. Cahill drank. From his unguarded conversation, Berger gained the impression that the new management meant to move the company to New York as soon as possible.

"BosWash," said Cahill. "Where the money is. Not in the boonies."

"California's boonies?" Berger asked.

"Well," shrugged Cahill and waved his hand. "Everything between."

At the head of the table, General Fraser said to Lucas, "I reviewed your personnel file, Lucas. I'm having them all reviewed, of course; but I looked at yours myself. You haven't had a real vacation since—"

"It's hard to do when you're building a business," said Lucas.

"It will be the policy of this company," said General Fraser, impatient with the interruption, "for every employee, particularly those in the executive suite, to take regular vacations. I want you to take the balance of August. When you get back, you'll have heavy responsibilities."

"Seems like an awkward time," said Lucas.

The general shook his head. "Later would be more awkward."

Lucas surrendered. "My daughter loves the beach. . . ." he mused.

"Saint-Tropez," said the general. "An impossible reservation this time of year, but I can get you rooms at the Byblos Hotel. I have friends. . . ."

The accommodations at the Byblos Hotel were the most expensive he had ever occupied, but Melanie was ecstatic. So was Jocelyn—almost. He considered it the greatest of luck that she had been able to take two weeks and join them for most of their three-week vacation. Their suite consisted of two bedrooms served by one bath, with a tiny sitting room between. The hotel, on the hillside overlooking the village, was their occasional refuge from the summer crowds that packed Saint-Tropez in season: a multilingual, youthful throng. Happily, guests of the hotel could claim fifty meters of the sand at Tahiti *Plage,* the best beach, a few kilometers from the town; and during the day Lucas, Melanie, and Jocelyn lay on padded wooden beach lounges, sipping the sangria served by hotel waiters, and constantly amused by the crowd that splashed in the cold water. Melanie played in the sand, wearying herself for the night, when Lucas and Jocelyn could make love, confident the little girl was sound asleep.

Melanie, at eleven, was not entirely a little girl. Her first day on the beach she was utterly humiliated by her one-piece bathing suit, in the presence of girls and women young and old wearing nothing but bikini bottoms. Before they left the town for the beach the next morning, Lucas found her a tiny bikini in a waterfront shop, and on the beach she shed her top and lay on her back on her lounge, deliciously conscious of the exposure of the almost imperceptible swellings that were to be her breasts.

Jocelyn, when she arrived, was reluctant to go top-less. She put her bikini bra aside only when she saw that she was almost the only woman on the beach with her breasts covered. Elegant in a hat woven of palm fronds, aviator's sunglasses, and studied, understated makeup, she was, Lucas realized, still a little uncomfortable wearing only half of an expensive designer bathing suit.

On the other hand, in the restaurant of the Byblos, or eating bouillabaisse at an open-air table on the waterfront, she was in her element: chic, noticed, self-confident.

For himself, Lucas accepted the custom of the town. He bought what he called a dyed-green jockstrap and reclined on the beach with his genitals covered but his nates uncovered and soon sunburned.

"I have a contract with the new Electroscript," Jocelyn announced during their first afternoon on the beach. She was nibbling on the lunch of omelet and salad brought to them by one of the hotel waiters. "A rather nice contract, from the general himself."

"I have some little influence left," muttered Lucas. He lay on his back, with his eyes closed, though he was chewing on a big forkful of salad that Melanie had put in his mouth.

"I come well recommended," said Jocelyn. "Not just by you and Arthur Ringold. He did a full evaluation of my company."

"Does he know you're here with us?" Lucas asked.

"He knows everything," said Jocelyn. "Snooping seems to be his forte."

"I don't think he's a very nice man," said Melanie.

"Did you know he's going to change the name of the company?" asked Jocelyn.

Lucas opened his eyes and sat up. "Hell. You're kidding. To what?"

"You know what 'ergonomic' means?" asked Jocelyn.

"*I* do," interjected Melanie with a grin. "It means making machines work so people can understand them."

"Jesus Christ!" Jocelyn exclaimed. "I had to look it up. 'Ergonomics—the science of man-machine interface.' Matt and Jim think the transcriber is deficient in ergonomics. They say they're going to add that element."

"Big deal," said Lucas.

"Which," Jocelyn said with pedagogic emphasis, "will make it a heuristic ergonomic speech transcriber. H-E-S-T. HEST. They're going to call the service HEST and change the name of the company to HEST."

"No wonder he wanted me out of the country," said Lucas.

"Actually, it's not a bad idea," she said. "They ran it past an outfit in New York that's in the business of finding distinctive new names for new services and products. Consultants. The consultants said it will sell. It's more distinctive than Electroscript. Easier to remember. Actually, the consultants did a market-research survey on it and came up with a report congratulating the new management on thinking of it."

"For which they paid?"

"Twenty-five thousand bucks."

Lucas grimaced, reached for the pitcher and poured himself sangria, and drank half the glass. "They wanted me out of the country for three weeks so they could make a lot of changes without consulting me. This is probably the least of it."

"What could you have done about it anyway?"

Jocelyn asked. "Let me remind you of an unpleasantness, my dear. You are an employee now. You work for General Matthew Fraser. If you'll take my advice, you'll resign your vice-presidency in favor of a consulting contract. As a consultant, you won't be an employee—and I don't think you're going to make a very good employee."

Most evenings they took dinner on the waterfront, where one evening they bought from an artist who circulated among the tables an India-ink-on-canvas abstraction of the sailboats along the mole. After dinner the three of them usually strolled the Quai Suffren, looking at the magnificent yachts backed up to the quai and watching barefoot girls maneuver for invitations aboard. They walked to the Place Carnot then and watched the men of the village playing *boule* under the strings of bulbs. At ten they walked back up the hill to the Byblos Hotel.

Melanie used their one bathroom first and was soon in her room with her door closed. Looking in on her a few minutes later, they would find her peacefully sleeping. Melanie understood that her father and Jocelyn slept together. He had essayed an explanation the day before Jocelyn arrived, but Melanie had interrupted him and told him gravely that she knew about things like that.

It was not easy for Jocelyn to accept the situation of their rooms. She did not like letting Lucas see her without makeup, with her hair unbrushed. She had inquired at the desk about getting another room but had been told there were none available.

"I'm sorry, Lucas," she said to him on their second night. "I'm having a period. I'm having some cramps and am really not up to—"

"It's all right."

She touched her lips with the wet tip of her tongue. "We've been without a chance since—"

"July," he said.

"I'm sorry," she said again.

"It's all right, honey."

"I've never given head in my life," she said.

"You don't have to."

"I thought about it on the plane, after I realized . . . You know? Would you like it?"

"God, yes," he breathed.

"Turn out the lights," she said.

She told him to stand naked by the window. From there they had a view of the pool, now lighted by torches burning in sconces on the walls. Two nude girls still lay on the chaise longues at poolside, apparently half drunk, laughing shrilly at whatever two fully dressed men were saying to them in French. Jocelyn knelt before Lucas. She was still wearing the white linen dress she had worn to dinner. For a while she toyed with his penis and scrotum, caressing them, hefting them in gentle hands, kissing them lightly. Then, abruptly, she sucked him into her mouth and began to massage him with her lips and tongue. He could not control himself and came to a quick orgasm, shooting deep into her throat, gagging her, causing her to pull his penis from her mouth, so that the last spasms shot the hot fluid over her cheeks and chin. She shook her head and rubbed her face in his pubic hair.

He learned to feign sleep in the mornings. She wanted to rise and contrive her makeup, style her hair, and apply her scents, before he woke and saw her in her natural, colorless state. He did see her, but he pretended he didn't. It was important to her that he didn't. She was a very ordinary-looking young woman until she prepared herself to face the world, and it was clear to him that her facade was her defense, in a way he had suspected but could hardly have believed before that two weeks in Saint-Tropez.

"Daddy," Melanie said to Lucas when they were alone, strolling along the edge of the surf one afternoon. "If you hit her with a little hammer, her makeup would chip."

11

1975

So MANY OF the California staff spent so much time in New York that HEST leased two small apartments in a building on Thirty-fourth Street, just east of Park Avenue South. During the last four months of 1974, Lucas flew the red-eye into Kennedy fifteen times, and reluctantly and a little resentfully made one of the shabby little furnished apartments a second home.

In October, General Fraser leased half a floor in the Pan Am Building and began the studied creation of the HEST executive offices. He hired designers. Every interior wall, all the ceilings, and all the floors were torn out, and when people began moving in, they moved into offices where electric cables still snaked across the concrete floors or hung loose from the ceiling, where dust and noise interfered with every function they tried to perform. Lucas saw the architect's blueprints and learned that an office was being created for him. He was told by the designer that General Fraser had selected all the furniture and that every vice president would have an office of identical size, with identical furniture, the only difference being the color of the carpets and drapes—and which of these four colors would Mr. Paulson prefer?

The New York staff took control of Electroscript and

made it HEST as if they had been working with the transcriber for years and knew every detail of the program and the business. Lucas found them a pushy, self-confident lot—though, he was compelled to acknowledge shortly, they were bright, well-educated, and, within some limitations, effective. They came to know him. They recognized him and spoke to him in the halls. He was—he would learn—a curiosity to them: a Midwesterner to begin with, then the founder of the business, an ancestor, yet only thirty-five years old. That he called General Fraser Matt—to his face as well as in conversation, as only Mr. Cahill dared to do—they attributed at first to his Midwestern informality, later to his iconoclastic personality.

The question was, what was this acknowledged founder of the business, this rather eccentric vice president, going to do? And just how important was he going to be?

His first title was vice president for product development. Operational control was taken from him in September. His area of responsibility and authority was defined on an organizational chart that he first saw in the UNI offices in Rockefeller Center. Gabe Lincoln was assigned to his department, but Martin Kent was assigned to operations, under Vice President Lars Gustavson. The consulting services of Professor David Berger were assigned to him. The consulting services of Merritt & Associates were assigned to market development, under Vice President Walter McConnell. Three of his California systems designers were assigned to product development, and so were two he had never met: one from UNI's computer services department and one newly hired, an MIT graduate named Bradley Gulliver. Lucas's vice-presidential office was to be in New York. He was authorized to maintain a departmental office in San Mateo, California. The only department with its principal office in San Mateo was operations.

Lucas gained a mixed reputation in the new company immediately, especially after his run-in with Richard Lillienthal.

"Excuse me." The shirt-sleeved young man had entered after one peremptory knock. He glanced at his clipboard. "You are Mr. Paulson?"

The interruption was not convenient. Lucas looked up from his new desk and nodded.

"I'm Richard Lillienthal, director of human resources."

"Well, which do you take me for, a human or a resource?"

"I beg your pardon?"

"I can't be both, a human *and* a resource. They're mutually exclusive terms, so you have to suppose I'm one or the other."

"Well, that's my title."

"Okay. Not your fault, I suppose. What can I do for you?"

The young man glanced around with an air of disapproval, maybe disturbed by the two bold prints Lucas had hung on his wall, rejecting all choices from the two-dozen prints approved by General Fraser for office decoration. "At your corporate level," he said, "you are entitled to a secretary, class 2. I'll hire—"

"Nope."

"I beg your pardon?"

"At this point I don't need a secretary in the New York office. I have a secretary in California, and she will be enough for the time being. Later on I may ask her if she wants to move here."

"Well, uh . . . of course, I'll have to interview her."

Lucas shook his head. "Won't be necessary. She does my work very effectively."

The young man took a deep breath. "All secretarial and clerical personnel will be hired by me, Mr. Paulson."

"Not *my* secretary, sonny. My secretary is hired by *me.*"

Lillienthal smiled tolerantly. "And, of course, you'll take care of any problems of employment discrimination that may arise, problems of fitting her into the corporate salary-classification scheme, and so on."

"Right. I'll take care of all that. Thank you, Mr. Lillienthal. Now, if you'll excuse me . . ."

The word went out: Paulson was a difficult man to deal with.

General Fraser installed his Japanese office in the Pan Am Building within the first six months, and immediately it was the famed inner sanctum of HEST. Employees who had seen it had a status denied those who had not. Those who had spent ten minutes there— rather than having had a glance—had better status. Few from inside the company were called there for meetings. It was the general's management technique that he conferred only with his vice presidents and an occasional director or manager, who passed his word down. With a fine sense of *noblesse oblige,* he walked through the offices from time to time, stopping at this desk and that to bestow a smile or to inquire into the progress on some bit of work.

Cahill rarely ventured out of the executive suite, where his office was near the general's; and it was *his* management style to call frequent meetings of the vice presidents, who were subordinate to him as senior vice president, to hear reports from all departments. These were shirt-sleeved meetings in the company conference room, with boxed lunches brought in by a caterer. General Fraser stopped in from time to time, often to eat an apple and a sandwich.

"Problem, Walt?" asked Cahill at the end of a presentation by Walter McConnell, vice president for market development. This was in a meeting held on Tuesday, March 11, 1975. "In a word . . . ?"

"In a word," said McConnell uncomfortably, "we haven't so far managed to get in."

"Fuckin' lawyers," said Cahill.

McConnell flushed and nodded.

Cahill, his nervous grin absent for once, bobbed his head repeatedly in a thoughtful nod. He sighed. "Matt will have to talk to them," he said finally.

"He's tried," said McConnell.

"UNI general counsel . . ." suggested Gustavson of operations.

Cahill shook his head. "Outside counsel," he said. "The firms that represent UNI and HEST . . . They—"

"Want to define the problem?" Lucas asked.

Cahill nodded at McConnell, who said, "We want to set up an initial job—use HEST to take the record in an important trial or hearing. We've got one in mind. The acrylics antitrust case is going to trial in June, in Philadelphia. Dugan, Schreib has agreed to use HEST in the courtroom. Judge Hilliard is agreeable if counsel for the remaining parties agree. We've got six other law firms to talk to. And we can't even get in the door at Tate, Janowski & McCulligan. I mean, they won't even talk to our representative."

Lucas shrugged at Cahill. "I had a good one all set up for you, and—"

"Matt didn't want to do that one," said Cahill curtly.

"That's Matt's mistake," said Lucas. "So, who's been talking to Tate, Janowski?"

"Bill Farley," said McConnell. "Philadelphia is his territory."

"What, uh . . . twenty-two years old?" Lucas asked.

"A Harvard Business School graduate," said McConnell. "His father is a vice president at Morgan. Top-notch young man."

"Yeah," said Lucas curtly. "Twenty-two years old, non-lawyer, with the company four months—"

"We have to build a staff, Lucas," said Cahill.

"You sent out a *boy*," said Lucas. "The kid never had a *chance*."

"Matt . . . himself . . . talked to the firm," said Cahill angrily.

"Umm, fine," said Lucas. "Matt's not a lawyer either."

"Matt's the president of the company," said Cahill.

"I don't care if he's Jesus Christ Almighty. He's not a lawyer, and he's given me ample demonstration of his ignorance of lawyering."

At seven that evening—Lucas having canceled a return flight to California—General Fraser ordered wine and drinks for Lucas and Cahill in his office. The general had removed his jacket and had loosened his necktie. He sat on his couch.

"I understand I'm ignorant of lawyering," he said, with a carefully measured smile. "I was of the impression that I knew something about it."

Lucas shrugged. "I know something of small-unit infantry tactics," he said. "But I know about as much of generalling as you do of lawyering."

General Fraser allowed his smile to broaden. "I'll let that one go," he said. "We'll play chess sometime and see what you know. For the moment, the problem is exerting some influence on this Philadelphia law firm. Were you telling Jim you could do better than I've done?"

"Wouldn't take much to do better than that, would it?"

The general's chin snapped up, but he suppressed his instinctive anger. "Want to put your money where your mouth is?" he asked.

"What am I betting?"

"Not much," said the general. "Your credibility."

"What do I get if I win the bet?"

The general shrugged. "Credibility," he said blandly.

Lucas discovered, to begin with, that the New York offices of HEST did not have a set of Martindale-Hubbell law directories. He ordered one delivered immediately to his office and wandered down the street to the library of the Association of the Bar of the City of New York to look up the firm of Tate, Janowski & McCulligan. He copied from the directory the names of the most senior partners.

Back at his desk, he called the senior partner of his old Kansas City law firm—Joseph Drake, the aged lawyer who had made the motion in a partnership meeting that Huggins, Dodd & Drake buy the first shares of Electroscript stock.

"I read good things about you, Lucas," said the thin voice on the telephone line. Lucas was surprised at how old Joseph Drake sounded. "We're proud of you."

"Well, thank you, Mr. Drake. If I'd stayed home and tended to business, I might have done better."

"I think you'd have done well at whatever you set out to do, Lucas."

They talked for a few minutes about lawyers in the firm, the ones that Lucas remembered and asked about.

"Mr. Drake, I've called to ask a favor."

"Of course. What can I do for you?"

"Have you ever heard of a firm in Philadelphia called Tate, Janowski & McCulligan?"

"Well . . . maybe. I don't know."

"I need an introduction there, to a partner who can make things happen."

"I'll get you one. Somebody's got to know 'em, if they amount to anything."

"I'll be grateful. I'm trying to teach a smartass a lesson."

"You're the man to do it, Lucas. Hah-hah. You're the man to do it."

The next day Lucas received a call from James Victor, a tax partner at the firm of Tugg, Perkins in Chicago. He had met Victor once briefly, though neither of them remembered it; but at the request of Joseph Drake, Victor was willing to introduce Lucas to Avery Rittenhouse, the senior tax partner at Tate, Janowski,

He met with Rittenhouse and two of his partners over lunch at the Barclay Hotel in Philadelphia—where the soft-voiced, white-haired lawyer acknowledged he was directly descended from the Rittenhouse for whom Rittenhouse Square was named.

"I suppose," said Rittenhouse when the subject of using the transcriber at the upcoming antitrust trial was broached, "our sense of the matter is that the firm does not want any side issues being raised that might possibly muddy the waters, as they say, or obscure the issues in what is going to be a long and expensive trial."

"At the end of any given day," said Lucas, "you can cancel. You'll see what the service is doing every day, and if you're not satisfied, you drop out. The most you could lose is inaccuracies in one day's transcript."

"Your company's young man told our office manager that the system was incapable of error," said one of the other lawyers, grinning.

"The only thing in this world I can think of that's worse than being an employee is being an *employer*," said Lucas.

"It is capable of error, then?"

"Of course it's capable of error. All I can tell you is, I don't think it will make as many errors as a human reporter. I think I can promise that. I can't promise any more."

"We can always back it up with human reporters," said Avery Rittenhouse.

"And double your costs," said Lucas. "I can't recommend that. In my judgment, you should go with one method or the other."

" 'Be not the first by whom the new are tried/Nor yet the last to lay the old aside,' " recited Rittenhouse with a quiet chuckle. "Alexander Pope."

" 'What is more mortifying than to feel that you have missed the plum for want of courage to shake the tree?' Smith," said Lucas with a nod and smile.

Rittenhouse laughed, joined by the two other lawyers.

"Well, Mr. Paulson," said one of the others. "You make your case well. We'll reconsider and let you know."

A week later, Lucas left with General Fraser's secretary a note telling him that Tate, Janowski & McCulligan had agreed to join the other firms in using

HEST to transcribe the trial record in the acrylics antitrust trial.

In the spring, General Fraser hired his first administrative assistant: Bunny Cardinale, a tall, slim, graceful girl who had failed in her ambition to become a ballerina but still tried to affect the air and the moves of a dancer. She tied her black hair tightly behind her head, carried her chin high, and wore long, loose skirts that flowed around her legs as she walked. She carried the general's messages for him, sometimes curt memos she hand-delivered, often questions she read from the notes she had scribbled on a steno pad. When it was observed by the corporate staff that Bunny smoked the general's handmade, monogrammed cigarettes, they began to treat her with caution.

One Monday morning in May, when Lucas had just arrived on the red-eye, she knocked on his door.

"Good morning, Mr. Paulson. I've been looking for you. I tried to call you in San Francisco last night. General Fraser suggests you put an answering machine on your home telephone."

Lucas smiled at her. "So I could get messages from Matt in the middle of the night?" he asked.

She returned his smile with her eyes. "Well . . . that's what he suggests."

"Suggestion noted," said Lucas.

"General Fraser asked me to tell you he would appreciate your joining him for drinks at a meeting he's holding this evening." She handed him a note. "That is the address."

Lucas shook his head. "I'm taking the Metroliner to Philadelphia this afternoon. The acrylics trial opens next Monday, you know."

Bunny Cardinale shook her head. "General Fraser doesn't want you to go to Philadelphia," she said.

"Why?"

"He didn't tell me, Mr. Paulson. He just said you were not to go."

"What's this meeting?" Lucas asked, glancing at the address, not recognizing it. "What's it for?"

"I don't know," she said. "It's a very small party. Just a few men."

"It's important, you say?"

"That's my understanding."

The address, he found when he got there, was of an old apartment building on East Fifty-third Street, a narrow, three-story brick building, obviously remodeled and improved, although white paint flaking off the brick lay like building dandruff on the sidewalk. A small costume shop occupied a storefront below sidewalk level. Worn stone steps with wrought-iron railings led to the door to the entry hall. There, Lucas found but one mailbox, one buzzer button, one speaker. He pressed the button.

"Yes?" a woman's voice.

"Lucas Paulson."

The buzzer sounded, the lock vibrated, and he opened the door.

"C'mon up." It was Cahill at the top of the stairs, martini in hand. "Hey. Party's already started."

Lucas climbed the carpeted stairs, noticing on the way up that the walls to either side were hung with framed theater posters. At the top, Cahill grabbed his hand, shook it firmly, and gave him a little shove through the door.

He had but an instant to glance around the small, cozy apartment before his attention was seized by the

179

girls: four of them, all stripped to their panties. He recognized them. They worked for the company. Two were secretaries, one a data processor. One sat on a couch beside a man he did not recognize. The other three stood with drinks in their hands, all conspicuously self-conscious but all bravely smiling.

Cahill held Lucas by the arm and spoke quietly to him. "Uh, you know Barbara Segal there?" He referred to the data processor, a small but heavy-chested girl who had made a point of speaking to him in the office halls for several months. "She's sort of paired with you for the evening. Informally. No obligation for either of you. Is that okay?"

Lucas sighed. "When in Rome . . ." he said.

". . . do as the Romans do," said Cahill. "I'll appreciate it."

Cahill gestured with his chin, and Barbara Segal came across the room to Lucas. She smiled shyly at him, blushing. "What would you like to drink, Mr. Paulson?" she asked.

"Have any red wine?"

"Open a bottle," said Cahill. "In the kitchen, Barb. I think there's a bottle of Médoc."

"I'll go with her," said Lucas.

"Uh, well, I'd like you to meet Len Stacey first," said Cahill.

Lucas had heard of Stacey. He was divisional vice president of United Northeastern, in charge of the division to which HEST was assigned on the organizational chart of UNI. Not a prepossessing man, he had nevertheless given Lucas reason to respect his ability to learn quickly and to ask penetrating questions. Lucas had exchanged memoranda with him but had never met him. He was cordial but anxious to return to the girl on the couch. He shook Lucas's hand and said he hoped to see him in the office during the week.

Lucas went to the kitchen, where he found Barbara Segal struggling with the corkscrew. He took it from her and opened the bottle.

"Did you get, uh, summoned to this?" he asked.

"Oh, no. I volunteered," she said. "I mean, they asked me and said I would probably be with you, so it was, like, okay with me."

"Okay," he said quietly. "No obligation. Whatever they expect, I'll say we did, whether we do or don't."

"I appreciate that, Mr. Paulson," she said. She spoke with a New York accent ("asked me" was "esked me"). Her mousy brown hair was cut in bangs across her forehead. Her skin was imperfect. Though her breasts hung loose and her belly was prominent, her body was taut. She was perfectly suited for quick and satisfying sex. "But . . . I mean, like, it's okay. Ya understand? Mr. Paulson, it—"

He grinned and slapped her lightly across the seat of her bikini-style panties. "Barb," he said. "Call me Lucas."

One more surprise waited. When General Fraser arrived, Bunny was with him, and she disappeared into a bedroom and shortly emerged stripped to her panties the same as the others.

The final guest, who came half an hour later, was Floyd Gosnold, vice president for long-range planning, in reality, the officer in charge of acquisitions, who had made the final decision to acquire Electroscript. He was a tall, dark, grim-visaged man, who accepted a drink with hardly a word and drew the last unattached girl immediately onto his lap on a chair in a corner of the room.

"Is there an agenda for this meeting?" Lucas whispered to Cahill.

"Yes," Cahill nodded. "Eat, drink, and make Barbara."

It was unlike the general, as Lucas guessed, for the party to be entirely without purpose. He guessed right. After a while, Bunny slipped up to him and dismissed Barbara with a gesture.

"Stacey asked that you be invited," she said quietly to Lucas. "Matt wants you to avoid any specific answers to any questions. You'll be meeting with both of them tomorrow, and Matt wants to be a part of any conversation that's anything but social."

Lucas laughed. "You look good, Bunny," he said.

She grimaced and yet laughed at the same time. "Shit," she said. With her trim, erect dancer's body, she had managed to maintain until now the same aloof dignity she affected in the office.

The apartment was the general's city retreat, where he spent nights his wife supposed he spent out of town. It was comfortably but functionally furnished, without much style: perhaps as a withdrawal from style by a man who put too much effort into it. Cahill said there was a library office downstairs. The bedrooms were upstairs.

A caterer had left food in the kitchen, and the girls served it. There was caviar and vodka, Scottish salmon, whole cold lobsters, salad, a chocolate mousse, coffee, brandy. They ate from the coffee table or end tables, or from plates balanced on their knees.

"Nice party, Matt," Lucas said when he had a moment alone with him, while Bunny was in the kitchen pouring a drink.

"Thanks, Lucas. Watch this pair from UNI. They'd like us to lower our guards and say something stupid."

"I thought I should be in Philadelphia this week."

General Fraser shook his head. "You're product development. Not your problem. When the time comes to take bows, you and I will go to Philadelphia. In the meantime, we let the people whose job it is take care of their problems."

"I got the contract for you. I'd like to—"

"Stay within organizational boundaries," said the general firmly. "That's the way we operate."

They ate and drank. Leonard Stacey drank too much and settled into peaceful withdrawl in the corner of the couch. The girl assigned to him sat solicitously beside him, sipped champagne, and watched him fall asleep. Floyd Gosnold made conversation about the business for a few minutes, then apparently decided it was inappropriate in the company of five bare-breasted girls and two drunk men—Stacey and Cahill—and he shrugged and quietly suggested to the girl nearest him that they go upstairs to one of the bedrooms. General Fraser stood then and with a toss of his head sent Bunny ahead of him to the stairway to the next floor. He cast a scornful glance at Cahill, who had drawn a girl onto his lap and was kissing her breasts, nodded once at Lucas, and followed Bunny.

"Where are your clothes?" Lucas asked Barbara.

"In the closet. But I . . . I mean, look, it's okay with me. I wouldn't have come if it wasn't."

Lucas put aside his glass and offered Barbara his hand to help her up from the floor, where she had been sitting beside his chair. "Some other time maybe," he said. "Some other way. I don't like the arrangements. Where do you live? I'll take you home."

When Stacey and Gosnold faced General Fraser and Cahill and Lucas across the conference-room table the next morning, it was as if the evening before had never happened. They had come to New York to demand the HEST business plans for 1976, 1977, and 1978. They wanted to know how much money the company would earn in each of those years and how much it would spend in each of two dozen expense categories, how many installations would be operational in each year and how much revenue each one would generate, how many employees the company would require each year, and what kinds of incentive plans had been established to insure company loyalty and performance.

"When, Mr. Paulson, will research and development be essentially finished, so we may regard the service as complete?"

"It will never be complete," said Lucas bluntly.

"How do you mean that?"

"Technology changes," said Lucas. "What we are doing now was technologically impossible two years ago. What we are doing now will be obsolete two years from now."

"Since there is no competition," said Gosnold, "it is hardly necessary to keep the system state-of-the-art."

"If it makes money," said Lucas, "there will *be* competition. And when competition comes along, our advantage will be that we are ahead of everybody else. To be ahead, you have to stay ahead. We must explore every technological development that can affect HEST and adopt anything that promises to make us faster, more accurate, easier to use, cheaper . . ."

"In other words," said Gosnold, "there will never be a time when we can congratulate ourselves and say we have a going system we can live with for the immediate future."

"That's exactly right," said Lucas.

*　*　*

That same day, after Stacey and Gosnold had left, General Fraser asked Lucas to come to the Japanese office for a drink.

"You gave them the word," the general said, lifting a Scotch.

"But I remember what the Greeks are said to have done to bearers of bad tidings," said Lucas.

Lucas, who had accepted a Scotch, sipped thoughtfully, and the general fell silent. After a long moment, the general began a discourse on the battle pictured on one of his painted screens. He explained the strategy and tactics, inspiring in Lucas only the thought that it would be a rare student, indeed, who could contradict him and that he might be making up his lecture as he went along.

"Ah." Someone had rapped on the door, and General Fraser went to open it. He knew who it was, since no one else was allowed to knock on his office door instead of stopping at his secretary's desk and being announced. "Hon-ey!" he exclaimed. "Daddy's girl! Come on in!"

The nine-year-old girl walked in, self-possessed and curious about the graying man with the California tan who stood in the center of the office. She looked up into his face, studying him gravely.

"Susannah," said General Fraser. "This is Mr. Paulson. He works for me. He is the man who started our business."

Susannah extended her hand. "I am pleased to meet you, Mr. Paulson," she said.

12

GENERAL FRASER STALKED into the conference room.
Jim Cahill, who was sitting at the head of the table, rose
and shifted to another seat. Walter McConnell, vice
president of marketing, reached to the ashtray in the
center of the table and crushed out his cigarette.
Prentice Halliburton, corporate general counsel,
turned over a page of his yellow legal pad, apparently
to cover the notes he had written. Foster Theisen,
senior partner from the firm that represented the
company as outside counsel, stood and extended his
hand to the general. Lucas Paulson nodded at the
general, and shoved back his chair and crossed his legs.

General Fraser shook hands perfunctorily with
Theisen, then sat down and scowled.

"Well?"

"It's a discussion draft, Matt," said Cahill. "It
isn't—"

"Is anybody telling me it won't go in the final draft?"
the general asked. He shook a cigarette from a box.
"Hmm?"

"All we can do," said Theisen gravely, "is make our
case. We prepare a memorandum—"

"Memorandum!" sneered General Fraser. "What
good's *that* going to do?"

186

"What alternative do you have in mind?" asked Theisen coldly.

"Well, I have a call in to Warren Burger," said the general.

"He hasn't returned it?"

"Not yet."

"You had better hope he doesn't," said Theisen.

"What's that supposed to mean?"

"You'll find out. You can't call the Chief Justice of the United States and try to make an *ex parte* argument against a report of the Judicial Conference."

"I can't, huh? Nixon called him to try to queer a case."

"Much good did it do him," said Theisen dryly.

"Much good may it do to shoot memoranda at them."

They were discussing a draft sent to HEST by the Director of Technological Systems Development of the Federal Courts Administrative Office. The draft was of a report being prepared for issuance by the Judicial Conference of the United States, discussing the impact of technology on the administration of justice. The draft contained a comparison between LEXIS and Westlaw, the two competing systems of computer-assisted legal research, a survey of computer systems for maintaining dockets and records, and a report on HEST. The draft said that the number of errors in transcription made by HEST made it unacceptable as an alternative to traditional methods of taking transcripts of trial testimony. HEST was invited to comment.

"If this son of a bitch is circulated," said General Fraser, tapping his finger on a copy of the draft, "we are out of business. Every goddamn judge in the

United States will read that we make too many mistakes, and we'll never get into another courtroom."

Lucas shook his head. "I wouldn't say that."

"You wouldn't? Of course, it was your goddamn system that fucked up, Mr. Product Development."

"I'll take responsibility for that," said Lucas, "and also credit for successful operation in the twelve courtrooms where we're running simultaneously right now."

The general tapped his finger even harder on the draft. "You trying to tell me this isn't going to hurt the business?"

Lucas shrugged. "It'll hurt. I don't think it will kill us."

"Oh. Well, I'm glad to hear it. Does anybody have any ideas better than shooting memoranda down to Washington?"

"Cancel your call to the Chief Justice," said Theisen.

General Fraser nodded. "All right. I'll do that. But I give you guys about forty-eight hours to come up with something, then I'm going down to Washington to talk to a few people."

Cahill called Lucas into his office, with Theisen and Halliburton. He hung his coat in the closet, rolled his shirt sleeves back over his forearms, and propped his feet on his desk. "You understand, of course, he really didn't try to call the Chief Justice."

"I didn't think he's that stupid," said Lucas. "I don't appreciate his thinking *we are.*"

"Ah, that's Matt's style," said Cahill. "He knows you didn't believe him."

"He can be tiresome sometimes," said Foster Theisen.

"He treats us like boys," said Prentice Halliburton.

"Yeah, but you're his staff," said Cahill. "Here you

are—Lucas Paulson, Prentice Halliburton, Foster
Theisen—three of the most capable men who could be
brought together to work on a problem like this; and
you *are* working together, because Matt hired you.
You're not the kind of guys he likes, necessarily, but he
hired you. Give the man credit."

Prentice Halliburton nodded thoughtfully, as if the
idea had not occurred to him before. He was a handsome, gray-haired, forty-year-old lawyer who had left
a major Wall Street firm to accept his position as general counsel to HEST. Although he was conspicuously an able lawyer, he was an innocent in many
ways.

"The trouble," said Cahill, "is that the test they ran
was, in the first place, on the system as it was in
October, and—"

"And in the second place, they cheated," said Lucas.

"That's how Matt puts it," Cahill agreed.

"The professors and the computer hackers of the
American Bar Association came back to haunt us,"
said Lucas.

"I don't follow," said Halliburton.

"I can rig a test," said Lucas, "that will prove
smoking cigarettes is good for you. And so can you."

"They screwed us," said Cahill. "The test was not of
how the system would work in a courtroom environment but of how capable it was of deciphering homophones. It was a shootout against an experienced
stenographer who could guess meaning from context."

"Homophones . . . ?" asked Halliburton ingen-
uously.

"The woman playing witness read the phrase 'sum of
the digits,'" said Lucas, "and the system transcribed it
as 'some of the digits.' One of the professors almost
choked on his chortling."

"You know," said Cahill. "Like 'ate'—'eight,' 'steak' —'stake,' 'one'—'won,' 'to'—'too'—'two.' And so on."

" 'Know'—'no,' " said Halliburton.

"Right," said Lucas. "They wrote a script to be dictated to the machine and a stenographer. It was absolutely salted with homophones."

"But why would they do that?" Halliburton asked.

"To kill us," said Lucas.

"You may find this hard to believe," said Theisen, "but there is a strong trade association of the court reporters. Obviously, we threaten the existence of their business, and they mean to destroy us if it is within their power."

"Court reporters?" said Halliburton.

"We once supposed," said Cahill, "that schoolteachers were all dear little old ladies with blue hair, a profession with ethics that would never let them strike. Now they are a menacing union with all the ethics of the teamsters. Yes, court reporters. And they have friends in the courts."

"Plus allies in the Luddites of academe and the ABA," said Lucas.

"So what can we do?"

"Write memos," said Cahill. He sighed and shrugged. "You can't muscle the judges."

"We can make a very good case," said Halliburton.

"Jim," said Lucas. "I want you to go to Washington with me."

"Matt wants you to stay out of it," said Cahill. "It's not product development's problem."

"I'm going," said Lucas. "Are you going with me?"

"He'll fire you," said Cahill.

"Like hell he will."

* * *

Lucas had rented an apartment on East Seventy-second Street. He had to pack that evening, Cahill having agreed to go with him to Washington on the shuttle early in the morning. When he unlocked his apartment door, about 6:45, he found the lights on and the rooms filled with the savory aromas of tomato paste and oregano and garlic. He was not entirely surprised. Bunny had a key and often let herself in.

She was in the kitchen, stirring the sauce. Two bottles of Chianti, in baskets, were on the kitchen table. The pasta, wrapped in paper, lay on the counter.

"I had to come," she said. "He almost drove me insane today."

Lucas stepped up behind her, slapped her gently on the rump, and nuzzled the hair at the back of her neck. "I'm glad you came," he said. "The son of a bitch is on a tear, isn't he?"

"When he came back from lunch he wanted a quickie on the couch. After that, he tossed me a folder of letters and memos and told me I had misunderstood his position on every issue they covered." She closed her eyes. "Lucas, I . . ."

"You want out?" he asked. "I told you I'd help you."

She nodded. "I can't take any more," she whispered.

"I'll talk to someone about you," he said. "I have a few friends."

His dining table overlooked the East River, and they ate their dinner in the light from the river and highway, with just one candle burning in the center of the table. Shortly before they finished, the telephone rang. It was Jocelyn, calling from California, mostly to tell him that his real-estate agent had an offer on his condominium in Sausalito. Jocelyn was wistful. She hadn't really believed, she said, he was going to sell it. Then she said she was coming to New York for a meeting on Monday and wondered if he would like for her to come on Saturday and spend the weekend with him. He told her yes, sure.

Bunny drank Chianti while Lucas talked on the telephone, and when he returned to the table she poured his glass full.

"The general thinks his daughter has the makings of a dancer," she said. "Because she's going to be tall and slender. Of course, he said he wouldn't want her to try to make a *career* of it. . . . Of course, that wouldn't do. I mean, she being the daughter of General Matthew Fraser and all."

"He'd like to marry her to the Prince of Wales, I imagine," said Lucas.

Bunny sighed. "You couldn't believe how much I wanted to be a ballerina. I really wanted that, Lucas. When I had to face it that I'd never make it, I auditioned for shows—you know, the chorus or anything, anything to get to dance on stage." She shook her head. "Struck out again. Finally, I tried for a part in *Oh, Calcutta!* You know the nude ballet scene? I danced stark naked for five months in one of the *Oh, Calcutta!* companies. It's the only time anyone ever paid me for dancing on the stage. How'd the general like his daughter to try *that?*"

"*My* daughter is going to be short and plumpish," said Lucas. "She's thirteen. In junior high school she is an absolutely all-A student. She scored in the top percentile in mathematics, in their scholastic aptitude tests. She can whip through algebraic equations that had me stymied when I was eighteen and resolved never to look at another one again."

"You should bring her here," said Bunny. "There are fine schools in New York."

He nodded. "If I can get settled, I mean really settled. You know, I travel so much. In the morning, Washington. Next week, California." He shrugged.

"What you need is a wife," said Bunny. "Uh . . . don't worry—I don't mean me. I mean—"

"I know. I've sacrificed a lot to this business we're in."

"More than it's worth, if you don't mind my telling you so."

Lucas nodded and reached for the wine.

When Lucas arrived at the shuttle terminal the next morning, Halliburton was with Cahill. "I had to tell Matt we're going to Washington," Cahill said. "He insisted you're out of your jurisdiction and said to tell you he wants our general counsel to do the talking."

Lucas shook Halliburton's hand. "Glad to have you along, Dick," he said, using the nickname Prentice Halliburton himself suggested.

"Matt's orders . . ." said Halliburton weakly.

"It's fine with me. No problem. Did you pack a hankie in your briefcase? We may have to stay overnight."

It was almost ten o'clock when they arrived at the H Street headquarters of the Federal Courts Administrative Office. David Rutledge, the Assistant Director of Technological Systems Development, who had sent them the draft for comment, met them at the reception desk and led them to his small, book-cluttered office.

"Judge Welsh will be joining us in a little while," said Rutledge. "He's the director, you know. And I understand there's lunch at the Army-Navy Club. . . . Is that right?"

"Right," said Lucas. "I'd like to make a couple of calls while we wait for Judge Welsh, if you don't mind."

When he returned to Rutledge's office a quarter of an hour later, the secretary said the group had assembled in the director's office.

Judge William Welsh was a spare man of sepulchral face and demeanor, tall, with little left of his sandy hair. He wore rimless eyeglasses, a dark blue suit, and a bow tie. He had been a judge of a district court in Michigan, had taken early retirement after a heart attack, and on recovery had accepted the directorship of the Administrative Office. His office was spacious, carpeted with Oriental rugs, and walled with bookcases filled with law books.

"I understand, Mr. Paulson, that you take objection to our evaluation of your computer system—and that you are the spokesman for your delegation. So. Why don't you state your case?"

"I am sure you know, Judge Welsh, that we installed HEST in the District Court for the Eastern District of Pennsylvania last year and that it made the transcript in the acrylics antitrust case."

"I know that," said Judge Welsh, "and I know it didn't work very well."

"Judge Cartwright was satisfied. Counsel were satisfied," said Lucas. "We had some problems. Some inaccuracies had to be repaired by hand, which our company paid the cost of doing. We made some changes in the system, and the installation is still working in Judge Cartwright's courtroom."

"I'm well aware of that. We've seen the invoices."

"Two other United States district courts are using it," Lucas went on. "In fact, there are three trials in progress this morning in federal courts, with HEST making the transcript. We are running this morning in five state courts, a public-utility hearing in Texas, and in two deposition-takings. This morning, eleven HEST installations are making transcripts. A little later in the day, the number will be twelve, when the business day starts in California."

"I find it a costly experiment, Mr. Paulson," said Judge Welsh. "On average, I'm advised, traditional court reporters can do the same work for 62 percent of what you charge."

Lucas shook his head. "That figure represents transcripts delivered, on average, six days after the testimony is given. If they provide overnight service, they charge about 89 percent of what HEST costs. And with HEST, the court and the lawyers can have transcripts in minutes. You can pull off the sheets and read what a witness said five minutes ago."

"I don't dispute that, Mr. Paulson," said Judge Welsh. "If, in an occasional trial, the lawyers want transcripts in five minutes and are willing to pay for it . . ." He shrugged. "Our report goes to the inaccuracies in computer-prepared transcripts, and I think that's a major issue."

"Exactly," said Lucas. "But I'd like the accuracy of HEST judged from its performance in a working environment. The judges and lawyers who have used it say they don't find any more errors in a HEST transcript than they find in a court reporter's transcript. That's the proof of the thing."

"Our tests demonstrated the contrary, that your machine makes many more errors than a competent stenographer," said Judge Welsh.

"If your test results differ so radically from courtroom experience," said Lucas, "that suggests there was something wrong with the test procedure."

"I'm not concerned," said Judge Welsh loftily, "with whether or not the test satisfies the company that sells the machine. I hardly expected it would."

"What if it doesn't satisfy the judges of the Judicial Conference?" asked Lucas.

The judge's thin white lips stiffened, he frowned, and he raised his chin. "You can raise that issue with them, if you wish," he said.

"Of course," said Lucas. "And I think I will. Uh, incidentally, Judge, I can't help but admire the set of red leather Supreme Court reports you have on your shelves there. Those are really handsome."

"Thank you," said Judge Welsh coldly. "Now, I believe I am to see you at lunch also, am I not? Perhaps you will excuse me until then."

"You didn't win any points there," said Cahill when they were in a cab and on their way to the offices of Biddle & Cromwell.

"I didn't expect to," said Lucas. "I wanted to find out something."

"Did you succeed?" asked Halliburton.

Lucas nodded. "They're not even *pretending* it was an objective test."

"Rutledge knows it wasn't," said Halliburton. "He spoke to me in the men's room. He also said to watch out for Judge Welsh. The old boy is accustomed to ruling from the bench, not to being disputed."

"Toward the end I had a sense you were needling him," said Cahill.

"More than that," said Lucas. "I gave him a swift kick in the ass."

"Why, for God's sake? That's Matt's game."

"I got tired of his air of superiority," said Lucas. "I knocked him off his pedestal."

"How? I didn't catch it."

"The set of law books bound in red leather," said Lucas. "The ones I complimented him on. It was a gift from a law publisher. Worth some five thousand dollars. The Detroit *Free Press* editorialized that it was inappropriate for a judge to accept a gift like that from a company that does business with the courts and suggested he send them back. But he never did."

"If he's got something like that in his background, how'd he get the directorship?" Cahill asked.

"Friend of Jerry Ford," said Lucas.

"How do you know all this?" asked Halliburton.

"A lawyer in Detroit was kind enough to fill me in," said Lucas. "If you're going into a battle with dirty fighters, Dave, it's a good idea to bring along your brass knuckles."

"How can you use that information?" asked Cahill.

"I've already used it," said Lucas. "I reminded somebody of it, and he called and reminded somebody else."

"Well, why are we on our way to Biddle & Cromwell?"

"Alex Brady set up our lunch," said Lucas.

"Who's Alex Brady?"

"Alexander P. Brady is the number-one antitrust lawyer at Biddle & Cromwell," said Lucas. "When I met him in Chicago he was a law clerk for Judge Stevens of the Seventh Circuit. He taught at the University of Chicago and wrote his books on trade regulation, which you'll find in every law office of any consequence in the United States. He's been interested in the transcriber since the early days, and last year I invited him up to Philadelphia to watch a day's trial in the acrylics case and see how HEST did with the transcript. He—"

"Matt has no idea," interrupted Cahill, "how much you're on top of this Judicial Conference business."

"I can't have Matt bulling around in a thing like this," said Lucas.

They gathered in a private dining room at the Army-Navy Club—Paulson, Cahill, and Halliburton from HEST; Alexander Brady of Biddle & Cromwell; Nathan Rastenberg of Gordon, Milstein, Ruggiero & Cooper; Judge Bryan Newnan of the United States Court of Appeals for the District of Columbia; Judge Enrico Feliciano of the United States Court of Appeals for the Third Circuit; Judge Harold Russell of the United States District Court for the District of Columbia; and Judge William Welsh and David Rutledge of the Federal Courts Administrative Office.

The waiters served drinks to the men assembled in the dining room, and everyone was introduced to everyone else. About one o'clock, they sat down for lunch.

JUDGE FELICIANO (a Philadelphian occasionally mentioned as a likely candidate for the first vacant justiceship on the Supreme Court of the United States): "Well, Cartwright tells me he's entirely satisfied. He showed me part of the transcript in the acrylics case, and I don't see how you could distinguish it from a transcript made by a steno."

JUDGE RUSSELL (dreaded by the Watergate defendants, his sentences were sterner even than Judge Sirica's): "I'd like to try the thing. I'm telling you, anything would be better than these court reporters."

JUDGE WELSH: "We tried to devise an objective test. We had the help of some well-qualified consultants."

JUDGE NEWNAN (an activist of the Judicial Conference and a catch by Nathan Rastenberg, who had brought him directly from his courtroom to this lunch): "Oh, hell, Bill. Who's qualified to pass judgment on anything so new?"

JUDGE FELICIANO: "Who were these consultants?"

JUDGE WELSH: "We had some professors—"

ALEXANDER BRADY: "The academic community has been anything but objective about the advent of technology in the sacred precincts. They were determined to shoot down computer-assisted legal research, and they've demonstrated a totally unobjective hostility toward the computerized speech transcriber."

DAVID RUTLEDGE: "We had some representatives of the bigger metropolitan court-reporting organizations. Washington . . . uh, New York, I believe, and—"

JUDGE FELICIANO: "You called in the foxes to judge the chickens?"

JUDGE WELSH: "It was only fair that they should have input."

LUCAS PAULSON: "So long as their input wasn't in devising the test."

JUDGE NEWNAN: "You object to the test itself?"

LUCAS PAULSON: "It was heavy on homophones. Naturally, that's a weakness of the transcriber. It was decidedly light on things that stenographers would find it difficult to cope with."

JUDGE NEWNAN: "Such as?"

LUCAS PAULSON: "Several people talking at once —which the transcriber can sort out because each person authorized to speak in a courtroom has a separate microphone and the computer sorts out the channels coming in from different micro-

199

phones. Accents—many of which the computer has been programmed to cope with, others of which it learns through its heuristic features. Specialized jargon—which can be loaded into the computer's speech dictionary prior to a trial in which that jargon is expected to occur. And so on."

JUDGE WELSH: "We've seen no evidence that the computer can handle all these things."

JUDGE NEWNAN: "Was the test set up to find out if it could?"

DAVID RUTLEDGE: "No."

JUDGE NEWNAN: "Well, exactly how was the test conducted?"

JUDGE WELSH: "We set up a HEST transcriber and employed an experienced courtroom stenographer. We read a text, and both the machine and the stenographer made a transcript. The machine made fifty-two errors. The stenographer made sixteen."

JUDGE NEWNAN: "What text? Where did you get this text?"

JUDGE WELSH: "It was prepared by our team of consultants."

LUCAS PAULSON: "Incidentally, did you pay these consultants?"

JUDGE WELSH: "No, they were volunteers."

JUDGE RUSSELL: "Jesus Christ!"

13

1977–1978

"I THINK THIS is a mistake," said Lucas. "I agreed to come here, but I think it is an error."

"They are your people, Lucas," said Jocelyn. "I don't see how you could refuse to meet with them."

"If there is one in the group, even one, who talks out of line—not just now, but ever—it's going to bring us a disaster."

"Worse for them than you. And they know it."

"There are too many of them," said Lucas.

"Well. You're here," she said a little impatiently. "Nobody forced you to come."

She turned off the highway and onto an unpaved road that climbed into a pine forest on the mountainside. She grimaced as the suspension of her Jaguar failed and she heard the clash of metal on rock. A wheel slid into a rut, and the transmission protested as she shifted down and spun the tires to fight her way out of the rut.

"I want to come back down before dark," she said grimly.

A mile or so up and around the mountainside, the road emerged from the pine forest and into a clearing. There, still well below the crest of the mountain, but with a spectacular view of the Pacific and many miles of coastline, stood a group of cabins and a lodge, all determinedly rustic. Jocelyn guided the Jaguar to a place among the other cars parked at the edge of the clearing, and she and Lucas walked the hundred yards up a grassy slope toward the lodge.

Dave Berger came out of the lodge, followed by Martin Kent, Gabe Lincoln, Patricia Bonneville, Les Harrington, Al Preston, and Jane Shnider. All of them were wearing blue jeans or shorts, sneakers, T-shirts; three of them had bottles of beer in their hands. They gathered around Lucas, and all of them shook his hand. They led him into the lodge, and Jane Shnider offered him a bottle of beer.

Lucas accepted the beer and sat down on one of the chairs facing the stone fireplace. He glanced around the one big room in the lodge. The place was a study in rusticity—lighted by bare bulbs strung across the rafters; furnished with a collection of maple chairs and couches upholstered with nubby fabrics, plus a big trestle table and benches; equipped with a hand pump on the countertop by the sink. Flypaper tapes also hung from the rafters. The place had a smell that suggested only occasional occupancy.

Jocelyn sat down beside him. She wore a tailored black skirt and a white silk blouse, her makeup was in place, and her hair was styled as always. Patricia Bonneville and Jane Shnider, who had never seen her before, stared at her with unconcealed curiosity.

"Well," Lucas said, noticing that everyone seemed to be looking at him with anticipation on their faces. "I guess somebody found a meeting place where Aunt Tillie won't pop by and recognize us. Where do we start?"

"We start," said Dave Berger, "by acknowledging the futility of the meeting. Any conspiracy that's hatched here is doomed to failure from the beginning."

"I wouldn't go quite that far," said Martin Kent. "We're here to explore our alternatives. Surely that's not futile." Kent had abandoned his IBM style since he left that company to join Electroscript, and this afternoon he was unshaven and sweaty in hiking shorts and shoes. He tipped a can of beer and took a noisy swallow. "Talk of a rebellion maybe, but—"

"You may as well understand," said Lucas. "You will not break the company. General Fraser will not change his mind, and the officers and directors of UNI will back him. I am sympathetic. I couldn't be more so. But you will not force the company to retreat. The general would let the company be destroyed before he would let himself be forced into backing down."

"Let's be completely objective," said Patricia Bonneville. She was a big, athletic young woman, unstylish, her face marred by an overbroad nose, thick lips, and a pinkish, coarse complexion. She had been Gabe Lincoln's assistant from the early days of Electroscript and had made important contributions to designing HEST's ability to cope with making multiple transcripts simultaneously. "How far does it set the company back if every one of us walks out? Maybe not including you, Lucas, and maybe not including Dave. How much would it hurt?"

"Lose the whole design team?" said Lucas. "It would take a year to recruit a new team and bring it up to speed. The company would lose a year."

"They can operate without us," said Gabe Lincoln. He had lost many pounds in the eight years Lucas had known him, and his beard was trimmed shorter and had begun to turn gray. "They might have some problems for a while, when the system develops a grinch, but they can operate it with the new people they've brought

203

in. What'll happen if we all leave is that development will come to a stop."

"Let's say that a little differently," urged Al Preston, a thin, tea-and-milk-colored black, the chief expert on vocabulary building. "We're not leaving the company. The company is leaving us."

All of them had received letters from Jim Cahill, notifying them that the company intended to open a new computer center in Westchester County, New York, early in 1978, and that thereafter HEST would be run from there and the San Mateo operation discontinued. All of them had been given ninety days to advise the company in writing if they would accept transfer to Westchester. Those who did not would be terminated when the move was made.

"I have to tell you," said Lucas, "that I did not oppose the move to New York. I'm sorry. I know it hurts most of you. But it makes business sense for the company, and there was no way I could make a persuasive argument against it."

"You didn't tell them we might all quit?" asked Jane Shnider. She was Martin Kent's chief assistant in communications technology and had followed him to Electroscript from IBM. A slight blonde, she lived with Kent in an apartment in Haight-Ashbury, and both of them remained married to their spouses. "You didn't tell them that they might have to put together a whole new team?"

"I had no right to say anything like that for you," said Lucas.

"Some of us are just out, then," said Patricia Bonneville. "I can tell you *I'm* not moving to New York. What happens to me if I move and six months later the company drops me?"

"You'll do all right, Trish," Lucas said. "Your talent

is going to be prized by somebody. You won't be out of work a month. I don't think any of you will."

"Well, I'm not goin'," said Gabe Lincoln angrily. "No way."

"The trouble is," said Les Harrington, "that this company has no place for creativity any more. Fraser's an old chicken-shit military officer, and the company's got his personality. What this company wants is neat ranks, marching in step. Well, the kind of people that march in step don't create anything."

"Except dust," said Gabe Lincoln.

"I came out here," said Martin Kent, "to talk about a strike. I came to see if anybody wanted to walk out Monday and let them see if they can run the system without us—that is, without this group here and maybe a dozen others who will go along but didn't come to the meeting. If we're not talking about that, I'm going on up the mountain."

"If you all walk out Monday," Lucas said to him, "the system will go down. Fifteen operations will be interrupted. Trials will be interrupted. The company will lose contracts, probably be sued for damages. Sales of new contracts will go to hell. The system will be down Monday. The system will be down Tuesday. Wednesday or Thursday they'll get it up again, running with somebody else on the controls. And gradually the company will recover."

"We'll all be out of jobs," said Patricia Bonneville. "We'll all have rotten reputations. And a year from now, we'll be a company joke. A year from now they'll laugh at us in New York, about how the California crowd thought they could fight the company."

"It just tears the guts out of me," said Al Preston bitterly. "I mean, we *made* this business—you, Lucas, and you, Dave, and Gabe and the rest of us—and now those New York pricks are going to take it away from us. I mean, the fact that we *built* the son of a bitch counts for nothing. Nothing . . ."

"Welcome to corporate America, man," said Gabe Lincoln bitterly.

They ate a picnic lunch on the trestle table, and Lucas circulated around the table, sitting with one and then another, chatting with them, putting his arm around them, patting their shoulders. He was moved. He guessed that Martin Kent and Jane Shnider would go to New York. None of the rest would, he supposed, and he might never see them again. He began thanking each of them, until he realized how final that sounded, then he stopped and just talked about what they had done and incidents that had happened and the future.

He was glum on the way down the mountain in Jocelyn's Jaguar. When they were on the highway, on their way back to San Francisco in late afternoon, she opened up to him.

"I didn't want you to know this until that back there was over, but I notified McConnell last week that I will not renew my contract with the company when it comes up in August."

Jerked out of his introspection, he frowned. "Uh . . . why?"

"They've hired an agency of New York flacks, the kind of slick advertising types that sell beer and pink plastic hair curlers. If I wanted to be subordinated to creeps like that, I'd work for that kind of agency."

"Matter of pride," he suggested quietly.

"Professional integrity," she said.

Lucas sighed and shook his head. "With the center here closed, I won't be back in California much," he said. "And you won't be in New York much. We're going to have to find—"

"Not necessarily," she interrupted. "Once a month, or once a week for that matter, isn't enough anyway. I'm seeing someone else. So are you."

"As a matter of fact, I'm not."

"I am. And it may be serious. He wants an exclusive, at least for a while. Why shouldn't I give it to him?"

Lucas stared at the highway rushing toward his eyes. "I have no right to tell you not to," he said quietly.

"Do you want to tell me not to?"

He nodded. "I wish I could."

"Why don't you?"

"I'd have to say I'm in love with you, that I want us both to give up everything else in the world and . . . I can't say that, Jocelyn. I can't ask you for that." He shrugged. "I haven't been in love—I mean, the great big lifetime thing—since I was in love with my wife, when I was a kid. I mean, I haven't felt that kind of lifetime commitment since I was twenty years old. I—"

"You respect me," she said wryly.

He shook his head. "Let's omit bullcrap. I just can't say to you, 'Commit yourself to me. Toss away everything else. You and I are it.' I can't say that—except maybe selfishly. Is that a cliché?"

"No," she said. "It's very honest. I appreciate it."

He looked away from her, fixing his stare on the highway once again. "Could *you* say it?" he asked.

She was silent for a moment. Then she shook her head. "But it's been great, Lucas," she whispered.

When Melanie's school took a spring break in March of 1978, her grandfather D'Annunzio put her on a plane for New York, and for the first time she made the flight alone. She was almost fifteen.

Melanie had become by then the woman she would be: striking for her expressive, dark eyes, her glossy, dark brown hair, a figure already filling out that would soon be heavy-breasted and broad-hipped. She might have been eighteen. Mature men cast appreciative glances, and she knew why. She was mature in understanding, too. And in self-esteem.

She was not surprised when a woman accompanied her father to the airport to meet her. Her father introduced the young woman as Connie. Melanie did not quite hear her last name, and she did not ask. Her father said Connie would accompany them on their vacation week in the Bahamas and, so they could get acquainted, would go with them to dinner this evening. Connie was a systems designer, her father said, and this afternoon she would show Melanie the new computer center while he went to a meeting he had to attend at General Fraser's house.

Melanie was disappointed that Connie was not Jocelyn, whose style had impressed her; and she was at first scornful of Connie's plain features, freckled cheeks, and soft talk. This Connie, as Melanie appraised her, was no great beauty and no great personality, but just a simple, outgoing young woman who plainly wanted to please both Melanie and her father. She was intelligent; none of his women ever failed in that respect; she spoke well and listened well, and much of her conversation was about computers. She was also, as Melanie immediately observed, stricken with Lucas Paulson.

Connie showed her the computer center. Melanie had seen the one at San Mateo, but it had been insignificant as compared to this one. Melanie was pleased that Connie was surprised by her knowledge of digital mathematics and computer logic. The people in the center congregated around the teenaged girl, the daughter of their vice president of product development, and were amused but impressed by Melanie's questions about megabytes, nanoseconds, and baud rate; and they walked away chuckling, wondering if they had just heard a well-rehearsed performance or been cross-examined by a prodigy.

The next morning, Lucas, Melanie, and Connie flew to Freeport.

Melanie spent hours snorkeling, then took her first scuba-diving lesson. She joined her father and Connie in champagne and took wine with her dinners. When she had gone to her room, after eleven o'clock, twice she slipped out and went walking alone in the edge of the surf in the moonlight—until a black policeman warned her it was not safe for young girls to walk alone on the beach so late. Another night she put on her most grown-up dress, a black sheath with spaghetti straps taut on her tanned shoulders, and went down to the hotel gambling room. She was bluntly propositioned.

The next night she did not leave her room until after midnight. Even then, she only stepped out on her balcony, clad in a pair of cotton pajamas, to breathe the salt air and to strengthen her resolve that someday she would live on a beach. The light in the next room—the room her father and Connie shared—fell on the concrete floor of the balcony. She was curious, and on an impulse she climbed around the wrought-iron barrier between their balcony and hers and stood in the shadows to the side of their sliding glass doors.

Only sheer curtains covered the glass, and Melanie could see her father and Connie naked on the bed. She was not surprised or distressed; she had long had in her mind a vivid image of what her father and Jocelyn must have done when they slept in the same bed in Saint-

Tropez. She sat down on the concrete under a glass-topped patio table, in the shadow of beach towels hung to dry, and watched.

She understood that what she saw was quite ordinary: two people sharing a simple, exultant moment. Even so, she was wide-eyed with fascination.

She had never seen a man naked before. The male organ between his legs was not like the one on Michelangelo's David; her father's organ stuck out from his crotch hair, long and thick; and, with the big soft thing behind it, it swung around as he moved. And Connie. Untidy hair grew all over her lower belly, and as she spread her legs wide and opened her slit she exposed fleshy inside parts, pink and shiny.

What they did was what Melanie understood that people did, but it was not as she had imagined. She had known he would push his organ into the woman's body, but she had not envisioned the labor that followed. One of them had tuned the radio in their room to a jazz concert. The wail and blare of trombones, trumpets, and saxophones seemed to set a wild rhythm for their tumbling and plunging. Melanie could hear their voices through the electric music, his in deep grunts that spoke pleasure as she had never heard it; Connie's in a low, warm laugh that spoke it better.

Once his organ slipped out of her, and Connie shrieked with laughter as she grabbed it and shoved it back in. She wrapped her legs around him then, and after that they heaved in unison.

Melanie felt the cold of the concrete through her light pajamas, first as a hard discomfort in her buns, then mysteriously as a new and pleasant stimulation. The tide was out, and the smell of new death on the air also stirred her. She began to touch herself with the cool tips of her fingers, slipping her hand inside her pajamas and touching first her nipples, finding it surprisingly pleasant to squeeze her breasts in her hands, then hurrying her hand down inside her waistband and to the smooth, slippery valley between her wet little lips. The touch sent lovely sensations through her whole body. Only a week before, maybe, she would have been troubled by those sensations, but she wasn't now; instead she sat there and stimulated herself, content, satisfied with her new knowledge, a little pleased with herself. When she saw her father roll away from Connie and the two of them lay on their backs with satiation evident on their faces, Melanie decided their feelings and hers must be something alike and that she would not postpone any longer than necessary the more complete pleasure they must have known.

The next day on the beach, she studied Connie with a newly critical eye, not certain that two people could do what she had seen her father and Connie do and not fall in love. She did not want Connie for her stepmother.

Half of Connie's face was hidden behind her huge sunglasses. Her belly had turned a permanent little roll on the upper edge of her bikini bottom, exposing a quarter inch of its lining as well as a few of her wispy pubic hairs. She had brought a gin and tonic to the beach, and although the ice had all melted and the glass was gritty with sand, she still sipped from it. She joined only occasionally in the desultory, heat-slowed conversation between Melanie and her father. She listened and smiled from time to time, but Melanie could not tell if her eyes were open behind her big sunglasses.

Melanie and her father talked about porpoises. Melanie had seen a film at school, suggesting their intelligence might be superior to that of apes.

"Maybe superior to ours," her father said placidly. Warmed by the sun, he welcomed his lethargy. "The

211

story is that they came out on land once, found it not as friendly an environment as the sea, and returned. If they had stayed out and competed with us, they might have beaten us."

Melanie laughed. "Maybe they'd make us put on shows for them. Jump through old tires. Bat balls around with our noses."

"Maybe they'd give us hamburgers for our reward," her father suggested, his smile spreading into a grin.

"Maybe they have a god who would've sent them a Christ to die for them," Melanie laughed.

"Maybe they've got no sins for Him to die for," said Lucas.

"What a disappointment for Him!" Melanie exclaimed, shrieking with unrestrained laughter. "No sins to die for! He'd be unemployed!"

"You two!" Connie protested. "That's disrespectful!"

Her father turned his face toward Melanie, his back to Connie, and rolled up his eyes and turned down the corners of his mouth. Melanie clutched her belly and roared with laughter.

November. Dressed in a tuxedo, Lucas worked his way to the bar and asked for a glass of red wine for himself and ginger ale for Melanie. She waited just beyond the crush at the bar, talking with Mrs. Lars Gustavson, wife of the HEST vice president for operations.

Melanie wore a knee-length, shoulderless white cocktail dress her father had bought her for the occasion; she wore a touch of makeup around her eyes and a dark lipstick, and her long hair was gathered and brushed into a swirl fastened high on her head. Mature as she looked, the bright wonder with which she viewed the party around her betrayed her youth.

The occasion was a dinner of the Anti-Defamation League of B'nai B'rith, for which HEST, like many corporations, had bought tables. HEST had bought two, and General Fraser had invited the wives of several of his vice presidents and Lucas Paulson's daughter. The dinner was at the Plaza, and it was preceded by a cocktail party in a room entered by descending a broad, carpeted stairway. Hundreds milled with their drinks, images of them front and back reflected by the gilt-framed mirrors that lined the walls. Senator Javits would be the after-dinner speaker, and Melanie had already met him and had been complimented by him.

"Some of these people!" Melanie whispered to Lucas when he handed her the glass of ginger ale.

"Familiar faces, hmm?"

That was why he had accepted Matt's invitation and had flown her in from Kansas City. She recognized film actors in the crowd, but there also were Broadway personalities, writers, composers, politicians, even statesmen—as well as top officers of major corporations. It was an opportunity for her to see something of the world that she had never seen before and might rarely, if ever, have occasion to see again. He himself was at a loss to identify some of the familiar faces that passed them in the throng.

"Nelson Rockefeller," Mrs. Gustavson said quietly to Melanie, nodding discreetly to her left.

Melanie covered her surprised grin with her hand.

"Lucas," said Jim Cahill. He gestured with his chin to one side. "Talk to you a minute?"

Lucas glanced at Melanie. She had been once more

213

engaged in talk by the bosomy Mrs. Gustavson, so he followed Cahill a few steps away from the group.

"Got a little problem," said Cahill quietly.

"What?"

"Webster's here. From Miami."

"So?"

"So we're a chair short at the tables. Matt wants Webster seated at a HEST table, for sure. That makes us one short."

"Meaning what?" Lucas asked darkly.

"Meaning Melanie," said Cahill. "After all, she's not with the company, she's a guest, and she's a child. Matt wants you to make some other arrangement for her. Take her somewhere. Twenty-one maybe. Somewhere."

Lucas's face had turned deep red. He seized Cahill by the lapels. *"No!"* he growled. "You tell Matt that when dinner is served, my daughter is sitting at the table where her place card is, and you tell him I will pick up anybody sitting in her place and throw him on the floor. Or, if it's a woman, I'll throw you to make room for Melanie. Or better yet, I'll kick *Matt's* ass. You tell him that, Jim. You tell him I'm mad enough and crazy enough to do it."

Cahill shook his head, his mouth wide open. "Lucas, for God's sake!"

"I mean it. Make other arrangements. You're good at arrangements. Make some."

Lucas moved protectively to Melanie's side as Cahill rushed to General Fraser, drew him aside, and whispered to him. He saw the general's face flush with anger, and the general turned toward him and mouthed the words, "Are you nuts?" Lucas smiled bitterly at him and nodded.

Someone touched his arm. He turned and found

Patricia Bonneville standing beside him, looking at him quizzically. "Uh," she said. "I was on my way over to say hello and seem to have witnessed a drama. Anything . . . ?"

He turned her away from Melanie—big, horsy Patricia, overdressed and overmade-up and awkward—and quietly and curtly explained to her.

"Hang in there, boss," said Patricia. "You got half an hour. I've got one idea. Don't do anything stupid till Trish has a crack at the problem." Then she hurried away.

Cahill slipped to his side. "Easy, man, easy," he whispered. "You said work on it. I'm working on it. Don't go near Matt, though."

Lucas took Melanie by the arm and led her around the room, letting her see as many of the people there as she could. She said she wished she had a little notepad so she could write down the names of all the famous people she did recognize. Ten minutes passed, and Cahill hurried by him, smiling wanly and nodding. Melanie had no inkling of the drama.

"Hey, boss!" It was Patricia again at his side. "Take a peek at the note I'm delivering to General Horse's-Ass."

The note, written on a sheet of Plaza notepaper, read: "Would appreciate it if you could spare Mr. Lucas Paulson and his daughter to be my guests at my table. Have long wanted to meet LP." Pinned to the note was the business card of Thomas Miller, chairman of the board of Consolidated Technologies. Patricia took back the note and strutted across the room toward General Fraser.

"What's that?" Melanie asked.

"Well," said Lucas. "It seems that you and I have been invited to be the guests at the table of the chief

215

executive officer of another company. CONTEKS, it's called. It's a bigger company than HEST, bigger than UNI. It's an honor, Melanie."

Melanie was seated across the round table from her father, beside Patricia Bonneville, whom she had met in San Mateo and remembered. Lucas was seated to the left of Thomas Miller.

"I can't tell you how very much I appreciate this, Mr. Miller," Lucas said when he was able to have a private word with his host.

"Trish explained your problem," said Miller. "I had extra places. I always take extra places for affairs like this. You never know what will happen."

Lucas shook his head. "What happened shouldn't have happened."

"I suppose there's no love lost between you and Matt Fraser," said Miller, "so you may not mind my telling you I've always thought of him as a second-rate intelligence. He's something of an organizer and manager, I suppose, but he has about him a cruel and arbitrary streak that I can't imagine he was taught by the army."

"He was a chicken-shit colonel, I can tell you that," said Lucas.

"Mmm. I hadn't heard about that. Incidentally, I owe you a debt of gratitude. Your letter was something of a surprise, but I took your advice and hired Patricia Bonneville, and she's turned out to be a real asset to us. Did Fraser turn loose any others that I should pick up for CONTEKS?"

"I'd have liked to see Gabe Lincoln with Trish, as a team. Unhappily, he's ill. In fact—I guess Trish knows it—Gabe is going to have to have coronary-bypass surgery, and even with that he may not have long to live."

"Yes, Trish knows. I'm sorry about Lincoln. I've

heard good things about him and not just from Trish. Anyway, she's given me something of a history of the speech transcriber, and I'm very pleased to have the opportunity to meet you."

"Well, I'm pleased to meet you, Mr. Miller. Wish I had met you earlier."

Miller smiled. "I always wondered why something as representative of high technology as the speech transcriber fell into the hands of a smokestack company like UNI."

"Evil stars," said Lucas. "A combination of unfortunate circumstances."

"Ah," said Miller, nodding. "Yes, I heard it was that way. So . . . We should keep in touch. Who knows what may evolve?"

14

1979–1980

AUGUST 10, 1979 was the fifth anniversary of the contract that employed Lucas Paulson as a vice president of HEST, and on that day the contract expired. The board of directors met that morning. Item on the agenda: the status of Lucas Paulson.

When he returned from lunch, he found a note on his desk saying that Arthur Ringold wanted to see him as soon as possible. He sent word to Ringold, who was in the directors' room in the executive suite; and in a few minutes Ringold came into his office and closed the door.

When they had exchanged pleasantries and Ringold had lit a Pall Mall, Lucas grinned and asked, "Well? I suppose I am unemployed."

Arthur Ringold laughed. "Technically, I suppose you are, for the moment. The board did not continue your vice-presidency. You are not surprised, I imagine?"

Lucas shook his head. He was troubled to see that Arthur had developed a palsy. His hand trembled as he manipulated his cigarette and lighter. Arthur had aged in the year since Lucas had last seen him.

"Matt was surprisingly complimentary toward you," said Ringold. "He moved that you be dropped as a vice president but said it was only because you did not exactly fit into the current management structure."

Lucas laughed aloud.

"No," said Ringold quickly. "He said he hoped to keep you with the company, only in a position that would permit him to use your talents and reputation more effectively than they could be used in the position you have held. He said it was really anomalous for you to be vice president in charge of any one department when your abilities go to everything the company does."

"Of course he doesn't want a vice president without portfolio," said Lucas.

"He's a firm believer in chain of command. You know that."

"And he hates what he calls insubordination," Lucas added.

Ringold sighed and put his cigarette between his lips and pulled hard on it. "Well, anyway . . . He suggested offering you a consulting contract, guaranteeing you two hundred thousand a year."

Lucas shrugged. "How very generous."

"You don't think it's generous?"

"No. It deprives me of participation in the executive-incentive plan and therefore of the big bonuses that will be paid to vice presidents as the company begins to make very high profits—which it will do within the next year or so. For two hundred thousand a year he binds me to a no-compete contract, which assures him I won't go somewhere else and start another transcriber. And, of course, I lose all authority in the company, especially the ability to protect my people. It's not generous at all, Art."

"Wait till you hear the rest of it," said Ringold. "I moved that you be elected to the board of directors at the next stockholders' meeting."

Lucas's face split into a broad grin. "You're kidding! You've got to be kidding!"

219

Ringold shook his head. "Not at all. And I got them to agree to it."

"How?"

"As you know, UNI now holds just 40 percent of the stock in HEST. After the big stock split, they sold off 35 percent of their original 75 percent to raise capital. Matt was uncomfortable with their doing that, but it was UNI's decision. Matt has bought about 1 percent, but the rest of the 35 percent has been bought on the over-the-counter market and is held by some fifteen hundred stockholders. Okay, so the company and Matt Fraser have, say, 41 percent. Among the three of us, you and Dave Berger and I have 25 percent. If we vote cumulatively, we can elect two of the eight directors— I'll stay as one, and you'll be the other. How does that appeal to you?"

"Matt will come to the stockholders' meeting with proxies from many of those small stockholders."

"Doesn't make any difference. The three of us still own 25 percent and are entitled to a quarter of the seats on the board. I announced that we wanted them."

Lucas smiled, then chuckled. "That must have given Matt fits."

Arthur Ringold pursed his lips and smiled. "Indeed," he murmured. "And Floyd Gosnold, too. So you are not shut out of management. In a sense, you are promoted. You'll be a participant, and since you are also a major stockholder, you will profit from whatever success the company has."

"And Matt—"

"And Matt will be unable to apply the word 'insubordination' to anything you do. So you hang on, take your two hundred thousand a year, and see what happens."

* * *

220

"Steady, boss. Pick up that right wing."

Lucas shot a tense glance at Trish, then he twisted the yoke too abruptly and overcorrected. The airplane rotated obediently on its axis, and the right wing passed through the horizon and pointed at the high clouds, while the left wing swung down and pointed at the Hudson River. He twisted the yoke again, not so much. The airplane leveled out.

"Okay, get her down to fifteen hundred," said Trish. "You'll have to hold altitude on this run, or the controllers will get sarcastic."

His mouth was dry as he eased the nose down and watched the altimeter. He had let the airplane get away from him for a moment. It was a Cessna Skyhawk, a high-winged four-seater, heavier and faster than the trainer in which he had gotten his license but still a simple airplane, easy to fly, as they all said; and he was embarrassed. He raised the nose just before the altimeter reached fifteen hundred and let the airplane wallow into a stabilized altitude within a few feet of what was assigned. It began to climb again, and he began to pull on the trim wheel, to trim it to hold altitude.

Out of the babble of voices from the speaker in the ceiling, he distinguished a call for him. "Skyhawk eight-five Quebec, contact La Guardia tower on one-two-six-point-five." He had amazed himself by how quickly he had learned to hear his calls out of the confusion of radio traffic on a busy frequency. They said it was instinctive, and apparently it was.

"Eight-five Quebec, Roger," said Trish.

She was handling the radios and now switched frequencies and talked to La Guardia. She had some four hundred logged hours as a pilot. It was her idea to fly the VFR route through the New York traffic-control area, a low-altitude corridor down the Hudson, over the George Washington Bridge, along the river between Manhattan and Jersey, and then out over the harbor. This corridor kept small airplanes well below the altitudes for the big jets' approaches to the New York airports and afforded a scenic fly-by of the city. It was, just the same, a challenge for a new pilot.

The Tappan Zee Bridge was behind them. The Palisades rose off their right. He could see the flat, water-bound expanse of La Guardia ahead and to the left, with a 727 lifting off in a steep climb to the northwest; it would pass well above and behind the Skyhawk. To the right was Teterboro. A Lear jet poised at the end of the runway like a runner on starting blocks suddenly rushed forward, sped down the runway, and hurtled into the air. It passed beneath the track of the 727, then turned up its nose and climbed fast, turning east, crossing the track of the Skyhawk more than a thousand feet above it.

"Watch your altitude," said Trish.

He had been looking at the jets, and his tense hand on the yoke had pulled it back imperceptibly but enough to cause the little airplane to climb a hundred feet. He put it down again, exactly on fifteen hundred.

"Skyhawk eight-five Quebec, descend to one thousand," said La Guardia.

"Eight-five Quebec, Roger."

The bridge loomed ahead, looking like a giant net spread across the river to catch little airplanes. Lucas's palms were wet as he turned the nose down and shifted his eyes back and forth between the altimeter and the bridge.

"Top of the tallest tower of the GW is 624," said Trish calmly. "Go between the towers. You'll clear by five hundred feet."

They had rehearsed this. Five hundred feet was plenty of separation, particularly for a little Skyhawk, churning along at a hundred twenty miles an hour; but the bridge looked big and close. He guided the plane toward the center of the span, where the cables hung closest to the deck.

"Got it made," said Trish. "Keep an eye on the chopper over there."

She pointed to a helicopter just over the Manhattan shoreline and flying upriver at maybe five hundred feet. The trouble with helicopters, as he had learned, was that they were like aerial puppy dogs; they didn't fly in straight lines and were apt to come at you from any direction, totally disregarding every traffic rule. This one was red and white, and it did turn and swing away over the river beneath them.

The Skyhawk passed over the bridge, the proximity exaggerating its flying speed. He took an instant to look at the traffic on the upper deck, then peered ahead and looked around for the helicopter.

"Skyhawk eight-five Quebec, descend to and maintain zero-five hundred. Contact Newark tower on one-two-seven-point-eight-five."

"Eight-five Quebec, Roger."

He took the airplane down, down until it was—as it seemed to him—skimming the green water of the Hudson, only five hundred feet above the surface. Buildings on Manhattan loomed above him now. A DC-9 turning sharply over the harbor ahead after its liftoff from Newark showed him why he was assigned to five hundred feet. He could not see Newark Airport, but its traffic roared over the harbor, turning and climbing, one jet after another.

"This is great for a back-seat passenger maybe, but I haven't got time to look," said Lucas to Trish, tilting his head toward the Empire State Building and the other towers of Manhattan, all rising well above his altitude. The World Trade Towers ahead, so close to the waterfront, looked like the guardians of a huge gate. "Frankly, it's a little scary."

"Watch your altitude," said Trish.

He was on his way to a two-day meeting at the Educational Testing Conference Center at Princeton. Trish had suggested they rent this Skyhawk and fly him to the meeting. She would return to pick him up on Friday afternoon and they would fly up to the Poconos and spend the weekend. He had agreed. On the ground, they could hike or even venture a horseback ride from their hotel. Trish would bring tennis rackets, he was sure, and she would shame him into playing her when she could find no other opponent, and then she would shame him more by beating him mercilessly. He had agreed to her plan, even the unspoken parts of it.

She pointed, and he swung the nose of the plane to the left to pass to the east of the Statue of Liberty.

"Eight-five Quebec. Understand your destination Princeton. Turn to two-five-zero degrees."

With a TWA 727 roaring immediately overhead, Lucas turned the Skyhawk to the new compass heading. This brought them past the Verrazano-Narrows Bridge and over Staten Island, over lush green golf courses. To their right lay industrial New Jersey—an obscured vista of docks, refineries, factories—under a dense layer of pollution.

He had signed a two-year consulting contract and

had been elected a director of HEST, as Arthur Ringold had promised. He had been relieved of all responsibility as a line officer, however, and the consulting assignments so far handed him had not been demanding. He was on his way to Princeton to lecture at a seminar for HEST sales representatives, to teach them a little about lawyers, the chief customers and prospective customers for the transcriber. It was typical of what he had been asked to do.

Lucas taught his seminar on Thursday afternoon, spoke at the dinner that evening, and taught again on Friday morning. The final event of the seminar was a luncheon Friday noon, which General Fraser and Walter McConnell were supposed to attend. When Lucas dismissed his assembly of salesmen and came out of the meeting room, he was confronted by James Cahill.

"Matt couldn't make it," he said. "Or McConnell. Watch out for who did come, though. He'll be with you as soon as he gets off the telephone."

"Who?"

"Len Stacey," said Cahill. "Matt's word to you is—be careful of anything you say to the guy."

Lucas grinned. "Soul of caution," he laughed.

Lucas remembered Stacey from that night in Fraser's New York apartment when they had amused themselves with young women from the office, with cold vodka and Beluga caviar. As a HEST vice president, Lucas had been supposed to communicate with officers of UNI only through General Fraser, but Stacey had often telephoned him with specific questions and had demanded his answers directly, not through channels. He had not telephoned since Lucas became a consultant.

Stacey was a tall, pleasant-faced man: bald, pink, freckled. His sandy-blond eyebrows were all but invisible, his lips were white, his eyes pale blue; his face seemed indistinct and bland. He was, though, as Lucas had learned, an incisive man, quick to learn and long to remember.

He sat beside Lucas at lunch. They spoke in generalities, pleasantries, and said nothing specific. Lucas introduced Cahill, who spoke to the marketing representatives on General Fraser's behalf and then introduced Stacey, who greeted them and told them they were the front line, the people who would make the company a success. When he sat down, he asked Lucas how he was going back to New York.

"I'm not, actually. A friend is picking me up in a small plane, and we're spending the weekend in the Poconos."

"How much out of your way would it be to drop me at Teterboro?" Stacey asked.

"Uh . . . I suppose we could do that. My friend is an experienced pilot."

"Good," said Stacey. He turned to Cahill. "That'll save me an hour or more. I'm flying out of Teterboro on a company plane for Chicago."

Lucas tossed his bag in the rear of his rented car, and Stacey slipped into the front seat. "I'm not going flying with you, you understand," he said as he slammed the door. "I wanted to talk with you out of Cahill's hearing. I'll take over the rental of this car and drive it back to New York."

Lucas glanced curiously at him and waited for him to say more.

"Floyd Gosnold is going to be elected president of UNI," said Stacey.

226

"I've heard that," said Lucas. "Began to hear it when he became senior vice president."

"Bother you?"

"Should it?"

"It should," said Stacey. "Gosnold doesn't like you and hasn't liked you since the day you told us the transcriber would never be finished but would eat up research-and-development money forever, just to keep up with the new technology."

"Well, that was the truth. What'd he want me to do, lie?"

"He didn't like it," said Stacey. "Still doesn't like it. It offends his sense of orderliness. He's a Harvard MBA, you know. His theory of management is to pry a highly specific business plan out of every manager, for this year and for two or three years after, and then to apply relentless pressure on every manager to meet plan. A business that requires constant tinkering, as he would put it, and can't know in 1979 what it's going to be doing in 1982 offends him. And, of course, so do you, personally."

"Oh?"

"From the beginning. I don't know why—maybe you didn't speak deferentially enough. Besides, Matt's fed him stories about how insubordinate you are, and Floyd doesn't like that either. He has a pronounced sense of hierarchy. When your contract ran out last summer, he wanted to dump you entirely. Matt wanted you around as a consultant, so he agreed to that; but when Arthur Ringold demanded a directorship for you, Floyd growled like a lion."

"I'm not entirely surprised," said Lucas. "The man is not subtle. So why do you tell me all this?"

Stacey drew a breath. "I'd like to separate HEST from UNI. Does that surprise you?"

"I think it's a good idea. It was an unfortunate match from the beginning."

Stacey nodded. "Because UNI is smokestack-oriented and run by smokestack managers."

"I have to give Matt this much," said Lucas. "He has shielded HEST from some of the worst manifestations of smokestack mentality. But not all. Not—"

"He hasn't been able to stop them from voting dividends on the HEST stock," Stacey interrupted.

Lucas nodded. "We should be retaining earnings, ploughing them into research and development. Otherwise, one of these days—"

"A new system will be developed and wipe us out."

Lucas sighed. "Well . . . I wouldn't put it quite that dramatically. But it is pure stupidity to skim off this company's earnings at this stage in its growth."

"You know why they're doing it," said Stacey.

"Sure. Earnings from the smokestack enterprises are down. UNI has to find money to put new hammers in the foundries. That's why UNI sold 35 percent of the HEST stock and reduced its 75 percent holdings to 40 percent—to raise capital."

"Put yourself in the position of some foundry manager in some squalid town in western Pennsylvania," said Stacey. "When he needed money to buy new hydraulic hammers, the company bought Electroscript. When he needed money to buy a new furnace, the company shoveled capital into computers. There he was, running an obsolete plant and struggling to keep his nose above the water, and the glamour boys of high tech kept demanding more capital. The company owned 75 percent of HEST. That was a whole lot more than it needed to control it. Sure they went for the money. And, don't forget, hydraulic hammers are things UNI management can understand."

"So you think now they're ready to sell the rest of it, huh?"

"I don't know for sure," said Stacey. "They might, for a price. But maybe—"

"You have a buyer?"

"Yes. I'm not at liberty to tell you who. The question is, Lucas, would you sell your stock, or would you give your proxy to my buyers? With the votes of your stock, Ringold's, and Dave Berger's, we would have 25 percent. If my associates bid enough for the publicly held stock, they could probably get enough to take control, even if UNI didn't go along. I think UNI might sell, if the price is right. But what if we could take control anyway?"

"Have you talked with Arthur?" Lucas asked.

"Yes. Ringold Corporation needs the money. Art will sell if he thinks we have enough other stock to make the deal work. Dave Berger says about the same thing."

"There's an old cliché that applies here," said Lucas. "'If you would assault the king, be sure you kill him.' If we go along with you and you fail, they'll shut us out absolutely."

"That's a chance we all take," said Stacey. "But I want to ask you another question. If we take over and start assembling a new management team for HEST, are you available?"

Lucas shrugged. "With the right deal . . . with the right company."

Stacey peered at the airport as Lucas turned into the lane leading to the hangar and runway. "I'd like to have you," Stacey said. "If I can assure my associates that you will come back into line management, they will be more inclined to make a tender offer. I can probably swing the deal without you," he said. "But you'd be

229

icing on the cake. I can't promise it, but we might make you president. Whatever the titles, I would be chief executive officer, and you could be chief operating officer."

"What about Matt?"

Stacey shook his head. "He's too expensive. In more ways than one."

Trish was big, strong, plain, and brilliant—and utterly insecure in the role of woman. For a defense, she played at being one of the boys. Occasionally, though, when her defenses were down, she revealed her discomfort with herself and was direct in her appeal for affection. At first, Lucas had been very careful about Trish, being uncertain of how hungrily she might grasp at any sign of affection, or what commitment she might read into the least intimacy between them. She had seemed to want to be a buddy, which he had accepted and encouraged.

Maybe it had been inevitable, though, that the occasion should arise when circumstances would dictate something very different. It had happened in her apartment two weeks earlier. They had been sharing a late-evening bottle of wine and some cheese; she had reached past him for the knife, accidentally touched him with her breasts, blushed deeply, and had been conspicuously aroused. She had offered herself to him: directly, bluntly, volunteering the assurance that she was realistic and would remain so. ("Hey, boss. Just recreation, okay? Just for fun. Just to cut another notch on the bedpost.") He had guessed she would be deeply humiliated if he refused, so he had gone to bed with her for a little while, in the dark, and after fifteen minutes they had returned to the bottle of wine.

The following weekend he had two more encounters with her—the second very much like the first, with Trish initiating their lovemaking but seeming to be quickly satisfied and afterward abashed and shy, as if she had exposed something she wanted to keep hidden. They had not yet spent a whole night together. In fact, she had made the reservations at the resort hotel, and he was not certain they would even share the same room.

She flew Lucas from Princeton to the airport near Stroudsburg, Pennsylvania, handling the airplane with practiced skill and complete confidence. She had, in fact, reserved just one room. She had also reserved horses for them to ride, and after they rode for two hours on the trails near the hotel, she swam laps while he sat at poolside with a drink and watched her. It was only when she had to dress for dinner and accompany Lucas to the candlelit dining room that she turned self-conscious and even timid. She wore flat shoes so as not to be taller than he; and her white cocktail dress, though she had bought it for this evening and had hoped the best for it, somehow emphasized just what she did not want to emphasize: her big bones and solid musculature, her forceful stride and gawky gestures.

"Jesus Christ, Lucas," she exclaimed nervously when they returned to their room after dinner. "What are we gonna do? Do you really want to sleep with me?"

"Sure," he said. "Why not?"

She sat down on the edge of the bed, letting her shoulders go slack. "Why not?" she asked. "That's what I came here for." She paused and sighed. "But I don't want you doing me any favors."

"Okay, it's a deal. I won't do you any favors."

"You could have any woman in the world," she said.

When he frowned and shook his head, she fluttered her hand and continued, "Yes, you could, just about. With me . . . Well. What you see is what you get."

"I like what I see," he said. He reached for her hands and took them in his as he stood before her. "I like you, Trish. I enjoy being with you. You and I are not in love with each other, but I admire you. You're a very special person. All you seem to lack is self-confidence."

"I've been robbed of it by experts," she whispered. "A succession of them."

"Well, let's see if we can't restore some of it. Come on, Trish. Let's you and I take a shower together."

She undressed hesitantly, blushing as she pulled off her underclothes. He had not seen her naked before, except in the shadows of her bedroom, with almost no light. The skin of her torso was white; her one-piece swimsuits had limited her summer's tan to her arms, legs, and face. Her big round breasts were solid. Her pelvis was like a bowl, filled with her belly. She was not fat. She was just a big woman, damaged in her self-esteem by a world obsessed with another style.

In the shower, he lathered her whole body, running his hands over her skin made slippery by warm water and soap. She closed her eyes and twisted sensually, drawing deep breaths. He pressed his middle finger between her legs, through her vaginal lips, and found her clitoris. He massaged it until she stiffened and writhed in the ecstasy of climax.

From then on, she was guided by instincts which both of them were surprised she had. When they stepped out of the shower stall, she dropped to her knees and began to lick the water off him, first his hips and belly, then his penis and scrotum, finally his buttocks, even running her tongue deep into his anus. When she felt him stiffen and gasp, she stayed there, pressing her tongue

in and exploring as far as it would reach, exciting him
with sensations he had never known before. Reaching
around his hips, she took his shaft in her hands and
manipulated it while she licked as far into his behind as
her tongue would reach—until he gasped and suc-
cumbed to a raging orgasm, spurting on the bathroom
floor.

"All I've ever had before were quickies," she whispered to him as they lay in each other's arms in bed. "I
just . . . accommodated guys. Most of them never even
bothered to try to make me come. That was what I was
going to do for you two weeks ago, our first time: just
make you feel good, because I like you so much. But
you . . . I came with you. You took the trouble. Jesus,
boss! I—"

"Shhh. How's *that* feel?"

"Oh, God!"

Lying awake beside him for hours, she offered her
breasts to be kissed, took him inside her as often as he
could rise to it, and kissed and caressed every part of
him to restore him. It was difficult to believe—but he
did believe—she had known nothing like this before
but offered him just what instinct suggested. She gave
him as much as any woman ever had.

When finally, just before dawn, she seemed about to
go to sleep, he ran his hand across her forehead to
brush her hair away from her eyes. "There's nobody
better than you, Trish," he said. "Absolutely nobody."

She sighed. "Thanks, boss," she whispered.

They ate breakfast at poolside the next morning,
sitting at a white-painted wrought-iron table under
potted trees, in the pleasant clatter of a resort-hotel
Saturday morning. They were easy with each other
now. She touched his hand on the table.

"I haven't even asked you about the meeting at Princeton," she said.

"I meant to mention one thing," he said. "I need a brief conference with Mr. Miller."

"I'm sure it can be arranged," she said. "He's an admirer of yours."

15

1980

"WHAT'S IT WORTH, do you think?" asked Thomas Miller.

"I expected you would audit it and find out," said Lucas.

They were having dinner in Miller's Park Avenue apartment, both in black tie, with a bottle of Château Lafite between them on the white linen tablecloth. The butler, in white gloves, bent over the table and served their plates: pheasant in a sauce of brandy and cherries, artichoke hearts, crisp green beans.

"One might pay a great deal more than an audit suggested," said Miller. "One might, that is, on the assurance of a knowledgeable consultant that it is worth more than the books could possibly suggest." He smiled slyly at Lucas. "Hmm?"

"It has only begun to scratch the surface of its potential," said Lucas. "I'll be frank. When I started it, I myself had only a vague idea of how complex and expensive the technology would be—or what it would be capable of doing once we had put it together."

"A machine that can listen to the human voice . . ." mused Miller as he looked to his fork and knife. "And can print the words it hears, even when they are spoken by a New Jerseyite or an Alabamian." He smiled again

235

and shook his head. "The potential is beyond the understanding of the UNI management."

Lucas nodded. "The meal is delicious."

"Thank you. I hope it is. I think you and I have something in common: we have learned to appreciate good food and good wine, that we *had* to learn it, in fact. Do I underestimate you? Forty years ago it was my best understanding that there were two kinds of wine: port and sherry, and one was white and one was red, though I was never sure which was which. At Thanksgiving and Christmas my mother put a bottle of sherry on the table with the turkey. Sweet sherry, it was; and before we ate, each of us drank a thimbleful of it. We thought ourselves rather sophisticated for that—and more than a little daring. I mean, wine, after all, on our dinner table!" He shook his head and laughed. "Sometimes, to be entirely frank, I regret the distance I've put between myself and those times and those people. Are your parents still living, Lucas?"

"Yes. My father still has his Chevrolet agency in Kansas City."

"And your daughter? That lovely young lady who was with you at the B'nai B'rith dinner."

"Melanie is a freshman at MIT. I'm very proud of her. She graduated valedictorian of her high-school class and was accepted at every university she applied to. I can't take much credit, actually. She's lived with her maternal grandparents."

"You never remarried?" asked Miller somberly.

"No. I might have, if I had found someone."

"You and Trish . . . ?"

Lucas smiled. "We respect each other."

Miller chuckled. "Euphemistically put. Forgive the personal questions."

"Not at all."

"Do you mind one more?"

Lucas shook his head. "If I mind, I won't answer it."

"What happened in Vietnam? Between you and Fraser? Do you mind telling me?"

Lucas sighed. "He was a lieutenant colonel when I met him. Battalion commander. And he was a . . . loud-mouthed martinet. He sent two companies to take a ridge, for no purpose but to kill the VC who were supposed to be up there. They weren't up there. They'd left. We didn't kill any—except maybe half a dozen. But he had a general coming, and he wanted to show him bodies, so he sent my platoon back up to carry down what bodies we could find. When we got back to the top of the ridge, just the one platoon now, we found the Charlies had come back in force. A fire fight developed. We were in trouble. So Colonel Fraser fixed it for us. He called down heavy artillery on us. He gave us ten minutes to get out, but then he didn't wait ten minutes. More of my men were killed by our 155s than were killed by the Charlies."

"Of course, he didn't admit his mistake," said Miller, frowning.

"Oh, no. It was all my fault."

"What's his attitude about it now?"

Lucas smiled. "I have no idea. He doesn't remember me from Vietnam. He doesn't identify me as the lieutenant who got on his shit list and was sent up a ridge to harvest corpses."

"He identifies you," said Miller, nodding emphatically. "You make him uncomfortable every time he sees you."

Lucas shook his head. "I don't think so. I really don't think he makes the connection. Even if he did, it wouldn't make him uncomfortable. I doubt he's ever admitted to himself that he did something stupid."

Miller lifted his glass and for a moment stared into his wine. "I don't think IBM would be interested in acquiring HEST. Nor would Xerox or Control Data. Small companies would be hard-pressed to raise the money—two or three hundred million, one would guess—and I think I pretty well know who has that kind of money or is trying to raise it. Stacey could be talking to a Japanese company. Do you think he'll talk to you again before they go public?"

"He has to. I gave him no assurance. Neither did Dave Berger. Dave doesn't particularly like the deal. He says it looks too much like a personal squabble inside UNI management."

"The professor has put his finger on one of the problems," said Miller, raising his chin high. "This proposition does look like a blood feud inside UNI. What's Stacey's real interest? Is he actually interested in getting HEST out of the hands of smokestack management, or is he chiefly interested in cutting Gosnold's throat? Beware of being made a pawn, Lucas."

"I don't like the idea of HEST being made a pawn, either," said Lucas. "Or Electroscript, as I'd rather call it."

"If you find out who's making the offer, let me know," said Miller. "Immediately. CONTEKS might bid. An interesting opportunity may arise."

In late afternoon, General Fraser liked to take off his coat and sit in his shirt sleeves, sometimes with his shoes off, too, in his Japanese office. Usually, after five o'clock, he allowed himself a Scotch (Glenfiddich) on the rocks and offered a drink to whomever happened to be with him. He had no wine to offer, so Lucas accepted a drink of Scotch. It was Lucas's habit, since he had become a consultant, to wear cashmere jackets and dark slacks to the office; and this afternoon he was comfortable in a gray cashmere jacket and black slacks, with Gucci loafers. The general sat in a corner of his big leather couch, with one leg stretched out on the cushions. Lucas sat deep in a leather chair.

"Just how much importance do you attach to corporate loyalty, Lucas?" the general asked.

"About as much as you do, I suspect," said Lucas. He took the question as the opening of a challenge, perhaps even an accusation.

General Fraser was relaxed, however, and continued in a conversational tone. "Good enough," he said. "But, seriously, do you suppose a man owes his loyalty to the company he works for?"

"If the company has earned it," said Lucas. "Loyalty should not be demanded or given on demand. It should be earned."

"And how would a company earn it?" the general asked.

"Not just by paying a man for his time," said Lucas. "It requires a good deal more. Mutual respect . . ."

"Well, what would you suggest a company do about a man who is trying to cut its throat behind its back?"

"Companies don't have throats to be cut," said Lucas. "People do. I assume you have somebody in mind. A cutter and a cuttee."

General Fraser grinned and chuckled. "Yes, I do. Fortunately, you and I are only tangentially involved. I do have somebody in mind, though. I'll ask you to keep the matter confidential."

Lucas nodded.

"If you haven't gotten it already, you will probably soon receive an offer for your stock in HEST. It will be from NDT—"

"NDT?"

"Nippon Digital Technologies. They are going to try to take HEST away from UNI, by buying your stock, Arthur Ringold's, and Dave Berger's, plus what they can get from the small stockholders. The offer will be attractive. They will probably get a substantial part of the publicly held stock. If they can get half of it, plus yours and Arthur's and Dave's, they will outvote UNI in a stockholders' meeting and take control of the company."

"So I should extend my loyalty to UNI?"

General Fraser laughed and shook his head. "I'm not stupid enough to think you feel the slightest loyalty to UNI. I wasn't talking about *your* loyalty."

"Ah. Good."

"I'm talking about Len Stacey," the general said, his voice dropping and his face darkening. "He's promoting this tender offer. He's in bed with NDT. Fortunately, in my years in Japan I became well acquainted with some of the principal officers of NDT. . . . You follow me. They are going to offer ten dollars a share for HEST stock. I need hardly tell you, it will make you a multimillionaire if you sell."

"Even after capital gain," Lucas agreed dryly.

"On the other hand, you'll be selling your share in the future of the company you contributed so much to build," said the general. "Ten dollars a share? Maybe it will be worth twenty in a year or two. How long will it be before it's worth fifty?"

"On the other hand," said Lucas with a small smile, taking a sip of his Scotch, "how much money can a man use?"

General Fraser lifted his own glass, whirled it to set the Scotch moving, the ice rattling. "I spoke of loyalty," he said. "It is one thing to set in motion a tender offer, in an effort to take control of a business. It is quite another to do so when you are an officer of the corporation that owns that business and wants to retain control of it. There is a conflict of interest, to say the least."

Lucas shrugged. "I suppose you are working your way toward a point, Matt," he said.

"All right," said General Fraser, betraying some annoyance at being prompted. "Len Stacey is an unethical son of a bitch. He knows Gosnold will kick his ass out of UNI as soon as Gosnold takes over. He wants to hurt UNI. Also, he wants a landing place, and he thinks the Japs will make him CEO of HEST. He may contact you and try to encourage you to sell to NDT. He may try to sweeten the pot with some kind of offer. I mean, he might talk about a better consulting contract or even another vice-presidency." The general shook his head. "Check his record. The battlefield is littered with bodies with his knife in their backs."

Lucas nodded. "Well . . . I only have five percent."

General Fraser frowned as he sipped from his glass. "You may control ten. I suspect Dave Berger will follow your lead."

"Ten . . ."

"And Ringold. Arthur has a good deal of respect for you."

"I begin to see your point, Matt."

"You got him by the short hairs!" laughed Arthur Ringold.

"Not really," said Lucas. "He's covering his back."

Lucas had flown to San Francisco to meet with Dave Berger and Arthur Ringold. They had their tender offer from Nippon Digital Technologies, Incorporated —$10.25 per share of HEST stock, conditioned on

NDT being able to acquire 45 percent. They sat in Dave Berger's cluttered professorial office on the Berkeley campus, using the hour before he taught a seminar on artificial intelligence.

"You know something," said Dave Berger. "The temptation is very strong for me to take my money and kiss off the whole business. Do you realize, Lucas, how much money we're going to get? Almost eighteen goddamn million dollars! What the hell? Why not take it and forget the transcriber? It was a job well done, and we'll be paid off."

"Let me ask you something, Dave," said Lucas gravely. "When you get your eighteen million, what are you going to do?" He glanced around the office. "You gonna quit here? Quit teaching? You going to go to some tropical island and live on the beach for the rest of your life? Or how about a nice flat in Paris? What are you going to do?"

"I'm going to stay right here and teach," said Dave.

"Good for you," said Lucas.

"I get your point," said Dave glumly.

"Anyway," said Lucas. "Ten and a quarter. What's it worth next year? And the year after? You pay your capital gain and you're going to have nine million. For twelve years' work. Five years from now you back your yacht against the quay at Saint-Tropez—right beside Matt Fraser's that's three times bigger." He shook his head. "I'm emotional about it. Maybe I'm wrong."

"For me, it's not so simple," said Arthur Ringold. "I don't own a single share of HEST. Not personally. Ringold Corporation owns it. And Ringold Corporation needs money. I won't be buying any yachts with the fifty-four million Ringold Corporation gets."

"You've decided to accept the offer?" Lucas asked.

"I have to, boys," said Arthur Ringold sadly. "I have

no choice. You remember I don't own a controlling interest in Ringold Corporation. My stockholders and directors will want to take the money."

"Even if the HEST stock is likely to double in value in less than five years?" Lucas asked.

Ringold nodded. "For myself, I'd stay in, even though my company is pinched. My directors won't."

Lucas sighed. "How badly will it hurt you, Art, if the tender offer fails?"

"We'll survive."

"You can always sell the stock later."

"Not for ten and a quarter," said Ringold.

"It will sell on the market for ten and a quarter within the year, I promise you," said Lucas.

"What do you have in mind?" asked Berger.

"If NDT gets the Ringold shares, they will have 15 percent. If they got all the stock in the hands of small stockholders—which they won't—they'd have 48 percent. Realistically, they might get 25 percent, making them a total of 40 percent. UNI has 40 percent. That leaves you and me, Dave, with 10 percent between us, in what some of my Midwestern friends used to call the 'catbird seat.'"

"What'll you do?"

Lucas grinned. "I'll think of something."

Melanie telephoned from Cambridge to discuss her summer plans with her father. She wanted to spend her summer on Block Island, working as a waitress in one of the old waterfront hotels. She knew another girl from MIT who was going to work there, and this girl had assured her that she could make and save a lot of money. Besides, she would be close enough to New York that her father could fly out and visit her on weekends. Lucas objected that her grandparents in

Kansas City would be disappointed if she did not come home for the summer. She told him that she did not want to go back to Kansas City—at least not to live there—ever again. He told her that she could move into his New York apartment and work for HEST or some other company. She said she wanted to try Block Island. He finally said okay.

He and Trish flew out the second week Melanie was there. He landed a small Piper on the one runway on the island, and they took a cab to the hotel.

The hotel was a nineteenth-century oceanfront hotel: a three-story, white-frame building in the center of town, facing the ferry slip where every day hundreds of tourists came ashore on the island and headed on bicycles and mopeds for its Atlantic beaches. Block Island offered few hotel rooms, and what there were were booked for months in advance; but it offered pleasant seafood lunches and dinners, served by handsome college students in airy dining rooms or on the long porches or in sidewalk cafés.

Melanie worked in one of the sidewalk cafés, in a small, hedged garden between a hotel and the street. Dressed in a short black skirt, white blouse, and red-and-white-checked apron, she hurried among her tables with the enthusiasm of youth and inexperience. She had only an occasional moment to say hello to Lucas and Trish. She was only free in early morning or late evening, but she seemed happy enough, and Lucas promised to fly out again, planning his arrival for early in the day, so they could sit down and talk.

When he arrived back in New York, waiting on his desk was notice of a meeting of the board of directors of HEST.

* * *

Arthur Ringold did not attend. Neither did Leonard Stacey. Six members assembled in the conference room near General Fraser's office: Floyd Gosnold, Terrence McGinley and Maynard Bruce of UNI, General Matthew Fraser and James Cahill of HEST, and Lucas Paulson.

Although General Fraser was president of HEST, Floyd Gosnold sat at the head of the table and rapped it sharply with an ashtray to demand attention. He scowled at Lucas, then bestowed much the same scowl on each of the others.

"The first item on the agenda—correction, the *only* item on the agenda," Gosnold mumbled, running his words together, "is the NDT tender offer. Matt . . ."

General Fraser crushed his cigarette in a glass ashtray. "Ringold Corporation notified NDT Friday that it accepted its offer of $10.25 per share," he said. "Small stockholders have accepted to the extent of 22 percent. That means NDT can acquire 37 percent of the stock, if it elects to pay the price—which it is not yet bound to do, since it conditioned its offer on acceptance by shareholders representing 45 percent. Assuming it does pay the price offered and take up the stock, NDT will vote 37 percent. I think we can assume a few more stockholders will accept the NDT offer, so its ultimate vote may be 39 or 40 percent. UNI has 40 percent. I myself have about 1 percent." He glanced at Lucas. "This means that Lucas Paulson and David Berger have become, in effect, the key stockholders. If they vote with NDT, NDT takes control. If they vote with UNI, UNI retains control." He fastened a baleful eye on the three directors from UNI. "By selling off 35 percent of the HEST stock, you put us at the mercy of our minority stockholders, gentlemen."

"Unless those two gentlemen split their vote," said Maynard Bruce.

"Professor Berger has given me his proxy and a power of attorney," said Lucas.

"So we know precisely where we stand," said Gosnold. "What do you want, Mr. Paulson?"

Lucas glanced at General Fraser, who with pursed lips stared at the notepad before him and rhythmically tapped it with his pencil. He glanced at Cahill, who met his eyes with a half-amused stare.

"I'm realistic," said Lucas. "I don't want anything outrageous. On the other hand, I may as well say before I tell you what I want that it is not negotiable. If you are not willing to meet my terms, then I'll take my chances with the new management."

The general's face had turned red. Gosnold's frown had all but closed his eyes.

"I want, for Dave Berger and for me," said Lucas, "a share of this company's executive-incentive plan. I want a ten-year contract, providing that Dave and I will be paid the same cash or stock or other benefits that are received by the best-paid recipient of benefits under whatever plan that recipient participates in—either of HEST or UNI. In other words, I want a share of this company's success."

"You want the same incentive compensation that General Fraser receives?" Gosnold asked indignantly.

Lucas nodded. "If he's the one who gets the most." He nodded again. "And to earn this compensation, I expect to participate actively in the management of the company. I don't care if you make me a vice president again. In fact, I prefer being a consultant. But I don't want to sit around the office doing nothing, just waiting for my checks to be delivered."

246

"I'm not sure how you draft a contract to cover this latter point," said Cahill dryly.

"Oh, you don't need to," said Lucas. "I think you'll find ways to make me active. You know I have a contribution to make. And since you're paying for that contribution, I imagine you'll ask me to make it."

"And in return for this," Gosnold asked, "you'll vote your stock with management?"

"When the contract has been signed," said Lucas, "I will advise our Japanese friends that Dave Berger and I do not accept their offer of $10.25 a share for our HEST stock."

At home in New York on a Tuesday evening five weeks later, Lucas received a telephone call from Jim Cahill. "Matt would like for you to pop by the townhouse, if you're not doing anything important. Just for a drink or two. Just the three of us."

Lucas walked the distance, on a late-summer evening, musing about the motive that might lay behind this friendly voiced invitation. It could not be casual. Matt Fraser did nothing casually, not with him, anyway. He wondered if young women from the office had been pressed into service for this occasion, as they had been the last time he had been invited to the townhouse.

The general was casually dressed, in slacks and a golf shirt. Jim Cahill had taken off his necktie and jacket but was still in a white shirt and the trousers of a business suit. They were conspicuously relaxed, sipping ice-cold vodka and nibbling on crackers. Cahill went to the kitchen as soon as Lucas had sat down, returning in a moment with the bottle of Stolichnaya from which they were drinking, and a lump of Beluga caviar.

247

"You know what I found out about you?" General Fraser said to Lucas. He nodded emphatically, and Lucas judged that he had drunk more than what was missing from the bottle of vodka. "You dicked Bunny." The general nodded again. "You and I shared a pussy for a while. I hope you kept your cock out of strange places and didn't plant any exotic biology in her for me to catch."

Lucas lifted his glass. "The same to you, Matt," he said.

The general laughed. "You have good taste."

"No, *she* does," said Lucas.

The general's smile weakened. "You know how I found out?" he asked.

Lucas shook his head.

"She *told* me. That's why she doesn't work here any more."

"That's why she doesn't have a key to my apartment any more," said Lucas.

General Fraser's smile returned, and he laughed again. "You son of a bitch . . ."

Cahill seemed uncomfortable with the direction of the conversation. "You want to talk to Lucas about the Senate hearings?" he asked the general.

The general shrugged. "You can tell him about it. Tomorrow," he said.

"You said you wanted more responsibility," Cahill said to Lucas. "We'd like for you to take up our cause in Washington, see if you can get more government agencies to transcribe their hearings with HEST. Beginning with the United States Senate. We'd like to get started with an important committee. You have contacts—"

"That's what you said you wanted," said the general

to Lucas. "Responsibility. Well, see if you can crack that nut."

Lucas nodded. "I'll give it a try," he said.

"Well . . . whatever you do, I can't fire you. You and your goddamn contract."

"I understand the UNI board of directors met this morning," Lucas said.

The general grinned. "That's why we asked you to come over," he said. "To share a little celebration."

"It came out well then," said Lucas, putting his spoon into the lump of caviar and transferring a generous serving to his plate.

"You'll love it," said the general.

"He's right," said Cahill. "You're going to love it."

The general's eyes narrowed. "Len Stacey," he said. "That son of a bitch is on the street. His Japs sold him out. Or maybe I should say *my* Japs did. They met with me two weeks ago, in Tokyo, and showed me documents that Stacey had delivered to them to encourage them to make their tender offer. The most important was a set of the functional specifications for the heuristic element of the system design. The son of a bitch was giving away the store."

"This morning," said Cahill, "Floyd Gosnold confronted Stacey with copies of the documents he had handed over to NDT. The board of directors authorized a criminal prosecution, unless Stacey resigned and surrendered every right he had under the company's incentive and retirement plans."

"He signed everything that was put in front of him," said General Fraser.

"But that's only half of what happened," said Cahill. "Matt . . ."

General Fraser laughed. "We know how much you

249

like Floyd Gosnold," he said to Lucas. "Well, congratulations. He's gone, too."

"Why?" Lucas asked, surprised.

The general clasped his hands behind his head and leaned back in his chair. "First he bought Electroscript. Floyd went to bat for that decision and pushed it through over a lot of opposition. Then he spent a lot of money on it. Then it began to make a profit and show a potential for making a great deal more; and at that point he damned near lost it. In fact, if not for what some of the directors called the loyalty of one Lucas Paulson—a man Floyd had condemned in intemperate terms in more than one board meeting—he *would* have lost it."

"Actually," interjected Cahill, "some of the board members were angry that he had put you, Lucas, in a position to—as they phrased it—blackmail UNI."

Lucas drew a deep breath and grinned. "And what about you, Matt?" he asked. "It would seem to me your position paralleled Gosnold's. I mean, you wanted to buy Electroscript. You spent money on it—"

"I was opposed to selling off 35 percent of its stock," said the general. "I was on record for that."

"Stacey had friends on the board," said Cahill. "They saw their man shot down in flames, and they took their revenge."

"So who's the new president of UNI?" Lucas asked.

"Sam Magnuson," said Cahill. "A capable man."

General Fraser drank vodka. "Odd how things sometimes work out, isn't it?" he asked absently to no one in particular.

16

1981

THE 727 BANKED steeply over Flushing and turned onto
the final approach course for La Guardia runway 31.
The orange lights on the expressways below shone
through the whirling snow, the first glimpse of the
ground for passengers peering anxiously from the windows; and soon they could see the streams of traffic, red
and white lights, at a standstill in both directions on
every roadway. People began to grumble. Getting
home, whether into town or out to the suburbs, was
going to be an ordeal. Lucas glanced at his watch—
7:45. It was going to take longer to get to his apartment
than it had taken to fly from Washington.

The 727 touched down. As it taxied toward the
shuttle terminal, snowplows worked the taxiways and
the tarmac of the ramps. The chief flight attendant
began her recitation about remaining seated until the
captain had turned off the seat-belt sign. Lucas ran
down his alternatives for getting home: a Carey bus, a
cab, even a rental car. It was going to make little
difference. Nothing was moving. The question was,
which was least uncomfortable? He was still trying to
plot some bearable way to get into Manhattan—and
had begun to face the possibility of being stuck for
hours in the airport—as he trudged through the corridor toward the main lobby.

"Hey, boss!"

Dressed in a leather jacket, blue jeans, and high boots, Trish waved and trotted toward him.

"Hey, you came back in a blizzard! Pay hell getting home."

"What are you doing out here?" he asked.

She seized his hand and rose on tiptoe for a kiss. "Oh, honey," she breathed. "I knew you'd be stuck. So I came out and . . . I've made arrangements."

"How'd you know what flight I'd be on?"

"Well, you weren't on the last one, and you weren't on the one before that. So you had to be on this one, which is probably the last one in tonight. If not . . . Well, Trish would have had to spend the night alone."

"Where? What arrangements?" he asked. He put down his bag and pulled on his overcoat. "How did you get out here in this mess, and what do you mean by arrangements?"

"Kommen Sie mit mir," she laughed.

He followed her out of the shuttle terminal. Laughing still, she waved and whistled until she caught the attention of the driver of a van. He blinked his lights and pulled up to where they stood, his windshield wipers barely clearing the heavy snow from his windshield. MARRIOTT HOTEL was lettered on the side.

"I told you!" she shouted at the driver as they climbed in. "I said he'd be on this one."

"It was either that or forget it, lady," said the driver, characteristically New Yorker in his half-sullen, half-facetious tone.

"For ten bucks more, you'd have waited out another one," she said.

"Nope. Would never have got back. Lucky if we make it now."

He negotiated the maze of roadways out of the

airport, the van sliding on pavement the plows could not clear as fast as the snow fell. Cars were off the edges. Crossing over the expressway, they could see the blinking lights of two emergency vehicles stuck in the stalled traffic. The driver made steady progress, even so, toward the gleaming red sign of the Marriott. In ten minutes, he deposited them at the door, and Trish gave him another ten dollars.

In the room, Lucas stood at the window and looked at the snow and the miles-long lines of cars below. "Nothing," he said, "like the care you get from a resourceful woman."

Trish, who had shed her jacket and jeans and was dressing to go down to dinner, stepped up behind him in her panties and bra and put her arms around him. "I couldn't just sit in my place all night, thinking about you stuck in the airport—or freezing in some car on the road for five or six hours. No way."

He turned and drew her up in his arms to kiss her. "You are somethin' else," he said.

Over rare roast beef and red wine in the restaurant, Lucas told Trish that his trip to Washington had been a mixture of success and frustration. He had talked with one senator and with six staff members.

"The senator," he said, "is an overburdened man, with too many responsibilities and minimal capacity to meet them. He'd make a good insurance agent, which is what he was fifteen years ago. He's genuinely interested in the transcriber but really can't get it through his mind what advantages it has. I couldn't help but like the man, but I was appalled at his limitations."

Trish cut a bite of thick, red, juicy beef and lifted it to her mouth with conspicuous delight.

"So far as Perkins was concerned, he made it very

plain what he wanted. To be paid off. He wasn't even subtle about it. He could line up the committee votes, he said. But he assumed the company would make it worth his while."

"What'd you tell him?"

"I told him the Senate could transcribe its proceedings with quill pens and shake sand on the pages for the rest of this century before he'd be paid off. Then he got loudly indignant and said he'd never suggested anything of the kind, that he was a man of the highest integrity, that never in his twenty-eight years on the Hill had anyone even suggested the slightest impropriety, et cetera, et cetera, et cetera. I told him I'd read Representative Ashbrook's confidential memorandum on him. That shut him up. Of course, it doesn't get us the votes."

"Oh for the life of a lobbyist," said Trish.

Lucas smiled. "Actually, I don't mind it as much as I thought I might. Washington sort of grows on you. It's the most provincial town you could imagine, but it has its charm."

She reached across the table and touched his hand. "I missed you," she said.

Back in their room, once more they stood at the window and looked at the stalled traffic. Standing behind him, Trish cupped her hands on his crotch and whispered in his ear that she wanted to give him a bath.

He closed the curtains, and they undressed. She kept her pubic hair shaved off now—because he had told her how much he liked that and had expressed satisfaction with it when he first saw her shaved. She stood with her legs apart as soon as she had pulled down her panties— giving him a display of her naked lips and the shiny pink between them. She hurried their bath inside the plastic shower curtain in the tub. When they were half dried, she hurried him to the bed. He knew why she had suggested she wanted him to have a bath.

Trish put both pillows under his hips, and he lay face down, resting his head on his arm, knowing his backside was lifted toward her. She caressed his buns with her hands, then kissed him there, and finally she pressed her face to his anus and thrust her tongue inside. It was what she had done, impulsively, their first night. Now she had learned to bring him all the way without touching his shaft with her hands—using them instead to spread him, exploring deeply with the moist, mobile tip of her tongue, finding and caressing what he had never guessed was erogenous. It was, in a special and different way. Making the place slippery with her saliva, she licked and penetrated with her tongue until he came to an extraordinary, almost painful orgasm.

He rolled off the pillows, onto his back, and she seized his shaft and sucked it hungrily into her mouth, drawing the last drops from him. She licked him, up and down his penis, all over his scrotum, keeping him erect. She rolled him on his side then and drew herself close to him, clutching his organ in her hands and rubbing it in her cleft. She rubbed it there, in that warm, wet place, without offering to shove it inside, until he climaxed again.

"That's twice without giving you anything," he whispered, gently pressing her hair back off her forehead.

"You're tired," she said. "I knew you were tired. And there's always the morning."

"There's some brandy in my bag," he said. "If you . . ."

She took out the bottle. He called room service and ordered a pot of coffee. They looked out the window again, at the traffic, and at the airport, which was now

255

closed, though the snow had ceased to fall, until the boy knocked. Trish waited in the bathroom while he received the coffee and tipped the boy, using the time to wash off and dust herself with talcum. He poured coffee and brandy for them.

"I'm grateful to you, Trish," he said quietly as he sipped coffee. "I mean, for coming out here tonight. It was more than thoughtful."

She sat on the bed, one leg drawn up, her coffee cup in one hand, the bathroom glass with a splash of brandy in the other. "You know why I came," she said solemnly.

He nodded.

"I wasn't going to say. I told you I wouldn't get this way." Her voice thinned and stopped, and she whispered. "But I'm going to say it. I have to. I love you."

"Why *not* say it, Trish?" he asked.

"It was supposed to just be fun. You would never have come near me after our first time, if I hadn't promised it was just for fun. You wouldn't have wanted big old ugly Trish falling in love with you."

"*Trish.* Stop that." He shook his head and sighed. "Forget that. I'm in love, too, Trish. With you."

She put aside her brandy and coffee. Her hands were trembling, and tears ran down her cheeks. "Why?" she sobbed.

"Why not? You're kind, thoughtful, intelligent, witty . . . And you're beautiful, Trish. In your own special way, you are beautiful. I mean physically. You are beautiful."

"Lucas . . ."

"We have so much in common. The same ideas. The same interests. What a partnership!"

"Oh, God, boss! Oh, God!"

* * *

256

Melanie came home for her spring break. Unconsciously, they had both begun to refer to his apartment as her home. Lucas insisted she fly home to Kansas City from time to time, but she had a room now in his apartment. Although she was at school and not home much, for the first time since she was an infant she lived with him.

His apartment—the fourth one he had lived in since he moved to New York—consisted of a long living-and-dining room with big windows affording him a view of the East River, a windowless library, two bedrooms, two baths, and a kitchen.

His living-room walls were hung with bright paintings and prints, which at night were lighted by spots from the ceiling track. The floor was varnished dark but mostly covered by Oriental rugs in assorted sizes and colors. His furniture was modern: two lounging chairs with ottomans, a comfortable leather-covered couch, a huge freeform, glass-topped table usually covered with books and magazines, a tall rack for his music system. Usually he left the drapes drawn back from the river-view windows. He enjoyed the changing light on the river panorama, from the bright sunlight of dawn to the orangish city glow of night.

Melanie was as untidy as he was, only her clutter was different: clothes more than magazines, underclothes and damp towels left almost everywhere. He was pleased, even so, that she had seized on the apartment as her home and made herself comfortable in it. It was good to hear her refer to it as "our place" and "our apartment."

Occasionally, Melanie smoked marijuana in the living room. She was casual about it. She smoked it because she enjoyed it, not because she thought she was making a statement. But then, returning for the spring break, she brought home cocaine.

"Hey," she said, putting aside her empty cup. He had made espresso with his espresso machine, because he knew she liked it; and they had drunk little cups with lemon twists in hot black coffee. "Hey, guess what I've got in my suitcase?"

"I could never guess," he said.

She tipped her head and narrowed her eyes, mocking a conspiratorial air. "Coke," she said.

"Cocaine?"

She nodded. "Just a little—what a friend of mine gave me."

Lucas's face hardened. "I don't like that, Melanie."

He could tell from her expression that she was genuinely surprised. "You don't . . . ?" she asked. "I mean . . . never?"

He shook his head. "The stuff is dangerous. I wasn't too upset about the grass. But coke is different."

"Everybody does it," she said lamely.

"Not everybody," he said. "But I don't care if Jesus Christ snorts it—it's a very bad idea."

"Is there medical evidence of that?" she asked skeptically.

"Enough," he said. "On the other hand, if you went in the chem lab and accidentally happened on a new enzyme, would you test it by swallowing it, since there is no medical evidence that it's harmful? Myself, I prefer not to ingest a substance until I see evidence that it's *not* harmful."

"Then why do so many people . . . ?"

"What a lot of people do is immaterial. A lot of people smoke cigarettes, too. A lot of people drink too much. A lot of people go to church and light candles, and you laugh at their stupidity."

Melanie drew a deep breath. "What do you want me to do with the stuff?" she asked.

He shrugged. "Use your own intelligence, make your own judgment."

She went in her room and got it, silently showed it to him, then flushed it down the toilet.

She was eighteen. During the summer she would work in the New York offices of CONTEKS. That had been arranged by Trish, who had spoken to Thomas Miller about her. He promised her a summer-end trip to Europe.

In September, the Securities Subcommittee of the Senate Banking, Housing, and Urban Affairs Committee opened hearings on SEC regulation of corporate mergers. A HEST terminal in the hearing room took the record of the proceedings. Lucas, who had secured the contract for HEST, was in Europe with Melanie when the hearings began. General Fraser, appearing on the evening news on all three networks, described the advent of HEST on Capitol Hill as "a major contribution by technology to efficiency and economy in government."

Venice was for Lucas and Melanie their last stop on their summer-end trip to Europe. They arrived there on a Friday and would stay until Wednesday. Melanie was enchanted by the city and asked Lucas for a promise that they would return as soon as they could. Rain fell two of their nights in Venice, but they discovered that a Venetian evening could be most beautiful in the rain.

One rainy evening they sat for dinner at a table overlooking a canal, and Melanie confessed to her father that she was not a virgin.

"Do you care?" she asked quietly, looking up at him

with the dark eyes that still reminded him of her mother.

"In the sense that I care about everything that affects you, yes," he said. "Otherwise, if it troubles you, it troubles me; if it doesn't trouble you, it doesn't trouble me."

She smiled, and the candle flame flickered in her amused eyes. "It happened two years ago," she said.

"There wasn't anyone you could talk to, was there?"

Her smile disappeared, and she shook her head.

"I haven't been much of a father."

"In many ways you've been the ideal father. You're my hero, you know."

"In what way?"

She grinned. "Look at yourself," she said. "You're forty-one years old. You're so rich you really don't have to work. But, of course, you want to. You do what you do extremely well. You've earned the admiration of just about everyone you've encountered in your life." She reached across the table and laid her hand on his. "And, just in case you didn't know it, you're one gorgeous hunk of man!"

Lucas laughed. "I still wish I'd been a better father, though."

"Well, it's worked out all right. Maybe I wouldn't have liked you as well if you'd been around all the time."

"We owe your grandparents a lot," he said.

"They're angels," she said. "And that's exactly why I can't live with them anymore."

He nodded, smiling warmly. "You opened the conversation on the subject of your virginity. Is there a problem?"

Melanie shook her head. "I'm often horny," she

said. "It's hard to get satisfied without complications. I like sex, but I can't afford to get a reputation as an easy lay. It's damn tough for a woman, you know that?"

"I suppose so."

She nodded. "Anyway . . . I've been surprised that you never married again. I thought sure I'd have siblings."

"Well, I may marry again," he said soberly.

"Trish?"

He nodded. "I think so. I have more in common with her, we share more mutual respect, than I've known with . . . Well—"

"Not with my mother," Melanie interrupted. "You don't have to be embarrassed about that. I understand about her, I think. She went ape over religion."

"It was more than that," he said.

"She was determinedly middle class, prosaic, provincial . . . She would have been an impediment to you."

"Trish won't," he said, anxious to turn the conversation away from Catherine.

Melanie sighed. "She's no ornament. I hope you don't mind my saying that. I can see the rest of it. Is she good in bed?"

"Outstanding. But I'm glad you can understand the rest of it. It will be a partnership."

"She's a career woman. You plan to have children?"

He nodded. "I'd like to start a second family, Melanie. Would you mind?"

"God, no. Go to it! You deserve the happiness. Incidentally, why isn't Trish with us on this trip?"

He shook his head. "I don't know. We'd planned on her coming. She was a little obscure about why she didn't. I'll want to find out when we get home."

Melanie raised her wineglass. "Congratulations," she said. "I hope it's everything you want."

Their return flight landed at Boston, and Lucas deposited Melanie in her new off-campus apartment before he took the AMTRAK train for New York. He arrived at home on Wednesday evening, September 9. Trish, who was expecting him, was in the kitchen when he opened the door and dropped his bags on the floor of the foyer.

They kissed. She was wearing a bra and a half slip and was barefoot. She held him to her tightly, and for a long moment she was silent, just holding him and breathing deeply.

"I brought you something," he said.

"You brought me you," she said. "That's what counts."

He kissed her again. "Has the world held together in my absence?"

"Perfectly. The Senate hearings are generating reams of paper all printed over with windy bullshit, which seems to fascinate the news media, as if they'd never seen such a thing before. CONTEKS bought Amalgamated. We're going into videotex in a big way."

"You'll lose a fortune on it," said Lucas.

"Tell Tom Miller that."

"I will."

"Aside from that," she said, breaking away from him and stepping back into the kitchen, "I have a lovely cold salmon here and am putting together some sauce. Wine is in the fridge. I hope that's not what they served you on the plane."

"Nothing so good," he said.

"Are you worn out?"

He shook his head. "Slept on the plane. Slept on the

train. I have no accurate perception of what day it is or what time, but I'm still bright-eyed."

Trish grinned. "I'll do something good for you," she said.

"I'll do something good for *you*."

She shrugged. "We'll see," she said airily.

They ate at the dining table, in the last warm light of the day. He gave her the antique gold necklace he had bought for her in Venice. She told him the details of the CONTEKS acquisition of Amalgamated, and he told her a few tales from his trip. They drank a bottle of *premier cru* Chablis, and for dessert she had chocolate-covered strawberries.

"I missed you," he said as they went in the bedroom.

"I missed you," she said.

Something was wrong. Though she was subtle, she was troubled, and she was concealing something she knew she would have to tell and dreaded telling. He did not press her. He could tell that it was something deeply troubling, that it would be cruel to force her to talk before she was ready.

In the bedroom, she sat down on the edge of the bed, still wearing her half slip and bra. "Wash it, honey, and let me give you a nice sucking," she said.

"You having a period?" he asked.

She shook her head.

"Well, then?"

Trish closed her eyes and exhaled a loud breath. "You don't know, do you?" she asked. "You don't know why I didn't go to Europe with you?"

"No. I want to know why."

"Innocent . . ." she murmured. She looked up into his face. "Lucas. I stayed home . . . to have an abortion. It was supposed to be two days after you left, so I'd be all recovered and ready for anything by the time you got back, and you didn't even have to know about it. The doctor was in a little car accident and postponed until Monday, day before yesterday. It wasn't so easy. I had a little complication. It's over, and it's all right, but I can't take you inside me for a few days."

He was not sure if his face was white or red. He felt as though he had been punched in the stomach. "Trish! Was it . . . *ours?*"

"Of course it was ours. Whose did you think? I got fouled up on my pills. Skipped. I had to stop and start over again on the next cycle. Of course, that makes you more fertile than ever. I knew . . ." She sighed and shook her head. "I was glad you were going away. That gave me time to take care of it."

"But, *Jesus Christ!* Couldn't you have told me? Don't you think I had something to say about it?"

She shook her head. "No."

"It was *ours,* dammit! Not just yours. Trish! Jesus Christ, that was . . . that was our son or daughter!"

"Well, I'm the one who'd have had to carry it. And go through childbirth. It was *my* decision."

He sighed heavily. "I'm not an abortion freak, Trish; but, goddammit, it was ours together and our decision to make together."

"I am an unmarried woman—"

"We'd have gotten married."

"Sure. That's how my parents were married, with my mother pregnant. And if he didn't throw it up to her the rest of her life, anyway he thought it: that he'd *had* to get married."

"I told you I love you."

"But you never spoke of marriage. You've stayed unmarried for fifteen years or whatever. I didn't know what you wanted. I wasn't going to force a proposal out

of you by telling you I was pregnant. Anyway, I didn't
want the baby."

"Why not?"

"I'm scared. Scared to be pregnant. Scared of having
it. Scared to be a parent. Besides, I'm thirty-two years
old. That's late for having a baby. I'm doing well with
my company. I've got my life half straightened out,
with a good job, a man I love to sleep with, and . . . I
don't want the commitment."

Lucas put his face down in his hands. He didn't want
her to see his tears. "It was *our* baby, Trish. You should
have talked it over with me. The decision was yours,
yes, but . . ."

She stared at him quizzically. Lucas was gently
shaking with sobs.

1982–1983

LUCAS SAT ACROSS the desk from Thomas Miller. The corner office in the Citibank Building seemed all windows, expanses of glass on two walls, offering a spectacular view of snow-covered Manhattan, all the way to the World Trade Towers and beyond, to the harbor and the Statue of Liberty. The office was sparely furnished, with one immense abstract painting covering an entire wall and the remaining wall hung with two angular brass sculptures. Miller's desk was a long table, most of its surface bare. It was dominated by an elaborate white telephone, offering Miller access to four lines, also capable of memorizing three dozen numbers. Miller poured coffee from a silver carafe into china cups.

"Odd that I should think you're wrong," he said to Lucas.

"You have your sources of information," Lucas replied.

"I suspect we are dealing with the same information, essentially," said Miller. "We reach different conclusions from the same facts."

"My real question is, what good is it? How will people use it? I know Edison said something of the kind about the phonograph, his own invention—that it probably had no commercial value—but I can't help wonder what the market is."

"You don't think the American consumer will pay for home banking services, home shopping services, and so on, on the television screen?"

Lucas shook his head. "I've gone to half a dozen presentations and looked at it. It's a lot of cute graphics and half-legible text on the TV screen, all in garish colors. The only service I've seen that looks marketable to me is the banking service, and that alone is not nearly enough to justify the cost, either to the consumer or the supplier."

"A lot of companies disagree. A lot are plunging in."

"Publishers," said Lucas. "Time, Inc. Times-Mirror. Others. For them, it's a defensive move. They figure the screen, with maybe an ink-jet or laser printer at the side, is the newspaper or magazine of the future. And it may be, in the next century. In this century, why should I pay ten dollars a week for an electronic newspaper when I can get the *Times*—a far more complete newspaper—on my doorstep every morning for four dollars a week?"

"You can get a newspaper edited specifically for you," said Miller. "You don't want sports coverage, you don't get sports. You want science news, you get science. And so on."

Lucas shrugged. "Maybe I'm old-fashioned. I'm not a big sports fan, but I get interested sometimes in something in baseball or football, and I want to read the sports news. When I flip through the paper, a wide variety of things catch my eye, and I'm glad my newspaper isn't restricted to a limited number of subjects I've specified."

"You playing devil's advocate?" Miller asked.

Lucas nodded. "To a degree. But I think the companies pouring tens of millions into videotex in this Year of Our Lord 1982 are going to lose their tens of millions. Uh . . . accumulating experience that will be useful to somebody later."

Miller raised his eyebrows high. "I've got four million in research-and-development costs."

"Market research?" Lucas asked.

"The results are entirely dependent on the question," said Miller. "When you ask people if they would like to have videotex, all of them say yes. When you ask if they would pay twenty dollars a month for it, most of them say no."

"That's because they don't know how they're going to use it," said Lucas. "It's like buying a personal computer. It's a wonderful thing to have, if you have a specific use for it. Otherwise, it's a complete waste of money."

"Businesses live on consumers wasting their money," said Miller with a faint smile.

"Temporarily," said Lucas. "And not on big-ticket items."

"Are you suggesting I drop the videotex idea?"

"I suggest you put it on hold for the short term," said Lucas.

"I was thinking of offering you the presidency of a subsidiary to develop and market it."

"I'm flattered. But I would decline with thanks. I'm sorry, Tom, but I think it's a dead end for the near future."

Miller reached across his desk with the carafe and poured more coffee into Lucas's cup. "Are you satisfied with the way things are going at HEST?"

Lucas shook his head emphatically. "No. They are not doing the research-and-development work that's going to have to be done sometime. The stock is still paying dividends, skimming off money we need to prepare for the future."

"That's because UNI has no future," said Miller.

"Hats and shoes," said Lucas. "Railroad-car axles. Milk and beer bottles. Horse collars—"

"Celluloid collars," laughed Miller.

Lucas nodded. "Button hooks. The company needs money, and it takes it where it can get it."

"The current recession hurts it badly."

"UNI has laid off almost twenty thousand workers," said Lucas.

"And HEST has hired . . .?"

"Five hundred. None of the same people, of course."

Miller rose and stepped to the window. He looked down at the street far below. "Incidentally, Lucas, I'm sorry to hear that you and Trish don't see each other anymore. It's none of my business, but you are two of my favorite people."

"She's a fine young woman," said Lucas stiffly. "We had a fundamental disagreement, and . . . But she's a fine young woman, and I wish her well."

Miller turned his back to the window. "And how's your daughter?"

Lucas was always glad to hear that question, and his voice betrayed his pleasure in answering it. "I couldn't be more pleased with her, Tom. She has yet to come up with a score under ninety-four on any of her exams or a letter grade under A. She's been offered a summer job at MIT, an assistantship, working with a professor of mathematics on a major book he's writing; and I think she'll take it and stay there."

"She's a smart girl, Lucas. She did good work for us here last summer."

"She knows far more about computers than I'll ever know. She's already a big critic of HEST. She thinks it's not programmed right. When she and Dave Berger get

269

started discussing the transcriber, I go find a book and read."

Miller grinned. "What's she think of videotex?"

"She thinks it's technologically primitive."

Miller laughed. "Interesting. Bring her around for lunch when she's in town. I'd like to see her again."

Melanie came to New York for a week at the beginning of the summer and for ten days at the end. There was no time for a vacation trip that year. It was not her father's schedule that interfered; it was hers. With the money she made during the summer, she bought her first car, and in the fall she drove down sometimes on weekends.

Twice she brought a young man named Craig, who slept with her in her bedroom. Later in the summer, she told Lucas she did not see Craig anymore. She talked about him. Craig, she said, had expected her to tolerate his having a sexual relationship with a young man at the same time when he was having one with her. ("No way. I mean, I'm open-minded, but . . . Uh-uh! Can you imagine being kissed by someone who had, maybe half an hour before . . . ? *Forget that!*")

On a Thursday afternoon in July, Lucas met in the HEST conference room with a monsignor, two priests, and a professor of computer science from Fordham University. They represented the Archdiocese of New York and wanted to discuss the possibility of installing a transcriber in St. Patrick's, to record the sermons of the cardinal archbishop. They wanted to know if it could be moved into a conference room to record various discussions. Lucas always enjoyed presenting the transcriber to people who were not familiar with it. He gave the little committee a demonstration. Their conversation was lively and interesting, and when the meeting broke up at four o'clock, he was sorry it was at an end.

He had an appointment to keep, however. He left the building and walked out on Forty-second Street. In a hot, glaring sun, he walked west, past Madison and Fifth Avenues, onto the part of Forty-second Street that had become a strip of sex shops and porno shows. The street was crowded with hustlers of every style. Shirt-sleeved policemen walked in pairs, necessarily oblivious, for the most part, to the selling that was going on around them. The street was littered. The hot air was redolent with a mixture of exhaust fumes and the pungent odors from the fast-food shops.

He was looking for a store, which he had been told he couldn't miss because of its big, colorful sign—THE RAINBOW SHOW. He found it on the south side of the street. It was on the second floor, up a wide flight of wooden stairs lit by neon tubing.

"Hey! There he is! Lieutenant!"

Lucas turned and broke into a grin as he recognized the big black man swinging around the end of a counter and coming toward him. "Sergeant!"

In the sixteen years since he had returned from Vietnam, Platoon Sergeant Elvin Kilbourne had lived a mercurial life. For a while he had lived on his partial-disability pension, at first just loafing on the streets, then enrolling at NYU, dropping out, trying a trade school, dropping out, taking a job finally as a taxi driver. He had spent two terms on Riker's Island, six months for a mugging, another thirty days for breaking and entering. That kind of thing was behind him now. He had come to work at the Rainbow Show in 1977 as a cashier and bouncer. Now he was one of two partners in the place.

Lucas knew his history. He had seen him from time

HAROLD ROBBINS PRESENTS

to time since he came to New York. Kilbourne had seen
his name in the paper and had called him, and since
then the two of them had met about once a year,
usually for late-afternoon drinks in an Eighth Avenue
bar that Kilbourne favored, where they were served
beer and bourbon and ribs and fried potatoes. Lucas
could never pay. Buying the lieutenant some bourbon
and ribs was the least he could do for the man who
carried him down the hill, Kilbourne said. He introduced Lucas to a dozen of his friends as the man who
had saved his life.

Kilbourne grabbed Lucas's hand. "Shee-it, man!" he
laughed. "You ain' change. You nevah change."

"Turned gray," said Lucas. "Which you're doing
yourself."

Kilbourne ran his hand over his graying hair. "Shee-
it. Won' live forever, thass fer sure." He nodded.
"Anyway . . . Hey, you ain' seen my business. Wha' ya
think this place? Supermarket of sex. Lemme show ya
'roun'."

The glass showcases in front were filled with sex
devices: dildos, vibrators, straps and chains, gags and
blindfolds, jars and tubes of supposed stimulants. Garish lingerie shared wall space with grotesque rubber
and leather clothing, including rubber masks that could
be locked on a subject's head with small padlocks.
Other cases and racks displayed films and videotapes.
The vast central area of the store was filled with racks
of magazines. In the rear was a darkened arcade for
peep-show machines. A man sat in a booth by the
entrance and made change for the stream of men who
wandered in.

"Got live shows," said Kilbourne, his voice betraying
some pride. "Over here."

272

He led Lucas through a wide door and into a second room of the establishment.

"This here's what ya call a rap show," said Kilbourne, pulling back a curtain and showing Lucas a pair of tiny booths, separated by a glass window like the one in a theater ticket-seller's booth—that is, with a small round hole in the middle. "Man pays five, sit down here, girl come in an' sit down there. Ten minutes she do what he say—take off her clothes, pose any way he say, talk with him 'bout sex, what she like, what he like. Only thing, he can't touch her. No prostitution. Jus' look an' rap."

Two of the booths were occupied. The other two girls available were a black and a Hispanic, the Hispanic girl very small and delicate. They wore flowered wrappers —he supposed for efficiency in stripping naked. Both of them were smoking. They stared expectantly at Lucas, and when it became apparent to them that they were not going to earn any money from him, they dropped their eyes and stared dully at the floor.

"Over here, live peep show," said Kilbourne.

He led Lucas to a small window on the wall of a round enclosure. Taking a quarter from his pocket, he inserted it into the slot beside the window. A steel blind slid up. On a cot in the enclosure, a young black couple lay naked. The girl toyed with the boy's flaccid penis, and he squeezed her breasts. They looked bored, though not embarrassed.

"Put in a quarter, get to look for two minutes," said Kilbourne.

Lucas looked past the couple, to the faces of men behind the dozen little windows around the enclosure.

"Efficient merchandising," he said, stepping back from the window.

"I know you ain' interested, Lieutenant, but anythin' you want . . . I mean, you know, free. An' I kin arrange somethin' better, too. I mean, jus' in case you want."

"Thanks, Elvin. As it happens, I've got my own."

Kilbourne laughed. "I bet you have! Well . . . Want to go for a drink, or talk here? Ya know, I got to ask you somethin'."

"Up to you," said Lucas.

"Talk here then," said Kilbourne. "Out for a drink some better time. I ain' got no office, so . . ."

They stood beside the enclosure with the little windows, in sight, too, of the rap booths, where now the little Hispanic girl had gotten a customer and disappeared behind the curtain of one of the booths.

"I got a problem, Lieutenant," said Kilbourne gravely. "Cops come in here couple weeks ago, busted one of my rap-booth girls, said she offered to sell a man some shit. You know, what you call heroin. Said she offered it to a narc, through the glass. They got it in they heads that I was behind it. Say I gonna be indicted. Narcotics rap. You know what that'd mean. Attica. Long time."

"I wouldn't want that to happen to you, Sergeant."

"Believe me, I wouldn't want it neither. Point is, I got a lawyer that says he can beat it for me. I don' know how he means to do it, got the fix in or what. But he says he can beat it. He wants ten thousand dollars. That's the quick of it. He wants ten thousand dollars."

"I'll lend you ten thousand," said Lucas simply.

"Would you? I be grateful. And I pay you. I mean, if I don't got to go to Attica, I can get it up in time and pay you back ever' cent."

"What's the name of the lawyer?" Lucas asked. "I have some friends that can look into the guy and see what else can be done. Anyway, you need ten thousand, you got ten thousand."

"Knew I could count on ya," said Kilbourne solemnly. "When it git down to kickin' ass, knew I could count on the Lieutenant." His voice failed. "Knew I could," he whispered.

As it turned out, Kilbourne was the victim of a shakedown. When Lucas put a first-class criminal lawyer on the case, the shakedown fell apart. The participants denied any part of it had ever happened. A police sergeant called it a misunderstanding.

Lucas took Melanie to Kansas City to spend Christmas with her two sets of grandparents. Her D'Annunzio grandmother was aged and ill and seemed to find it wearisome to speak English. She spoke to Melanie in Italian, and fortunately Melanie could understand most of what she said. The two Paulsons were well, though Lucas's father was becoming forgetful. The trip turned Lucas and Melanie thoughtful. Lucas remarked on their flight back that one day they would come home for Christmas and not all four of her grandparents would be there.

In February 1983, Lucas brought back to HEST a contract with the Justice Department. Then he arranged for the White House to install a terminal to make printed records of selected presidential conversations and the transcript of certain meetings. At the mid-winter meeting of the American Bar Association, Lucas Paulson was the speaker at one of the principal luncheons. Subsequently he was invited to deliver a guest lecture at the Harvard School of Business.

The summer of 1983, he bought a Beechcraft Bonanza and a cottage at Siasconset. He hired an instructor to teach him to fly the Bonanza, a far more complex and faster airplane than he had ever flown before; and with the instructor he flew it to Kansas City once and to Florida, to familiarize himself with the sophisticated electronic navigation systems it carried. He began to fly regularly to Nantucket, living in his cottage on weekends, walking on the Nantucket beaches, and fishing.

Melanie remained on campus again that summer, taking extra courses and working on a software-design project: an integrated word processor, spreadsheet, and data-management program for micro-computers. Lucas flew to Boston on half a dozen Friday afternoons, picking Melanie up at the Bedford airport and flying on to Nantucket. He flew her to White Plains one week, and they drove into New York. Over lunch with Thomas Miller, she described the integrated software to him, and he told her it was worth millions of dollars.

One Friday afternoon she brought along a young woman, a graduate student in nuclear engineering, who carried no change of clothes but a heavy bag of books in which she immersed herself the entire weekend. Melanie confessed to Lucas that she had supposed the young woman might be so impressed with her father that she would sleep with him, at least the second night of the weekend. They laughed.

Another time Melanie brought a soft-spoken young professor named Briggs, who was much embarrassed to spend two nights sleeping on the same sofa bed with her in the cottage living room, while her father slept in the adjacent bedroom. She told Lucas later that Briggs had refused to undress and had slept all night fully clothed, which she thought was funny.

Their father-daughter relationship changed that summer. She would always be his daughter, of course, but that summer he found her adult enough to be his friend. He enjoyed her company and knew he would want it even if his parental duty did not suggest they be together. Her perceptiveness, which he had always known and admired, was coupled now with maturity of judgment. He loved her as his daughter, but his respect for her as a person was even greater now.

The last weekend of the summer they were alone. They had dinner in town on Saturday night and returned to the cottage about eleven. Melanie wanted to walk on the beach for a while, and he went with her, strolling in the dark, listening to the crash of the waves almost invisible on a moonless night. They talked.

"Would you like it if I find a job in the New York area?" she asked. "I mean, so we can live closer together?"

"Sure I would," he said. "And with what you've achieved at MIT, I think you can find what you want just about anywhere."

"I'd like to live near to you," said Melanie. "For once . . ."

She groped for his hand, and for the rest of the walk she held it tightly in hers.

They returned to the cottage. He offered her a final drink, and she said she would take a brandy. While he was in the kitchen, she went into the bathroom. He was sitting on the couch, in the light of a single shaded lamp, when she came out. She had changed into a light, lavender-colored shorty nightgown, and she sat down beside him.

"I'm . . . Somehow I'm wide awake," she said. She flipped her hair with both hands, whipping it back over her shoulders. "It's been a good day, but I'm not tired."

"Neither am I, particularly," he said.

She sipped. "I've loved these past two weekends," she said. "Nobody but us . . . It's been great."

He nodded.

For a long moment they were silent, staring vacantly into their brandies. Their heads were full of thoughts. Melanie spoke first.

"You're lonely, aren't you?" she asked quietly.

He glanced up from his brandy. "I suppose so. I don't think about it much, but—"

"You could call Trish," she said bluntly.

He shook his head. "No."

"Forgive me, but . . ." She drew a deep breath. "I think you were wrong about that."

Lucas sighed. "Too judgmental?"

"Yes. And worse than that. I couldn't say this when you first told me about what happened—you weren't ready to hear it—but I can't promise you I wouldn't do the same thing she did in the same circumstances. Anyway, even if she was wrong, she was entitled to be forgiven."

"Maybe I was stupid," said Lucas. "I've thought about it."

"So you could call Trish."

"No, I couldn't. We said too many hurtful things to each other."

"I didn't know about that."

"I didn't tell you that part."

"Did you really love her?"

"Yes. And she loved me, I'm sure. That's why we made it so bad—because we were so disappointed with each other."

"So . . . It looks like I'll never have siblings," said Melanie, straightening her back and smiling at him.

"Don't be too sure," he laughed. "I still have a roving eye."

1984

LILA FRASER—MRS. Matthew Fraser—was drink-
ravaged: unfocused, throaty-voiced, withdrawn. She
was a tall blonde. Her face was coarsely wrinkled, and
she wore thick black mascara and heavy blue eye
shadow as if to distract attention from the watery
vacancy in her eyes. Silver bracelets jangled on her
wrinkled arms, and a silver-and-turquoise necklace was
looped around her neck. She wore black velvet tore-
ador pants and a white silk blouse. Her eyes followed
the general constantly.

"It is very nice to meet you, Melanie," she said.
"Welcome to the family, so to speak."

"Thank you, Mrs. Fraser," said Melanie.

"We *are* a family. Aren't we, Lucas?" Lila Fraser
asked uncertainly, pleading for assurance.

"Of course we are," said Lucas.

Melanie, graduating summa cum laude from MIT,
had received attractive offers from a dozen companies,
less attractive offers from a score of others, as well as
offers to join the faculty at two universities. The offer
from HEST had been substantially more lucrative than
any of the others, and she had decided to take it. Her
father did not concur with the idea, but she thought she
saw in the offer an implication that she would be

allowed to work with Dave Berger to reprogram HEST for the new technology, to bring it into the '80s, as she put it; and the prospect intrigued her. Lucas's thought was that Matt had offered her a job to put another hook into him, to hold him in line. He could not be sufficiently specific to sell Melanie that idea. Besides, she said, with her record she could move on to another company anytime. Finally, with the HEST job she would be in New York—or in Westchester, at least—and close to her father. That was something both of them wanted.

Their invitation to dinner had said Melanie was guest of honor, to mark the occasion of her joining the company. Three vice presidents were there, two with their wives; and a pair of German bankers from Hamburg were probably under the impression that *they* were the guests of honor.

"I am very thick-skinned," Melanie had said aside to Lucas as they arrived and she took a Jack Daniels on the rocks from the houseboy. "I'll bet you have to be in this company. If it gets too tough, I'll get drunk and see how they like that."

"I will offer you no advice, my dear daughter," Lucas had said. "Play it however you want. I have perfect confidence in you."

Melanie was unable entirely to avoid Lila Fraser, who seized on her from time to time and led her away to be introduced to someone, twice to someone she had already met. Jim Cahill approached Lucas.

"I am astounded," he said to Lucas. He poked around in his martini with his fingers, trying to pick out an olive. "I can't believe you let her do it."

"Are you under the impression I have any control over her?" Lucas asked.

"Matt's motive isn't really bad," said Cahill. "He's

pleased to be able to tell the world he captured this year's top graduate from MIT. Also, you might take it as a peace offering."

"He can forget that," said Lucas curtly. "He and I are not at war, and there's no peace to be made. What I don't like about him, I'm not going to like any better because Melanie works for the company."

"She got a very generous package from the company," said Cahill.

"I am sure she's worth it," said Lucas.

Cahill managed finally to get two fingers on his olive, and he popped it into his mouth, together with his fingers to lick off the gin. "You know, you've limited Matt's corporate benefits. Since the company has to give you everything it gives to him. . . . You follow?"

"I understand he wants a golden parachute," said Lucas. "If Congress passes the Deficit Reduction Act of 1984 in its present form—"

"It could have disastrous tax consequences for anyone with a golden-parachute contract," Cahill completed the sentence. "We've been watching that."

"Why does he need a golden parachute?" Lucas asked. "Is there another takeover attempt on the horizon?"

"Not specifically," said Cahill. "But UNI will sell if it gets a good offer. So, of course, will Ringold. And Matt could find himself out of a job. As could I. Is there any possibility, Lucas, that you would accept an amendment to your contract, to let Matt and me have golden-parachute protection without the company having to extend the same to you? After all, you don't need it. In a takeover situation, you'll undoubtedly sell your stock, which takes care of you. Anyway, you could probably move on to another company—"

"So could you," said Lucas. "You're not General Fraser's doormat."

Cahill drew a deep breath. "Right now I'm his messenger. The question is, will you consider an amendment to your contract?"

"The answer is yes," said Lucas. "I'll consider it. I don't need a golden parachute, and I won't insist on one just because you and Matt get one. Uh . . ." He was distracted by a young woman in tennis whites who had just come into the room. "Uh, on the other hand, the new law is going to define a company's outlay for golden parachutes as a non-deductible expense, which means anything along those lines is going to cost the company dearly. As a director I will have to vote on it, and I don't see how I *can* vote *for* it."

Cahill nodded thoughtfully. "I'll carry the word," he said.

"Is that Matt's daughter, for God's sake?" Lucas asked.

Cahill turned and looked. "Oh, yes. Susannah. Quite grown up. She's eighteen. Just finished her sophomore year at Smith."

"I wouldn't have known her," said Lucas.

He watched her. Her father was frowning at her, critical undoubtedly of her appearing at his party in her short skirt and sweaty blouse, socks and tennis shoes; but she seemed able to cope with his disapproval, shrugging at him and grabbing a glass of champagne off the houseboy's tray. She wore her blonde hair long, all the way down her back. She was tall like her mother, slender, and graceful. Lucas stared.

Maybe she noticed. She walked across the room and spoke to him. "You're Mr. Paulson, if I remember correctly," she said.

He nodded. "And you're Miss Fraser."

She grinned and wrinkled her nose. "I'm Susannah," she said.

"And I'm Lucas, of course. How long has it been since I've seen you?"

"Three years," she said. "*I* remember."

"You have me at a disadvantage. Anyway, I'm glad to see you again. I won't bore you by remarking on how you've grown up."

"It seems to surprise some people," she said.

He laughed. "Not me. I'm an optimist."

"I've got to go up and change," she said. "I've been informed I can't sit at the dinner table in these clothes. I'm going to demand that my mother seat us together, though. Unless the Germans over there have a charm I don't detect, you're the only man here tonight who won't bore me."

She came down half an hour later, dressed in a long, full, swishing white skirt and a raspberry-colored knit blouse that dipped in a scoop over her breasts. Her father frowned again, this time apparently because it was too plain that she was wearing no bra. She had spoken to her mother and sat down at dinner to Lucas's right.

She told him over dinner that she was studying French and had arranged to spend the fall months at the University of Luxembourg. She expressed great interest in his airplane and said she would like to fly with him sometime. Speaking under her breath, she joked about her father's military bearing, about her mother's drinking, about Cahill's sycophancy, about McConnell's conspicuous insecurity at this table . . . about, in short, nearly everyone at the dinner. She was an entertaining companion.

"Matt was really pissed at the way his daughter threw herself at you," Melanie said during the drive back to the city.

"Oh? I enjoyed her very much. If I couldn't sit with you, it was a privilege to sit with her."

"Matt made a nasty little comment," said Melanie. "Something to the effect that Susannah had a way of attaching herself to whomever she thought was the best-looking man."

"I'm having lunch with her next week," Lucas said blandly.

The board of directors of HEST met two weeks later. On the agenda was a proposal for an amendment to Lucas Paulson's consulting contract, to allow the company to extend golden-parachute protection to General Fraser and James Cahill without having to extend the same to Paulson.

Under the terms of a second proposal offered to the board, General Fraser and James Cahill would receive compensation in the amounts of $1 million and $750,000 per annum, respectively, for ten years, in the event control of the corporation passed from its present stockholders, directors, and officers to an acquiring corporation. Furthermore, the company agreed to assume and pay any tax liability incurred by the two officers on this income. The purpose, as the general explained in a statement to the board, was to discourage raids on the company, in the first place, and second to afford him and Cahill income protection in the event another company acquired HEST and wanted to install a new president and senior vice president. Such corporate arrangements were not uncommon.

Lucas was recognized. "I am willing to accept the amendment to my consulting contract," he said. "This proposal was drafted by counsel and reviewed by my attorneys, and I am willing to sign it. If the board elects to grant golden-parachute protection to Matt and Jim, I do not insist on something similar for myself. Nor does Dave Berger, who once again has authorized me to act in his behalf. On the other hand, I oppose the golden parachutes and will vote no on that. The Deficit Reduction Act of 1984, which the president is going to sign, will impose a severe tax penalty, both on the recipients of golden-parachute payments and on the companies that make such payments. It will cost the company many millions of dollars. In fact, I'd like to know if the total cost has been calculated."

"It will cost nothing unless the company is taken over by somebody else," said General Fraser.

"You can see $17.5 million immediately," said Lucas. "Which in the Act is defined as outside the ordinary and necessary expenses of doing business and is therefore rendered a non-tax-deductible expense. Besides that, the penalty on recipients, which this proposal commits the company to pay, is very substantial. I'm not sure how much it is, but it could raise the cost to $25 million."

"Payable over a period of ten years," said General Fraser. "By somebody else."

"Not necessarily," said Lucas. "As we well know, the way the stock is held, several combinations of shareholders could join to effect a change in management. The rest might remain shareholders. In any event, a $25 million golden-parachute liability reduces the value of everyone's stock. It will just result in a lower offer by the would-be takeover bidder."

"Do you plan to accept a bid?" the general asked testily.

"I didn't accept the last one," said Lucas.

"But you don't promise you won't accept the next one?"

"No, I don't promise it."

The three directors placed on the board by UNI asked for a recess so they could telephone Sam Magnuson, the president of UNI. They returned in fifteen minutes and voted no. Lucas voted no, and the proposal failed.

"What I don't understand," said Susannah, "is why he thinks he should have a million dollars a year for ten years after he loses his job—*if* he loses his job. He has his army retirement pay. He has a package of benefits —you know, medical care and so on—from the army. He has mother's money. He has . . . I just don't understand it, Lucas."

They were eating lunch in La Bibliotheque on Tudor City Plaza, overlooking Ralph Bunche Plaza and the United Nations, at a table by a window wall, and a few minutes before had watched a crowd of Afghan protestors burn a Soviet flag. Susannah, who had arrived on the train from Rye station, was wearing a short white wraparound skirt and a Save the Whales T-shirt. Her golden tan contrasted with her blonde hair. As usual, she wore no makeup. She had drunk two gin-and-tonics and was sipping cold white wine with her lunch.

"I mean, he came home calling you the awfullest names," she went on. "He said you're his enemy! Can you imagine that? I thought only paranoics have *enemies!* And, of course, mother went into hysterics. Jesus!"

Lucas shrugged. "I'd forget it if I were you, Susannah," he said. "Matt bears some heavy burdens as president of a company. He has a right to get emotional now and again."

She laughed. "He called you a *prima donna*. When I told him a prima donna had to be a woman, he told me to shut up." She laughed again. "He said he spotted your arrogance the first time he met you."

"He doesn't even know when he first met me."

"When? Tell me about it."

Lucas shook his head. "Maybe someday."

"Oh, foo," she said. She looked down at the plaza, at the last of the demonstrators chatting amiably with the last of the cops who had come to contain and protect their demonstration. "I hate to waste time talking about my father and all his hang-ups." She returned her eyes to him. "What about Nantucket?"

He drew a breath. "Well . . . Melanie can go."

"Fine. Then I'm Melanie's guest."

"Where are your parents supposed to think you've gone for the weekend, while you're spending it on Nantucket with Melanie and me?"

"Boston," she said. "With my girlfriend Alicia Guest. If they should happen to call—which they won't—Alicia will cover for me."

Lucas tapped the table and sighed. "I'm not comfortable with this idea," he said.

"We've talked about flying. And seeing Nantucket. Of course, if—"

"Don't say, 'Of course, if you don't want me . . .'" he interrupted. "I do want you. I love the idea of taking you to Nantucket. But your father would—"

"I don't give a damn," she said. "And you don't either."

"All right," he conceded. He grinned. "We'll have a great time."

But when Melanie came for dinner that night—she was now living in her own apartment in White Plains—

287

she asked, "Why? Just why are we taking Susannah Fraser for a weekend on Nantucket?"

"I don't know," said Lucas. "Because she wants to go, I guess."

Melanie was in the kitchen, pouring herself a Jack Daniels. "The girl's eighteen. She can go anyplace she wants, whether her father likes it or not. And you know I don't care if Matt pops a cork over it. Still, I'm . . . curious. Are you and this girl-child developing a relationship? Am I entitled to ask?"

"Yeah, you're entitled," he sighed. "I've had to ask myself."

Melanie stepped into the kitchen doorway. "She's eighteen!"

Lucas nodded. "So I keep reminding myself."

"She has a crush on you," said Melanie. "I can understand that. I'm not sure I can understand your reciprocating."

"She's a lot like you in many ways, Melanie. She's mature for her years."

"Sure."

"I've taken her to lunch a few times—"

"You take her two or three times a week."

"I took her browsing through print shops in the Village. It was what she wanted to do. We took—" He paused to chuckle. "Believe it or not, we took the Circle Line cruise. I'd never done it before." He stopped again and frowned. "It was fun, Melanie."

Melanie's eyes softened, and she nodded. "Okay," she said. "You deserve a little fun, God knows. And who am I to advise my father to be careful?"

Friday dawned bright, but by mid-morning the sky was gray, and shortly a drizzle set in. Lucas phoned the flight service station from his office and was told that Westchester Airport had a mile and a half visibility and a five-hundred-foot ceiling, Nantucket had a mile and five hundred, Martha's Vineyard had three-quarters of a mile and was closed. The forecast was for more of the same the balance of the day and all day Saturday. He had no way to call Susannah and tell her their flight to Nantucket was off. He called Melanie, who already knew; she had looked out at the weather.

He went home at noon, thinking maybe Susannah had left a message on his telephone recorder. She had not, but as he was slicing a tomato for a sandwich, the door buzzer sounded. It was Susannah.

She dropped her blue nylon duffel bag just inside his door. She grinned widely, happily. "I didn't even look for you at the airport," she said. "I knew Nantucket was off." She brushed a wisp of her hair off her face. "So! Now what do we do with the weekend?"

"Uh . . . we can't go. I mean, fly; we can't fly. Anywhere. Melanie is just going home."

Susannah laughed. "Well, *I* can't. I'm supposed to be in Boston, remember?"

She picked up her bag and looked at him curiously, her eyes asking him what to do with it. "Gonna offer me a drink?" she asked.

"Yeah." He reached for the bag, carried it in, and put it down by the dining table. "Gin and tonic?"

"Wine. If you're having wine . . ."

She walked around his living room, looking at his paintings, at the view of the East River, and the books on his glass-topped table. It was her first visit to his apartment, and she was unabashedly curious.

She was wearing a pair of well-worn and well-faded blue jeans, stretched so tight across her bottom that her

289

two buns were separated and tautly molded by almost threadbare, light blue denim. Her hair hung down over a white T-shirt emblazoned with a yellow-and-orange sunburst.

He poured wine from a big bottle of white Bordeaux he kept in the refrigerator. "I suppose," he said, "I could try to get us reservations at a hotel in the Poconos, or maybe even on the Cape. It's tough this time of year. I can call Melanie."

She came into the kitchen. "If you call Melanie," she said, "I'll go home and make up some kind of excuse for not being in Boston."

"Well, Susannah, I—"

"But you *won't,* will you?" she asked softly. "And you won't call some stupid hotel." She sighed. "Please," she whispered. "You won't. . . ."

She stepped closer to him and put her hands on his arms, and she looked up into his face. He bent forward and kissed her lightly on the mouth, then pulled up.

He shook his head. "Do you know how old I am, Susannah?"

"You're forty-four," she said. "Big . . . goddamn . . . deal."

"You're *eighteen.*"

"Well, I'm not a virgin, if that's what you're worried about," she said crisply. She reached for one of the glasses of wine sitting on the counter and turned to walk back into the living room. "I understand your caution. You think you're obligated, because you are— yes, I know, you're old enough to be my father. So okay. You've discharged your obligation. You've reminded me of how old you are and how young I am. So I know. It's on record. I know."

"Well—"

She spun and faced him. "If you want me to leave,

290

say so. I'll go. If that's what you really want. If you don't . . ." Her voice softened, and she blinked as if to stop tears. "If you don't, then quit telling me how old you are. And spare me the conventional wisdom. And by the way, what *I* want is to stay right here all weekend."

"I don't want to hurt you, Susannah."

"Then don't tell me to leave."

He reached for her, took her in his arms, and ran his hands through her hair. Then they kissed: hard, fervently, erotically. He cupped her buns in his hands and pressed her hips to him, so she felt his throbbing erection. He pulled her T-shirt out of her jeans and ran his hands up under it, over the skin of her back. She pulled the shirt over her head and turned her back to him, so he could take her breasts in his hands. He held them, squeezed them, and nuzzled the back of her neck, and he guided her toward his bedroom.

She thrust a pillow under her hips, to elevate them toward him, and lay on her back, spread, waiting for him to pull off his clothes. He rose on his knees between her legs, and she reached for his penis to guide it into her as he let himself down over her. She pressed it into herself, and he penetrated her, only a little, between constricting lips that seemed to tighten against him.

"Oh, ooh!"

"Am I hurting you, Susannah?" he whispered.

"A little, but . . . just . . . easy!"

He pushed, and her flesh resisted. She grunted and nodded, and he pushed again. Sweat broke out on her face, but she nodded again. He pushed again, and suddenly he slipped through and his shaft eased all the way into her, until their bellies touched.

"You've done it before, have you?" he whispered breathlessly.

"With boys . . . Never with a man like you. Go on. Don't talk. Just do it, darling, *do it!*"

Before he was finished, she was rising to his strokes, thrusting her hips upward against his downward thrusts, driving him deeper and harder into her. When he climaxed, she wrapped her legs around him to pin him against her, with his shaft deep inside. She moaned, and her face and body had flushed a bright pink.

On December 11, he received a wire from Luxembourg:

> GREAT GOOD NEWS. MOTHER NOT COMING. WILL YOU
> MEET ME IN PARIS? SUSANNAH.

He wired back:

> BETTER THAN THAT. I HAVE FLIGHT TO LUXEMBOURG
> DECEMBER 20. WE WILL DRIVE TO PARIS TOGETHER.
> HAVE HOTEL RESERVATIONS. TELL MOTHER YOU WILL
> BE AT HOTEL REGINA, PLACE DES PYRAMIDES. LUCAS.

For six weeks they had enjoyed a fiery love affair, taking every opportunity they could find to spend hours in bed together. Only once again had she pretended to spend a weekend with a friend. But afternoons, evenings, even mornings, she had come to his apartment. At the end of the summer, when she was supposed to go to Europe to study, she had offered to cancel the trip to be with him. He had urged her to go. They would be apart five months, he said, and if after that time they had not developed second thoughts about their affair, then they would know it was strong enough for them to commit themselves against everything that would be thrown against them. She had agreed. She had flown to Europe the first week in September.

She wrote him three or four letters a week. After a month she began to suggest he come over at Thanksgiving. He resisted. She settled then on Christmas—he would not ask her to spend Christmas alone in Europe? He telephoned and told her he might come. In October she wrote that her mother was toying with the idea of coming. She wrote that she would discourage her mother by saying she had been invited to spend Christmas in Paris with a French family.

"La ville lumière," she said as she stood at the tall, broad window of their suite, looking west across the Rue de Rivoli toward the Eiffel Tower glowing in the mist of a rainy December evening.

He stepped up behind her and clasped his hands in front of her, locking her close to him. *"Joyeux Noel,"* he said.

She had dressed for dinner, in a black knit dress, tight around her hips, loose above. She wore also a necklace of diamonds and emeralds he had bought for her at Tiffany's before he left New York. She had combed her hair into a swirling pile, fastened in place with a diamond-studded clip: another gift from Tiffany's. He lifted her breasts, which were unconfined under the soft, knit wool.

At Venegende on the Boulevard St. Germain, they dined in gaslit *fin de siècle* elegance. Susannah ordered, showing Lucas both her French and her taste—escargot followed by pure white sole in a delicate sauce, with two bottles of old and musty white Bordeaux. After dinner, they walked to St. Germain des Prés in the rain, and found that, two days before Christmas, hopeful artists still peddled their works under plastic covers on the wrought-iron fences. Susannah bought a tiny watercolor, not much bigger than a postage stamp, of a vase of flowers. Their cab returned them to the Hotel Regina just before midnight.

Their bedroom was furnished with two narrow twin beds—the man at the desk said there were no double beds in the hotel. They clung to each other each night, nude under their feather bolster; and Susannah said she was glad he could not roll away from her.

"Why don't we forget it all and stay here for the rest of our lives?" she whispered to him in the dim light of their darkened room. The all-night traffic of the Rue de Rivoli whispered past, under their windows. "We can afford it. I mean, *you* can. We don't have to go back. Everything back there is so petty."

"We'd love it here less, as time went by," he said.

She sighed. "Promise me anyway that I won't spend Christmas apart from you next year."

"I promise you that, Susannah," he said.

1985

A Few More Warm Spring Days

19

LUCAS AND SUSANNAH had at first expected to fly back from Nantucket on Sunday afternoon. Over their dinner at the Jared Coffin House, they had agreed to postpone the flight until Monday afternoon. Monday, though, had dawned wet and foggy, and the rain and fog had hung in all day. It was Tuesday morning before he could fly back to Westchester Airport, where Susannah's car was waiting in the lot, and she could return to Northampton, Massachusetts, to Smith College.

On Wednesday morning, Lucas walked from his apartment to his office, taking his usual route down Lexington Avenue, into Grand Central Station on the east side, down to the bakery shop on the lower level to buy two Danish, finally up into the station and up the escalators into the Pan Am Building. It was his habit to arrive at his office not much after 8:30, when few people other than the receptionist and the mail-room boys were there. Lois, his secretary for the past five years, would arrive at nine, to find he had already made coffee. Usually they sat down together on the couch in his office and drank coffee and shared the Danish he had brought up.

"I was called to a meeting with General Hideyoshi Monday afternoon," she said when he had poured the

296

coffee. Hideyoshi was her name for Matthew Fraser—a reference to the Japanese martial artifacts in his office. "With him and Cahill."

"What did they offer?" Lucas asked.

She shook her head. "I assume you will give me a first-rate recommendation if I need it."

Lucas smiled. "We're not going anywhere, Lois," he said.

"If we do," she said.

He nodded. "If we do."

Lois Levenstein was a hard-spoken young woman, hard, too, in the misfortune of her florid, pitted complexion and coarse features, also in her solid, muscular figure. An office joke was that she had only barely lost in the tryouts for the job of left tackle on the Giants' defensive line. Her hair was bleached the color of dry straw, and her skirts were always tight across her hips.

"We stayed Monday evening and went through your files," she said. "I was ordered to help them find what they wanted."

"Cahill and . . .?"

"Cahill and McCluskey."

"Any surprises?" he asked.

Lois laughed. "Yes. That they didn't ask for half of what we thought they might. We copied a lot of stuff for nothing."

"How about disks?" he asked.

She glanced at his credenza, where an IBM personal computer sat beside the red box of a LEXIS/NEXIS terminal. "No. They didn't even ask what you might have on disks. For a high-tech company, this one is oddly computer-illiterate."

For more than a year, Lucas had been operating a program, about half of his own design, that interfaced his personal computer to the office word-processor system. Whatever Lois typed for him on the System 6, she immediately transferred to one of his small floppy disks. He had carried away on little disks a copy of every document he had written since the fall of 1983.

"Any reason to think Matt knows who was with me over the weekend?"

Lois shook her head. "I don't think he could have hidden it, if he had known. He talked to me about you in sort of fatherly terms, about what a bright guy you are, about how much he hopes you'll stay on . . . that kind of talk."

"Today could be the day," sighed Lucas. "I can't say I look forward to it."

"They're out in Westchester today," she said. "Big meeting."

"Who?"

"Hideyoshi. Cahill. Professor Berger. And a man from Chase Manhattan."

"Browning?"

"Yes, that's his name. They sent a limousine for him, to take him out to the house. Gail spent half the afternoon yesterday shopping for a particular wine the general wants to serve this man Browning."

"Okay. Any calls I need to worry about?"

"Just two I think you'll be particularly interested in. Elvin Kilbourne called Monday afternoon. And—" She could not suppress an evil smile. "Nelson Duncan. He said he'd be on the red-eye."

Lucas put a finger to his lips.

"Can I redecorate that office?" she asked slyly. "Throw out all that Jap crap?"

"We'll have to," he said. "That all belongs to the general."

From his window he could see the spire of the Chrysler Building, and, sitting with his feet on his credenza, he watched a man emerge from the hatch on one of the eagle-headed gargoyles at the sixty-first floor, as Margaret Bourke-White had done with her camera in the 1930s, and, as she had not done, crawl almost to the end. Though the man was attached to a safety harness, it made Lucas's stomach turn to see him there, and he turned away.

He activated his NEXIS terminal and did a quick check on Browning, the man from Chase Manhattan. The first story the NEXIS computer brought up was a *New York Times* account of the man's daughter's engagement to a young lawyer from Milbank, Tweed. Subsequent stories identified him as a vice president of the bank and either quoted him or noted his presence at various meetings. He was an officer of the Harvard Club, so maybe he had been a contemporary of Matt Fraser's at Harvard.

At 10:30, judging he might be in his store by then, Lucas called Elvin Kilbourne.

"Hey, Lieutenant. I see yo' name in the paper."

"Thank God it's my name this time and not yours, Sergeant."

"Shee-it," laughed Kilbourne. "Shee-it, man. Be no reason put *my* name in the paper."

"Good. Let's keep it that way, Sergeant."

"Ain' up to me. Them mothers come 'roun', wan' clo-ose me up, that's when I be git in the paper."

"Okay, Elvin," said Lucas. "This time it's me."

"Point is, Lieutenant—you got trouble? Sounds like some fuckers tryin' to screw you, way I read it."

"No. No trouble."

"Sound like trouble. Sound like they be kick yo' ass, Lieutenant—that same mother that called the 155s down on our heads. I'd like to have his ass. Some way."

"I'm workin' on that, Sergeant," said Lucas.

"Goo-ood. You know you got my prayers, Lieutenant. I don' figure they be any way I kin he'p, but . . . you know where to find me."

"I know where to find you, Sergeant. And thanks for calling."

As he reviewed his mail, his black telephone rang. That was his personal line, the one he paid for himself; even Lois did not have an extension. Matthew Fraser had the only other entirely private line in the office. Lucas swung around and picked up the telephone.

"It's me, honey. I couldn't . . ."

"I'm glad you called, Susannah," he said softly. "Everything okay?"

"Yes. Everything's fine. A couple of my friends made a pretty good guess where I was and covered for me."

"In other words—"

"The shit hasn't hit the fan yet. I thought you'd want to know."

"Well, I'd rather we made an announcement."

"Right," she said. "We're going to make an announcement that will shake the town."

"I'll see you . . ."

"Saturday. Maybe Friday night. Okay?"

"Okay. Be careful."

"Sure. I love you, Lucas."

"I love you, Susannah."

"'Bye . . . for now."

"Good-bye, baby. Be good."

He put down the telephone. For a moment he could not pick up the mail again and focus his attention on a dozen petty inquiries from people who should have gotten their information from sources that were readily available to them. For that moment his mind filled with his warm memories of the weekend. They had been friends and lovers. It had been perfect, and when Monday morning had dawned wet and foggy, with even the commuter airlines grounded, they had laughed happily and gone back to bed. Later, they had walked on the misty beach and listened to the sea birds and the roaring of the riptide. Most of their talk had been about places they had seen and now would share. Whatever else they had to think about, they put aside.

He'd had one bad thought. Lying in bed beside her on Sunday morning, when she was peacefully asleep and lightly snoring, somehow the thought had come of Catherine, who had been just nineteen, too, when he first lay in bed with her, and he remembered her sleeping just like this, carefree for one important moment and leaving him with the best moment he had of her: a memory that now returned to intrude.

His other telephone buzzed. He picked it up.

"Mr. Duncan on the line."

He met Nelson Duncan at Chelsea Place, a restaurant far down on Eighth Avenue, where they could enjoy a first-class meal and were not likely to encounter anyone who would know either of them.

"I can't believe this place," said Duncan when they were seated and the waitress had brought the bottle of wine Lucas had ordered. "When the cab stopped, I made him check the address again."

Although they had entered the restaurant through what seemed like a second-hand furniture store and had walked through an almost abandoned bar before descending the stairs to the dining rooms, the place was spacious and light and airy, and their waitress was quiet and knowledgeable. The cuisine was Italian, chiefly, and they ordered pasta with scampi and mussels.

Their conversation had soon turned to Matthew

Fraser. "He was a brigadier general then," said Duncan. "I was a major. He'd had combat experience. I hadn't. He was a Harvard man. I had graduated from the University of Iowa, and he was not subtle about making me understand that was my misfortune. But he liked me, or seemed to. Besides, I could speak Japanese, and he couldn't." Duncan stopped and shook his head. "He took me with him on some wild nights." He frowned and sighed. "It's funny how you can like a man even when you know he holds you in contempt."

"Welcome to the wide world of being held in contempt," said Lucas. "There are very few people he doesn't hold in contempt."

"There was a girl who used to work for him," said Duncan reminiscently. "A second lieutenant. I don't know why, but it was important to her to make a career in the army. He took every advantage of that poor kid. He summoned two of us to his apartment one Sunday afternoon. Another major and I. The lieutenant was there. She'd been sunbathing on his terrace, apparently, and all she had on was a pretty skimpy bikini. He wouldn't let her get dressed. I mean, he firmly discouraged her, and she was afraid to buck him. He made her serve us drinks and then sit and take notes of our meeting, in that little bra and the little strip of nylon across her hips that hardly covered her hair."

"Matt can be a bastard," said Lucas.

Duncan glanced around the room. "Which," he said quietly, "is no reason why our bank should not back him with a part of the cash he needs for the merger." He lifted his glass of wine and frowned into its red depths for a moment. "He's a successful bastard."

"Is he?"

Duncan looked up. "You're on the short end of the stick. You're the man he wants to cash out. You—"

"Not really," said Lucas. "What he really wants is to cash-out UNI. And, of course, Ringold. That's what he needs for control. Getting rid of me is just icing on his cake."

"I should be so lucky as to be gotten rid of on the terms you're being offered," said Duncan, picking up a bread stick and stabbing his butter with it. "You'll be a millionaire many times over."

"That was the point of the last fifteen years," said Lucas.

"But you don't like the idea of being muscled out of the company and the business you created."

"Something like that."

Duncan bit off a piece of the bread stick. "Exactly what is your relationship with HEST? That is, if you don't mind my asking?"

"I own 5 percent," said Lucas. "I'm a director. I have a consulting contract that pays me $230,000 a year. Does that correspond to the information you read on the company's SEC filings?"

Duncan smiled. "It corresponds," he said.

"Over the years they have gradually diminished my role, until today I really have very little to do with the way the company is run. My input is not asked for anymore."

"You're a chronic pain in the ass—according to Matt Fraser. An iconoclast."

Lucas sipped red wine. "I'm honored," he said.

"Gentlemen," said the waitress. She had their food and began to serve. She was an attractive girl, probably a student, and she was direct in her smile and the conspicuous attention she gave Lucas. Duncan, who was an overweight, balding man, a little older than Lucas, pretended not to notice.

"So precisely what is your interest?" Lucas asked as

soon as the waitress had left the table. "You looked me up, telephoned me, flew here from California—was it just to see me?—and here we are. Why?"

Duncan pulled his chin back against his chest. "I'm meeting General Fraser tomorrow. But the bank wanted me to talk to a . . . dissenter. Shall we call you that? A dissenter? General Fraser is trying to raise $1.1 billion. He has bank commitments for about $700 million. Somehow it all seems a little too smooth, and we wonder just how closely the New York banks have investigated. I wanted to talk to Arthur Ringold, but suddenly it seems he's not a dissenter anymore."

"Well, if Fraser has agreement from UNI and Arthur Ringold," said Lucas, "he has all he needs. The $700 million he has committed will buy enough stock to take complete control. He can take over without another $400 million from your bank."

Duncan, studying the food on his plate, shook his head. "His commitments are not all that firm. If our bank declines to go along for the additional $400 million, one or more of the others may withdraw their commitments." Duncan looked up from his plate and smiled. "As you well know."

"So you want me to tell you why you should not commit $400 million," said Lucas.

Duncan nodded. "I want *someone* to tell us why not. We've been subjected to some well-rehearsed presentations as to why we should."

Lucas covered his smile with a fist. "Suppose I tell you I can't offer a single reason as to why you should not."

Duncan shrugged. "That will weigh. It may not tip the balance, but it will weigh in it."

"What does the bank want?" Lucas asked.

"The same thing any bank wants when it makes a loan: reasonable assurance that it will be repaid."

"The business is sound," said Lucas. "Revenues are up. Market projections are encouraging. And actually, the market projections don't even begin to take the potential into account."

"A machine that hears speech and prints what it hears . . ." mused Duncan.

"It's used for trials and government hearings and so on," said Lucas. "We started in that market because that's where the money was. But think of the things it can do! There's an engineering firm in Dallas that uses HEST to write specifications and reports. In Washington there's a paraplegic lawyer who dictates memos and briefs to the machine in the evening. During the afternoon he talks to people and reads cases and documents; and in the evening, when his firm's HEST station is not being used for depositions, he talks into the microphone and turns out polished written materials. NBC is starting to make transcripts of its news broadcasts. We are just beginning to crack the potential—"

"But there's a worm in the apple," said Duncan. "Isn't there?"

Lucas nodded. "Yes. I think so. And, oddly enough, it's not Matt Fraser's fault."

"UNI has been taking too much cash out of HEST," said Duncan. "The stock pays too high a dividend."

"Money that should have stayed in," said Lucas. "For research and development."

"But the general denies that's a problem," said Duncan. "He admits that research and development have been shorted, but he says there's no competition, so . . ."

"Remember the old story about Christopher Columbus?" Lucas asked. "He showed the Spanish grandees how to stand a hard-boiled egg on end—by tapping it on the table and cracking the shell—and when they protested that anyone could do that, he replied, 'Of course, now that I've shown you how.' Well. We showed the world how to create a heuristic ergonomic speech transcriber, and now anyone can do it. The technology is quite straightforward. Except in the bells and whistles, there are no secrets and nothing that could be patented or copyrighted. With enough money and about a year to work on it, anyone can do it."

"And they could better HEST?"

"Well . . . maybe. The problem is, the research-and-development budget has been shorted to let UNI skim off cash. In the high-tech world, standing still is slipping back."

"The UNI management is oriented to basic, heavy industry," said Duncan. "Some ways, it's antediluvian."

"So is Matt Fraser, don't forget," said Lucas. "He's of an old school, an older generation. Matt believes in hierarchy, in subordinates that say, 'Yes, sir.' But that doesn't work in high-tech. My daughter graduated summa from MIT and came aboard with a first-year salary of $55,000. It was her best offer, but she could have gotten $40,000 at half a dozen places. One week out of college! She would never say, 'Yes, sir' to Matt Fraser or to anyone else. She'd tell him to shove it and walk off to a new job—which she would find in two or three phone calls. HEST is full of people like that. A would-be competitor who comes along and makes them a better offer will get them: half or more of Matt's key people. They feel no loyalty to him or the company.

They'll take their expertise where they can sell it on better terms."

"What about their no-compete agreements?" asked Duncan.

"Good for one year. *If* they're enforceable, and they are not necessarily enforceable."

"In other words," said Duncan, "if you are cashed out, you'll take your team with you and set to work to build a competitive system."

Lucas shook his head. "No. Honestly, no. I built one HEST. It wouldn't be any fun to build another."

Duncan picked up a garlic-drenched shrimp by the tail, bit it in half, and chewed on it. "All right. The worm in the apple is that any first-rate team of system designers could build another HEST, given the necessary capital."

"There is another worm," said Lucas.

Duncan smiled again. "I surmised as much. Delaware corporation law."

Lucas nodded. "HEST is a Delaware corporation. Under Delaware law, minority stockholders in a cash-out are entitled to an appraisal—particularly when officers and directors of the corporation are also officers and directors of the corporation that is offering cash for their shares. A court will order an appraisal and stop the cash-out if the offer is too low. It may be that $28.25 a share is generous compensation for the present value of the business, but HEST has only begun to exploit the technology. The unexploited business opportunities inherent in the heuristic-ergonomic design may make the stock worth two or three times their $28.25."

"Even granting that competition may invade the field?"

"Even granting," said Lucas. "After all, HEST has

at least a year up on any potential competitor. What's more, it has a good name and, one would suppose, some client loyalty."

Duncan grinned broadly. "If a court orders an appraisal and the appraisers fix the value at, say, sixty dollars, Matt's one billion won't buy the store."

"That's a possibility."

Duncan seized the body of the shrimp between his teeth and pulled the last of it out of the shell. "Is some minority stockholder going to demand an appraisal? And sue for it, if it's refused?"

Lucas smiled. "Oh, I suspect someone will."

The next day, General Fraser sat down to lunch with Nelson Duncan in the big downstairs dining room at the Harvard Club. Duncan, who had eaten there before, had been tempted to tell the general that he would meet him for lunch anywhere in town except the Harvard Club; but he let himself be dominated by his sense of duty and reluctantly sat down at one of the gloomy oak tables to partake of a meal he knew would be undistinguished. The general, conspicuously content, glanced around the room, making a quick survey of fellow Harvardians present, as he lit one of his monogrammed cigarettes. A man across the room nodded at him, and the general smiled faintly and returned the nod. He took a single, deep draw on his cigarette, then put it aside in an ashtray and picked up his Glenfiddich on the rocks.

The general was feeling comfortable. Nelson Duncan was not only an important banker but a former subordinate from his Tokyo days, and he was amused to see that Duncan had not entirely lost the habit of deference to two-star rank.

"Whatever happened to Lieutenant Bikini?" Duncan asked.

"Career officer," said the general. "She's a major now, I believe. Cute little chick, wasn't she? Timid in bed, but biddable."

"Weren't they all," said Duncan wryly.

"None like the Vietnamese," said the general. "None in the world. One of those petite Viet girls in her *ao dai,* with the tricks some Frenchman had taught her . . . The legs they had! The skin! The perfume." He shook his head. "You wanted one from the better classes, of course. . . ."

"Yes. Otherwise their teeth were bad," said Duncan. "I remember you emphasized that."

General Fraser laughed. "We learn from experience, Nelson," he said. He picked up his cigarette. "There's no teacher like experience."

Duncan's mood shifted as he lifted his glass and sipped white wine. "Changing the subject, General, what's the stockholder reaction to your merger proposition?"

General Fraser let smoke escape from between his lips and teeth, and again he put his cigarette aside. "There was never any question," he said. "We knew UNI would go along before we made the offer. We assured ourselves of Ringold last week. That makes 55 percent. I own 2 percent myself, and I believe Dave Berger's going to accept his money, in spite of some reluctance. We've had some acceptances from the small stockholders. There's no problem."

"What if some stockholder demands an appraisal?"

The general shook his head. "We'll refuse. We've made a generous offer."

"What if a stockholder sues? As I understand the

law, any stockholder can ask for a court-ordered appraisal. Of course, if the court's appraisers assigned a higher value to the stock, you'd have to pay that value to all the stockholders."

"Well . . . I don't think anyone is going to sue," said General Fraser.

"Lucas Paulson?" asked Duncan.

The general shook his head. "No. I don't think he'll do it. Anyway, if he does, we'll beat him."

"How can you be sure?"

General Fraser stiffened with indrawn breath. "Nelson," he said. He stopped and let the deep breath go, and he put his fingers together on the table before him. "You have before you an application for a loan from our company. Because of that I can reveal to you confidential information that I could not otherwise ethically reveal. For the same reason, you are ethically bound not to repeat to anyone what I am about to tell you. Agreed?"

Duncan closed his eyes and nodded. "Agreed."

"Yesterday we sent to Mr. Lucas Paulson a registered letter. In it, we advised him that company auditors have raised some tough questions about the way certain funds were handled during his tenure as president of Electroscript. We advised him that, unless satisfactory answers can be found for some of these questions, the company may have to bring suit against him to recover a very substantial amount of money, probably well over a million dollars."

"That's harking back to ancient history," Duncan objected. "Electroscript was absorbed in—"

"We didn't know about some of this until very recently," General Fraser interrupted. "But the retired comptroller of Ringold Corporation brought a lot of things to our attention, which we decided the auditors had to look into. I knew, of course, that Paulson treated Electroscript like a personal fiefdom, but I'd had no idea to what extent he treated its funds like his personal property. To cite the worst example, there is evidence that Paulson let contracts to companies other than the low bidders—and took kickbacks from the companies that got those contracts. To cite a smaller example, there's evidence that he kept on the payroll certain friends of his that did no work. Also, there's evidence that he put some of his girlfriends on the company payroll and shacked up with them in hotels all over the country at the company's expense. Oh, there's a mess coming out, Nelson."

General Fraser did not notice, probably, that Duncan's lips had become thin and white or that his eyes had narrowed. "I'm going to have to know, General," he said, measuring out his words as if he were mixing a complicated cocktail, "just how likely you think it is that accusing Paulson of ten-year-old defalcations will prevent him from bringing suit for an appraisal. I assume it *is* a tactic, that you don't really mean to accuse Paulson formally or try to sue him for a million dollars."

"That's a little blunt, Nelson," said General Fraser crisply.

"Bluntly, I have to know," said Duncan. "I have to know what likelihood there is that a court is going to order you to pay more than $28.50 per share for the HEST stock."

The general picked up his cigarette. "Our letter to Paulson makes it a whole lot less likely," he said. "You can call it a tactic if you want to and imply that you don't approve of it, but be realistic, Nelson; if we can

311

defang Paulson, we've defanged the most likely dissenter. What's more, my lawyers tell me that if he does sue, there's a chance we can have his suit dismissed immediately, on the showing that he's come into court without what they call clean hands. I'm not entirely clear on it, but they tell me that under this doctrine of clean hands, in effect, you can't come into court complaining that the company's cheating you if you yourself have been cheating the company. And the way I understand it, we can raise that issue at the first hearing."

"I'm skeptical."

"All right. Look at something else then. Look at his credibility. . . ." The general smiled. "You see what I mean? An accused embezzler—"

"How good's your evidence?" Duncan asked. "Just what is it, anyway?"

"The testimony of the retired comptroller," said General Fraser. "A perfect witness: a retired FBI agent."

"Is that all? What about the books?"

"I'll admit there are ambiguities. Aren't there always? The accounting records confirm what I've told you, but I suppose Paulson will have some explanation. He'll have some rationalization for every discrepancy."

"Anyway, you can tie him up in litigation for a long time," said Duncan dryly.

General Fraser nodded. "We can sweat him. Let him sit in a witness chair and explain every peculiar item. We can subpoena the girlfriends, too, and ask them what they were doing for Electroscript when they stayed in resort hotels and submitted expense accounts approved by Paulson."

"And you expect the prospect of that to scare him out of suing for an appraisal?" asked Duncan grimly.

The general shrugged. "Maybe. This is war, you

understand, Nelson." His cheeks reddened. "It's war between me and that egomaniacal son of a bitch."

As he held Susannah in his arms and kissed her, Lucas lifted her skirt and slipped a hand into her panties, so he could caress her bare bottom. As he ran his hand over her smooth, cool flesh, she giggled and groped for his crotch.

"While we can, honey," he said. "Our guests will be here any moment."

"I'd have come sooner but . . . Mother insisted I had to go into Neiman Marcus with her and try on a summer outfit she saw last week and thinks I simply *must* have. I couldn't just take off, without making her suspicious."

"She's not already? You're sure?"

Susannah shook her head. "No. She's completely loyal to my father. If she had the least idea what's going on, she'd tell him. If she knew—"

"Gangbusters," said Lucas.

"Gangbusters," Susannah agreed.

It was early Thursday evening, and they were in the long living-dining room of Lucas's apartment, standing at one of the big windows that looked down from four stories on the East River. The room crossed the entire front of the building and was almost forty feet long. Lucas had removed the walls that had divided it into two rooms. The walls were white, the ceiling was crossed by tracks mounting a dozen white spotlight fixtures, and the walls were hung with an eclectic group of paintings and prints. Only a few scatter rugs lay on the wide, dark-finished boards of the floor; and the furniture—most of it in stainless steel and leather—was placed to leave much open space. He had wheeled in a Lucite bar cart, and a bottle of Bordeaux sat open, breathing, in the midst of the bottles of gin and whiskey and the ice and glasses.

"I have to tell you something before anyone else comes," Lucas said to Susannah. "Your father has threatened me with a nasty lawsuit."

"I wouldn't take that too seriously," she said. "Since I was a kid I can remember him always threatening to sue somebody about something."

"I want you to know, because it's going to produce an emotional reaction in the others. He's had the company auditors accuse me of misusing company funds years ago. They're talking about a million dollars or so."

"He can't stand the possibility he might not be able to make you do what he wants you to."

Lucas held her close to him and caressed her hair. "I wish it didn't have to be like this, Susannah," he said.

She looked up solemnly into his face. "So do I. But . . . I love you."

"*I* love *you*."

Melanie arrived a little before seven. As always, she and Susannah appraised each other for a long moment: Susannah, tall and trim in a slim black cotton knit dress that clung tight on her figure; Melanie, shorter and fuller, wearing a white skirt and long-sleeved pink silk blouse. Dave Berger came a little later, bringing a bottle of Château Mouton-Rothschild—and he was at no pains to conceal his appraisal of either of the young women.

Lucas poured drinks for all of them: a martini for Berger, Jack Daniels for Melanie, glasses of the red Bordeaux for himself and Susannah.

"I want to show you all something before we go out to dinner," Lucas said when they were seated around his glass-topped coffee table and were sipping their drinks and munching peanuts. "I'd like to give the subject no more than fifteen minutes' conversation, and I'd like your promises that none of you will mention it again after that fifteen minutes is over." He took out his registered letter from HEST and let each of them read it.

Melanie's face darkened. "I will hand them my resignation Monday morning," she said angrily.

"Lucky you," said Susannah. "How do you resign from being a daughter?"

"This is crazy," said Berger. He had grabbed the letter off the table and was reading it a second time. He glanced at Susannah. "Forgive me, hon," he said to her, "but your father has lost his mind." He tossed the letter back on the table. "That's the end of their deal with me."

Susannah began to cry. Lucas pulled her into his arms.

Lucas fixed his eyes first on Melanie's face, then on Berger's. "I don't want any of you doing anything foolish," he said. "I mean it."

"I am resigning Monday morning," grunted Melanie through clenched teeth.

"I have one request of you then," said Lucas. "Stay away from anything that could be interpreted as a violation of your no-compete agreement. I don't want them suing you, too."

"And watch your no-disclosure obligation," added Berger.

"As to you, Dave," said Lucas. "Don't do anything dramatic. Not for the sake of dramatics, anyway. I don't need that kind of help."

"Do you need *any?*" asked Berger.

"Well . . . I don't need my friends getting themselves hurt by rallying around the flag."

"I don't see any flag raised to rally around," said Melanie. "Dad—"

"All right," he interrupted. "I have a couple of announcements. Number one—a suit was filed in chancery court in Wilmington this afternoon, asking for an appraisal of HEST, Incorporated."

"You . . .?" asked Berger.

"No, not me," said Lucas. "Mrs. Emmadine Clarke of San Mateo, California."

Berger's mouth dropped open. "Gabe's . . .?"

Lucas nodded. "The widow of Gabriel Lincoln, since remarried. She inherited two thousand shares from Gabe, the stock he received through his profit-sharing plan."

"You . . . ? She's fronting for you?"

"No. Not for me. She doesn't like the deal, she doesn't like Matt, and she figures her stock's worth three times what they're offering. She called and talked to me about it, but she's not a straw woman for me."

"What if her lawyers foul it up?" asked Berger. "What if Matt goes to her and settles some way?"

"Both are possible. But for the time being, the merger is stopped. It gives us a little time."

"Time to do what?" Melanie asked.

"I'm not ready to say yet," said Lucas. "But time anyway for something else important. I said I had *two* announcements."

Melanie's eyes shifted immediately to Susannah. "You—"

"On Monday when we stayed over on Nantucket," said Lucas, "Susannah and I applied for our marriage license. We will be married a week from Sunday, on Nantucket. Each of you is, of course, invited."

* * *

Friday morning.

"Matt regards the Clarke woman's suit as yours," said Jim Cahill with a measured, unfriendly smile.

"No, he doesn't," said Lucas calmly across his desk, where he was signing a dozen letters as they spoke.

"What do you mean, he doesn't? He certainly does."

Lucas shrugged. "I don't think Matt's that stupid," said Lucas. "He's checked, and he knows there's no connection."

"Her husband worked for you in the early days."

"I have seen the woman perhaps twice in my life and have had one telephone conversation with her," said Lucas, looking up from his letters. "She telephoned me when she got your offer of $28.50 a share and asked me if I thought she should sue you. I said yes. That's the substance of the only contact I've had with her in ten years."

Cahill had his shirt sleeves rolled back over his forearms, the white shirt rumpled and his tie loose. "Did you tell her you thought her stock was worth more than $28.50?"

"Yes, I did. I think it is."

"If you'll read the Delaware cases, you'll see that the courts will not take into account a speculative element of the value. The stock is selling for $27.00, occasionally $27.25, when there's a market for it."

"It's worth more," said Lucas flatly.

"Well . . . I won't argue the point. You are aware that Melanie quit her job this morning."

"Yes. I knew she was going to."

"Matt feels it would be better—in view of the questions raised about your handling of Electroscript and so on—if we terminate all your current assignments. We can't, of course, cancel your contract, which

317

still has some years to run—we can't, that is, unless we sue to cancel it, if it's found you did, in fact, misappropriate Electroscript funds. In the meantime, we think we have the right to insist you vacate your office and return any company files you have in your possession. I may as well tell you also that we've given your secretary notice. Her loyalty is to you personally and not to the company."

"Matt never misses an opportunity to be nasty, does he?" asked Lucas coldly. "Okay. I'll move out. But you had better remember something. I'm still a director. There's nothing you can do about that, either."

"We're aware of that."

"All right. One more thing. I want a letter, signed by Matt, advising me of the termination of my consulting assignments. I won't move a step out of here until I've got written notice of the change."

Cahill nodded. "Have it your way."

Lucas smiled. "I intend to," he said.

At seven-thirty Friday evening, the doorman sounded the buzzer in Lucas's apartment. "There is a car and driver here for you, sir." Lucas pulled his necktie tight, checked the set of his dark blue suit in the hall mirror, and went down to the limousine. He declined the chauffeur's offer of a drink but agreed that it would be pleasant to listen to a tape of a Mahler symphony on the car's stereo system. He settled back in the deep, soft seat, meaning to glance through *Forbes* and *Fortune* during the drive, but he was too lulled to concentrate and napped comfortably as the car sped toward Connecticut.

In Stamford, the limousine threaded through some mean streets and turned toward the water, entering finally a private enclave where the driver was waved in by a gate-house guard. Pulling into a parking garage beneath an office building, the chauffeur came to a stop at the exit from the garage to the docks. He led Lucas down a ramp and along the planks of a floating dock to a yacht moored near the end.

Autumn Mate was the name of the sixty-five-foot Chris Craft. Thomas Miller emerged from the main salon and extended his hand toward Lucas. Miller made no concessions to the nautical; he was dressed much as Lucas was, in a dark blue business suit. Thick white hair crowned his leonine head, and his face was deeply tanned.

"Lucas! Welcome aboard! I'm glad you could make it."

"I wouldn't miss it," said Lucas.

"Come on in and meet my wife," said Miller. "Also one of my wife's nieces. No problem for us. The women will leave us alone after dinner."

The main salon of the boat was a comfortable living room, furnished in the overstuffed and brocaded style of an English country house. In this, too, there was little concession to the fact that they were aboard a boat on saltwater. The water slapped against the hull, and the big yacht rolled slowly and only a little on the swell from the sound; but the women, like the men, were dressed as they might have been in a Manhattan apartment and were sipping drinks from crystal cocktail glasses.

"This is my wife, Faye," said Miller. "And her niece, Laura Henning. Mr. Lucas Paulson, ladies."

The women were both thin and tall and blonde, the wife in her fifties, the niece in her early thirties, Lucas judged. Both wore linen dresses, one white, one pink, with loops of pearls around their necks.

"A drink for the gentleman?" asked a steward who

had come in from another part of the boat. "And, can I refill you, Mr. Miller?"

Lucas asked for a Scotch on the rocks.

"We weren't planning on taking the boat out tonight," Miller said to Lucas. "I hope you don't mind."

"Not at all," said Lucas.

"We'll have dinner," said Miller. "Then you and I can get down to business. I hope you'll stay overnight, in fact, and you can go in to the city with me in the car in the morning. The guest stateroom is equipped with a kit—shaving stuff and all that."

"I'll be pleased, though I should probably call my daughter," said Lucas.

"Of course. And I'll get you to the Pan Am Building by nine-thirty, barring a disaster in morning rush-hour traffic. Okay?"

"I'll be in no hurry," said Lucas. "I was fired this afternoon."

The two women's faces automatically assumed expressions of sympathy, but Miller grinned. "Good," he said. "And did you resign your directorship?"

"I haven't yet."

"I'd recommend you do so immediately," said Miller.

Lucas nodded, but he glanced uneasily at the two women.

Miller noticed. "Faye and Laura know most of what's going on," he said. "We can talk in front of them. When we get down to the nitty-gritty, we'll bore them, so they'll dismiss us to my on-board office for that."

Lucas smiled at the two women. "I hope I don't bore you before then," he said.

The steward came in with a Stolichnaya for Miller and Scotch on the rocks for Lucas.

"You know the suit was filed Friday afternoon," said Miller.

"Yes."

Miller picked up his glass but held it without drinking. "The lady was happy to cooperate. I'm glad you thought of her. She was a good choice."

"Matt has already accused me of setting her up as my straw woman to sue him for me."

Miller nodded. "Uhm. I expected that. Let him try to prove it. She knows what to say."

"As I recall, she was intelligent," said Lucas. "I haven't seen her for a very long time."

"My people were favorably impressed," said Miller. "Well, anyway . . . You have a drink at last. A toast. Ladies . . . To a long and mutually satisfying relationship with our friend Lucas Paulson."

Lucas sipped Scotch. "And may I offer a toast, too," he said. He raised his glass. "To the white knight!"

20

"WELCOME HOME, MR. Paulson. Barometer thirty-point-oh-eight, winds zero-five at nine-zero, gusting to fifteen. Make straight in for Runway Six, report three miles."

"Thank you, sir. Will report three. Good weather for a wedding, wouldn't you say?"

"Couldn't ask for better. And congratulations to you, Mr. Paulson."

"Thank you again, sir."

He glanced into Susannah's beaming face, and she reached over and squeezed his hand, even though it was on the throttle, easing off power and increasing the sink rate as the Bonanza stabilized on its descent toward Nantucket.

"Nothing like being famous," remarked Dave Berger from the seat behind Susannah.

"Nothing like being welcome," said Melanie.

It was Thursday morning, the sixth of June. The sky was pale blue and cloudless, with a layer of haze hanging low over the Atlantic and diminishing visibility only as they descended into it. The shoreline remained distinctly visible, and Lucas was confident he would find the airport and the runway with no trouble, but he switched his navigation instruments to the Nantucket localizer and glanced at the indicators for a confirmation of his position.

Dave Berger reached for Melanie's hand and squeezed it. They had never shared the slightest physical intimacy, nor had the thought ever occurred to either of them; but they were genuinely affectionate toward each other and had been for some years, since she had stopped calling him Uncle Dave. Melanie was tense, and Dave was comforting her.

As they descended through the thin haze, the Nantucket shoreline faded from view, then returned, then faded again. Lucas was comfortable with his approach. The only other traffic in the area, a Piper Lance, had just been cleared for landing and was within a minute of touchdown.

Susannah was proud of the man she had chosen to marry. The hair beneath his dark blue Yankee baseball cap was almost white, though he was only forty-five years old; but he was strong and youthful, both of his body and of the set of his mind. His eyes were concentrating now, behind his sunglasses, as he flipped switches and pulled handles, with practiced, confident hands, guiding the airplane toward the Nantucket runway. It was difficult to resist the impulse to throw her arms around him and kiss him.

The landing was smooth. The Bonanza rolled out on the center line of the runway, and Lucas guided it off to the left, into a taxiway toward the ramp. His Beetle was waiting in the parking lot, but Melanie, who knew the limitations of the Volkswagen, had rented a car. Lucas and Susannah alone took the Beetle; Melanie followed with Dave and the luggage in a rented Chevy.

"Where the hell's he going?" Melanie asked rhetorically when Lucas did not turn right and out Milestone

Road toward Siasconset but left, toward the town of Nantucket.

"Where are we going, honey?" Susannah asked at the same time.

Lucas only smiled as he drove into town on Orange Street and turned toward the wharfs at the end of Main Street. After parking the Beetle at the curb, he led Susannah, now almost dancing with excitement as she guessed where they were going, onto the Old South Wharf where the ocean-going yachts were moored in ranks.

"Ah. Here," he said, stopping at the stern of the *Autumn Mate,* Thomas Miller's sixty-five-foot Chris Craft, which was backed up to the dock. "Our honeymoon cottage. Ours for a week, with a captain to run it. A wedding present."

She clung to his arm, flushed and voiceless.

The captain, named Peter, carried their luggage from the Chevy to the boat, while Lucas and Susannah, Melanie and Dave, explored the salon and galley and staterooms. The master stateroom, in the stern, was equipped with a king-sized bed. Flowers in vases brightened and scented the salon. The galley was stocked with champagne and all else necessary for a week's cruise.

"Mr. Miller said to give you this as soon as you arrived," Peter said, handing an envelope to Lucas.

The note in the envelope read: "Look over the attached, which was sent to me by a friend in California, then forget it for a week. Have the best of times. Tom."

The enclosure was a Xerox copy of a telegram from Nelson Duncan to the president of Bank of America. It read:

STRONGLY RECOMMEND NO ACTION AT PRESENT ON
FRASER TECH LOAN APPLICATION. HAVE REASON FOR
DISSATISFACTION WITH BUSINESS ETHICS F T MAN-
AGEMENT. WISH TO REPORT IN DETAIL.

Lucas saw no reason to show the telegram to Dave or
Melanie, certainly not to show it to Susannah.

Two friends of Susannah's came from Smith College
to be her bridesmaids at the wedding. The elderly
Congregational minister they had contacted on the
foggy Monday morning when they applied for the
license acceded with enthusiasm to their request that he
perform the service on the rear deck of the yacht. The
girls from Smith, wearing pastel-blue and pastel-green
frocks, with hats, marveled open-mouthed at Susannah's groom and at the boat. They stood with their
backs to the rail and soberly listened to the service.
Melanie was thoughtful, almost grim, standing at her
father's side. Dave stood behind Susannah, as if he
were her father.

Susannah's calf-length wedding dress was white—a
silk sheath under a sheer full skirt, a bodice seeded with
tiny pearls. Beneath a little cap also seeded with pearls,
her blonde hair hung down her back to her waist. She
wore a pale pink lipstick and no other makeup. The
ring Lucas slipped on her finger was a plain gold
wedding band. She stared into his eyes, with tears on
her cheeks, as she whispered her vows. When the
minister pronounced them husband and wife, she
kissed him fervently, then clung to him for a full
minute.

Melanie had ordered a wedding cake delivered to the
cottage in Siasconset but had been able to call the baker
in time to have it brought to the boat instead. Her gift

was a silver creamer and sugar bowl on a silver tray engraved with the date of the wedding. Dave Berger gave a half-dozen antique silver spoons with gold bowls. The two girls from Smith gave Susannah and Lucas a tablecloth and napkins.

Since Peter, the captain, said the boat could pull out of Nantucket Harbor any time, including after sunset, Lucas and Susannah conferred, then asked all their wedding party, including the minister and his wife and Peter, to join them for dinner at the Jared Coffin House.

From the hotel, Susannah sent a telegram to her parents:

> LUCAS PAULSON AND I WERE MARRIED THIS AFTER-NOON. PLEASE SHARE MY HAPPINESS. SUSANNAH.

The *Autumn Mate* pulled away from the wharf a little after sunset the day of the wedding, but it went nowhere that night, only to anchorage a couple of miles out in Nantucket Harbor. The next day it began a leisurely circuit of the islands: Tuckernuck, Martha's Vineyard, Cuttyhunk, then across the sound to Block Island, where Lucas and Susannah went ashore on their third day and rode bicycles to the beach, then on to Montauk and along the Hampton beaches, then again to Martha's Vineyard, where they dined ashore, and ultimately back to the wharf at Nantucket.

Peter was in daily radiotelephone contact with the office of Thomas Miller, but his instructions, from both Miller and Lucas, were to pass along no messages from anyone but Melanie. Melanie sent none.

Lucas had not anticipated the measure of happiness Susannah would give him. He had known her body for some time; his surprise was not in that. He had recognized her bright intelligence, augmented by a mysterious intuition that resulted in amazing perceptivity. He had seen ample evidence of her capacity for giving and receiving love. What he had not perhaps fully anticipated was the infectious nature of her optimism. With her, he recovered something he had almost forgotten.

Mornings, as the big motor yacht crossed open water between the Vineyard and Block Island or between Montauk and Nantucket, they ate their breakfast on the rear deck where they had been married, at a table set up by Susannah in defiance of the wind and spray and rolling of the boat. Afternoons, if they were at anchor, she ventured into the cold water and swam around the boat, or they fished, or on one rainy afternoon she took it upon herself to teach him backgammon. Evenings at anchor, after Peter had retired to his stateroom in the bow, she bared her breasts in the candlelit salon, that Lucas might look at them during long, unhurried dinners. Nights, in the luxurious master stateroom, she surprised herself, by her own admission.

She insisted that *he* shave off her pubic hair, if he wanted it off. He had told her, some time before, that he wished she would shave it; and now she offered herself to him, freshly showered and damp and ready. She had brought scissors and a woman's electric shaver. He told her a wet razor would be better and took his own down from the cabinet, with a can of Gucci shaving foam. Susannah watched with some degree of gravity as he snipped away the thick bush of hair and left her with a prickly stubble; but she giggled as he soaped her and drew the sharp blade over her, baring her soft white skin. She gasped as he bent down and ran his tongue over her naked pubes and between

327

her lips. She would not let him stay there. She drew him up and kissed him lovingly, clutching him tightly in her arms.

All week they talked. It was as if they had never before had the time, even in Paris, to talk together all they wanted. They said nothing of what they had to face when they returned to New York.

The tape on Melanie's telephone recorder was filled when she arrived home two days after the wedding. Jim Cahill had called eleven times, and there were two dozen hang-ups. Cahill's message was to call him as soon as she heard his message; but she didn't; she sat down to lunch. Soon the telephone rang.

"Cahill," he said brusquely when she picked up the instrument.

"Jim."

"Where's your father?"

"I don't know."

"Would you tell me if you did?"

"No."

"I'm with Matt in his office. He has the Massachusetts state police looking for Susannah."

"He'll be in deep shit if they find her," said Melanie.

"What do you mean by that?"

"She's nineteen years old. She was married to my father by the minister of a thoroughly respectable church, in the presence of many witnesses. It was a *wedding*, Jim; and if Matt wasn't invited, it was only because he's an insufferable ass. If he has the police interfere with anything in any way, Mr. and Mrs. Lucas Paulson will flay him alive in a court of law—besides making a public idiot of him. You tell him to cut the crap. I'm calling a lawyer right now, and if, when he inquires in Massachusetts, there's really any kind of complaint out against my father, the crucifixion will begin. You tell Matt that for me."

"Melanie—"

"I'm on this line, too, and by Christ you listen to—"
She hung up.

She called Horace Baxter, of Todd, Glennwellen & Marsh. Her father had already prepared Baxter for the anticipated outburst from General Fraser, and asked him to receive a weekend call if necessary. Baxter knew what to do. He called her back in an hour to say that no police agency in Massachusetts had any complaint against Lucas Paulson or any report that Susannah Fraser was missing. On the other hand, inquiry had been made yesterday of the town clerk in Nantucket as to whether or not a marriage license had been issued, and the old minister had received an angry call from General Matthew Fraser. The minister had told the general he had married a handsome man and a beautiful girl aboard a magnificent yacht, on which the happy couple had sailed away, leaving no word as to where they were going or when they would return. The minister could not recall the name of the yacht.

"But no criminal complaint? You're sure?"

"No. There never was one. Anyway, I told the police agencies to check the marriage-license record and talk to the minister if they had any question. They're laughing, to tell the truth. Irate fathers are a joke with them. They get a dozen complaints a day from the fathers of legal-age daughters who've married against family wishes."

"What'll Matt do?"

"Blow. Steam. What *can* he do?"

"I'll kill him," General Fraser had said. "I swear to Christ, I'll kill him." He had said it so many times that it had become a coarse abrasive against Jim Cahill's remaining respect for him—which was rapidly wearing down.

The general paced his office, driving his fist repeatedly into the palm of his other hand. Cahill sat on his couch, a martini glass sweating on the low table before him, watching and listening and wondering if the man would ever wind down.

"He could have had the fuckin' business. I'd have *given* him the fuckin' business! But not . . . Jesus Christ! Not *Susannah!*"

"Matt . . ."

"He only did it to get to me," the general grunted—something else he had repeated endlessly. "That son of a bitch has hated me and looked for a way—"

"Matt . . . Susannah is an intelligent young woman."

The general swung around and confronted Cahill with wild fury in his eyes. "Christ!" he yelled. "What difference does that make? Of *course* she's a smart girl, but so have a dozen others been—I mean, a dozen others that oily son of a bitch has got his cock into. You've watched him operate. Or have you been blind? Paulson . . . Paulson, for some reason I've never been able to understand, can dick any girl he sets his sights on. Shit, Jim! Haven't you seen it?"

Cahill shrugged and reached for his drink.

The general dropped heavily into the chair behind his desk. "You know what I'm carrying in my mind?" he muttered. He nodded. "A picture. I can't get it out of my mind. Susannah. My little girl! *My little girl!* That son of a bitch is putting his cock in my little girl! You can sit there and sop up gin . . . How would you feel if—"

"Matt—"

"Goddamn lawyers can tell me it's not a kidnapping. Goddamn lawyers can tell me she's old enough to marry anybody she pleases. But I'm telling you that son of a bitch tricked her into running away with him on some goddamn boat, God knows where; and it goddamn well tears me apart having to carry in my mind the picture of my daughter, my little girl, being dicked by that son of a bitch. It's an ugly goddamn picture, Jim, and I'll get that goddamn son of a bitch if it's the last thing I do."

Lucas and Susannah returned to his apartment—which he insisted was *their* apartment now—to find that Lois Levenstein had spent several days there during the week they were gone. She had established a temporary office for Lucas. His small computer was on the coffee table. She had rented an electronic typewriter and installed it on the dining table. She had arranged for his private telephone line from the Pan Am Building to be transferred to the apartment. Supposing he and Susannah would want their home disrupted as little as absolutely necessary, she had not rented filing cabinets but had stacked boxes of files in odd corners and laid out current files and correspondence in folders on the windowsills.

They arrived one midafternoon to find Lois seated behind the typewriter, talking on the telephone, while the other telephone, beyond her reach across the room, rang.

Susannah picked up the ringing phone. "Mr. Paulson's office," she said brightly, winking at Lucas. "No, this is Mrs. Paulson. No, it would not be convenient to take a call from Mr. Cahill right now. Tell him

331

he may call back. No. He'll have to call back." She put down the telephone. "That son of a bitch already," she laughed.

Lois hung up the other line. "Arthur Ringold is in town," she said. "He wanted to come this afternoon and have dinner with you. I told him tomorrow morning was the first time you had available. You have a call from Thomas Miller, which he wants you to return as soon as possible. Melanie wants to know when you're here. Dave Berger . . . Uh, Cahill a dozen times a day. Aside from that, welcome home. And congratulations to you both."

Lucas grinned at the hard young woman, dressed now as she had not been allowed to dress in the HEST offices: in tight maroon corduroy pants and a knit shirt. Susannah had met her, but Lucas introduced them again.

The across-the-room telephone rang. Susannah was closest. "Mr. Paulson's office. Who? Mr. Theisen. Of *what* firm? All right. Let me check."

Urgency and necessity defined their lives for the next several weeks. Melanie spent her days in the apartment and finally, at Susannah's suggestion, moved into the guest bedroom so she would not face the commute back and forth to Westchester. There was no time to establish an office anywhere else. Lucas established himself on the couch. Susannah went out and bought extension cords so the telephones could be placed within his reach or moved to the dining table for her or Lois to answer. The phones rang constantly. Messengers delivered documents to the door. Visitors came—Arthur Ringold, David Berger, Martin Kent, assorted lawyers and accountants. Reporters came to interview Lucas.

Boys from delis brought sandwiches and apples at lunchtime. They ate their dinners from cartons delivered from restaurants. Sometimes the phones rang after midnight.

Lucas was gratified by the way Susannah took to all this—with fascination and excitement. She answered the telephones, pecked away at the typewriter when Lois had to be relieved, served drinks to visitors and chatted with them when Lucas had to interrupt conversations to take a call. She began, too, to explore the mysteries of Lucas's little computer, trying to organize some of the accumulating documentation with a database program. Besides, she read every document that came, every one that was produced to go out, and listened to every conversation, to learn as much as possible as quickly as she could.

The second night they were home, Susannah called her mother. Three days later, Lila Fraser came to the apartment. It was early evening. She stood hesitantly in the door when Lucas opened it. She had apparently fortified her courage with a drink or two, probably in one of the stand-up bars in Grand Central, and her eyes were liquid and vacant. Her lipstick was smeared, and her cream-white linen dress was wrinkled.

On this one evening they had cleared the dining table, Melanie had arranged to have dinner out, and Susannah had prepared dinner for her mother and Lucas. Lila accepted two before-dinner drinks, then drank wine with her dinner. She became tearful.

"Your father will never forgive you, I'm afraid," she said to Susannah. "I'm not sure you will ever see him again."

Susannah ignored the comment. She pointed out the window, to the East River, to the marina beyond the

FDR Drive, where the *Autumn Mate* was moored. "See the big white boat?" she said to her mother. "That's the yacht we were married on."

One evening a week later, Susannah stood at the window and stared at the *Autumn Mate,* watching men boarding and wondering which of them was Lucas.

Lucas boarded about seven. He was greeted on deck by Thomas Miller, who introduced him to one of the CONTEKS vice presidents and to a corporate attorney. It was a warm evening, and the four men took their cocktails on deck, at first chatting amiably and watching the river traffic.

Miller, with a little tilt of his head, invited Lucas to stand apart for a moment at the rail. "That was a brilliant job you did on Fraser's Bank of America loan. Whatever you said to Duncan—"

"I didn't say much. Where Matt made his mistake with Duncan was in supposing he and Duncan were friends. Matt has always been oblivious of the negative impact he makes on people. Anyway, it is my impression of Nelson Duncan that he's a pro and made an honest, objective judgment. Of course, the lawsuit—"

"Without the Bank of America loan, they don't have enough cash to buy their controlling interest," said Miller. "They've offered UNI part cash and part notes."

"Would Sam Magnuson take a deal like that?"

"That's what we're going to find out shortly," said Miller.

A little after seven-thirty the party from United Northeastern Industries came aboard—Samuel Magnuson, chief executive officer; Douglas Forbes, comptroller; and Theodore Jefferson, chief corporate counsel.

For a few more minutes they all stayed on deck, enjoying the view of the river in the orange light of early evening. Then Miller suggested they go below. They entered the main cabin and sat down around the big table that had been unfolded and set in place for the meeting. Miller spread open a leather portfolio and opened the meeting.

"Sam. Doug. Ted. Thanks for coming. Let's get the subject for discussion on the table. On behalf of CONTEKS, I am offering to buy UNI's stock in HEST, Incorporated. That's conditioned, of course, on your selling it all. To be entirely frank, I control a hundred thousand shares already, that various people have picked up for me in the past year. I have commitments from Lucas Paulson and Professor Berger. With your 40 percent, CONTEKS will take control of HEST with an absolute majority of its voting stock. That's the story. I've mentioned everything but the price. We'll give you cash, or stock in CONTEKS, or a combination of the two."

Samuel Magnuson was a Boston banker, a Brahmin: a bulky, florid, white-haired man. He was a Harvardian, and he spoke in the flat accent of Boston and Harvard. "What price do you offer?" he asked.

"General Fraser," said Miller, "seems to believe you will sell *him* UNI's stock in HEST for $28.50 a share."

"We are under no binding commitment to sell to him," said Magnuson firmly.

"Sam, he has told the banks that you are," said Miller evenly.

Magnuson lifted his chin. "I suspect you know the situation," he said glumly.

"I think I do," said Miller. "Fraser offered you $28.50 a share, cash, for your entire 40 percent. You accepted that offer, and it *was* a binding commitment.

335

Then Bank of America pulled out of Fraser's funding consortium—"

"Followed by First National," said Forbes, the UNI comptroller.

Miller nodded. "Right. When those two banks pulled out, it left Fraser short of cash. Now he's offering you cash for part of your stock and HEST corporate notes for the balance."

"And we haven't decided whether or not to accept that amendment to the deal," said Magnuson.

"So you're under no binding commitment and can consider an offer from CONTEKS."

"Well, there's a moral issue, Tom," said Magnuson. "We have a long-standing and cordial relationship with General Fraser. He built HEST, after all."

Miller glanced at Lucas, communicating his appreciation of the irony. Then he nodded at Magnuson. "Of course," he said.

"Except for the Deficit Reduction Act, we would have given the general a golden parachute," Magnuson went on. "It's our feeling that he deserves it. Is it your intention to change management if you take control of HEST?"

"I'll make no commitment that we won't," said Miller.

"That makes it difficult for us," said Magnuson. "There is a matter of loyalty."

Miller turned over some of the papers in his portfolio. "Quite a few analysts seem to think UNI needs capital," he said, frowning over a sheaf of computer printouts. "If you sell HEST to Fraser Technologies, Incorporated, you'll get—what?—$200 million in cash, $200 million worth of corporate notes."

Magnuson nodded.

"If CONTEKS offers you $28.50 a share, you will

336

have $400 million cash. How much is your loyalty to the general worth, Sam?"

Magnuson glanced uncomfortably at his lawyer and comptroller. "My God, Tom. That's a damn hard way to put it."

"I'll put it even harder, Sam," said Miller. "Your stockholders will never stand for your taking cash and notes from Fraser when CONTEKS is offering cash. Neither will your board."

"You're muscling us," said Magnuson.

"Do I have to?"

Magnuson nodded gloomily for a moment, then shrugged. "UNI needs cash. No denying it. That's why we made a deal with Matt Fraser in the first place. I suppose HEST corporate notes are sound, but they're not cash; and a $400 million shot in the arm is twice as good as a $200 million one."

"Then we have a deal?"

Magnuson nodded. "I'll call my board together Monday." He reached for his glass and took a swallow of the vodka martini from which he had before sipped slowly, as if now he was relieved and could relax. "You place a lot of confidence in HEST," he said. "You going to put a lot of new money into it?"

Miller smiled and shrugged. "I will rely on the judgment of my new chief executive officer."

"Yes, I'd do that if I were you," said Magnuson. He nodded toward Lucas. "Some of the rest of us should have, a long time ago."

On Thursday morning, with a white-bright sun streaming in from the east, Lucas, Susannah, Melanie, and Lois were in the apartment. There was a buzz from the lobby. Lois went to the speaker to see who it was.

"Son of a bitch! Master Jim Cahill in person! Must be

a message from Hideyoshi. Maybe they want to surrender."

Cahill came up. His olive-green, summer-weight suit was rumpled already. His tie was loose. He accepted a cup of coffee and sat down wearily on the couch.

Susannah stood at the window looking at him. Lois and Melanie had gone to Lucas's library. Susannah, wearing white shorts and a lime-green T-shirt, regarded Cahill with a mixture of curiosity and hostility.

"Congratulations to you both," Cahill said, looking up at Susannah.

Susannah frowned, taken by surprise. "Thank you," she said quietly.

"I wish I could tell you your father is . . . in a better mood—I mean, more receptive to your marriage. But—"

"I spoke with my mother again yesterday," said Susannah quietly.

Cahill nodded. "Well, don't be too hard on him, Susannah. He's taking an awful beating."

"Nothing he didn't bring on himself," she said coldly.

Cahill shrugged. He turned toward Lucas. "Matt got the word from UNI last night," he said. "He couldn't believe it. They sold him out, Lucas." Cahill nodded. "They sold him out."

Lucas shrugged. "I won't disagree with that."

"It will break him," said Cahill. He glanced up at Susannah, who still stood, arms folded, listening. "I don't know if you understand what I mean, but Matt faces bankruptcy. He'll have his army retirement pay. He may lose the house in Westchester and—"

"No, he won't," said Susannah. "The house is mother's. Anyway, he's—"

Cahill spoke to her. "To be sure, Fraser Tech would get the Ringold stock; we took an option on it. Matt borrowed two million personally to buy that option. Now—"

"Exercise the option," said Lucas. "Buy the Ringold stock at $28.50. It'll be worth twice that in six months."

Cahill shook his head. "The market is still holding at $27.25. Which means the option is worthless. It's worthless even if Matt could borrow enough to exercise it, which he can't."

"Did Lila sign Matt's note?" Lucas asked.

"No. So then the house . . . Thank God."

"Why'd you come, Jim?" Lucas asked. "What do you want?"

Cahill glanced at Susannah, then returned his eyes to Lucas. "I assume you'll be the new president of HEST."

Lucas nodded.

Cahill bit his lower lip. "What are you going to do about Matt? Put him out on the street?"

Lucas shook his head. "I don't know," he said. "I—"

"What would *he* have done if he'd won?" Susannah asked.

"He'd have put Lucas out on the street," said Cahill.

"Then?" she asked, lifting her chin scornfully.

"I don't know, Jim," Lucas repeated firmly. "I don't know what we can do. What would Matt accept? Would he work for me?"

Cahill shrugged. "I have no idea. I don't speak for Matt anymore."

"Then what about you, Jim?" Lucas asked.

"I'd like to stay," said Cahill. "You once said I could move on without much sweat, and I suppose I can, but I've got a lot of years and fatigue invested in this business."

339

"Come talk to me after the stockholders' meeting," said Lucas. "I may ask a lot of you to stay on."

Cahill rose. "If you don't mind a suggestion, I think I'd call your mother if I were you, Susannah. Matt's at the townhouse. He got pretty drunk last night, and I suppose he's sleeping it off. Well. Thanks. And congratulations."

The telephone rang at ten that Thursday night. Susannah answered and turned, stricken, to Lucas. "Honey . . . Something's happened to Melanie!"

Lucas took the telephone.

"Mr. Paulson? Are you the father of a young woman named Melanie Paulson? This is Dr. Wilson at Lincoln Hospital. Your daughter has been in an automobile accident. The emergency squad brought her in twenty minutes ago. I think you had better come here, Mr. Paulson. I'm sorry. It looks pretty bad."

Susannah begged to come with him, but he begged her to stay in the apartment. Someone should be there to answer the telephone, he said. Weeping, she agreed to stay.

He rushed out on the street. There wasn't a cab in sight, and he trotted toward First Avenue.

"Paulson?"

"Yes . . ."

He felt a dull, crushing pain at the back of his head, and he felt his knees strike the pavement; then, perhaps mercifully, he blacked out. From time to time, and for a brief moment, he came back. He knew he was put into a car. He knew he was in the back seat with two men. He knew the car was moving.

"Well, well," laughed one of the men as his face swam into focus. "I do believe Mr. Paulson is coming around." He slapped Lucas hard across the face. "Wake up, you bastard!"

"Who . . . ? My daughter . . ."

"Stupider 'n he looks," the man laughed.

"Worries 'bout his daughter, though," the driver grunted.

The first man slapped his face again. "Daughter!" he sneered. "You understand about daughters, do you, Mr. Paulson?"

His head ached. His knees stung. And now his lips were broken and he tasted blood. He tried to focus on the streets outside the car. As nearly as he could tell, they were headed west, crossing Manhattan toward the Hudson. The car was an old Chevrolet. It stank of raw gasoline.

The men . . . He couldn't make them out. They were white. One was bearded. The one who had slapped him was wearing a stained undershirt, and big tattoos scarred the white flesh of his arms.

"Where . . .?" he whispered.

"Jus' for a little drive out in Jersey," the tattooed man laughed. "Look at the scenery. Check out the mosquitoes."

"You gonna remember it, Paulson," the driver growled.

There was one on each side of him, each a big, hulking man. One of them stank of sweat. One wore sandals. The driver lit a cigarette.

"Why?"

The tattooed man slapped him. The palm of his hand was hard and heavy, and it snapped Lucas's head to one side. His ear ached and rang. "Shut up, you bastard," the tattooed man said.

Lucas licked his lips, feeling them swollen and

smooth and slick with blood. He hung his head forward. The tattooed man popped open a can of beer and tipped it back for a long swig. He was to the right. He was bigger than the bearded man on the other side.

They turned south, maybe on Ninth Avenue; Lucas couldn't tell. It was a dark and squalid neighborhood. They would go south to the tunnel probably. Then over to Jersey . . . They could kill him there, if that was what they wanted.

He tried to clear his mind. He kept his head down, so the tattooed man would not slap at him again. He pretended he was still only half-conscious. He set himself in motion, weaving, hoping they would think he was slipping out again. If he could . . . He had to try something.

Lucas put his right arm across his face, as if to wipe off blood. With all the force he could muster, he drove his elbow into the tattooed man's ribs. Once, twice. The man roared and spat beer. Lucas chopped him in the throat. Then he swung at the bearded man to his left, driving a fist against his face. He reached past him and grabbed the handle of the door. He shoved the door open and pushed the stunned bearded man out. He scrambled after him, hardly feeling the tattooed man flailing at him and hitting him on the back.

He was on the street, on his knees, on the pavement. The Chevrolet shrieked to a stop. Lucas rose and ran. People on the street, blacks mostly, stared and gaped as he ran, with the three men from the car pounding after him. He yelled, but no one moved to help him. He ran toward a red neon sign. He didn't know why he ran for that, but it was a symbol of something, of people assembled, of refuge maybe, and he ran as hard as he could.

The neon sign in the window said BUDWEISER. He reached the door only one pace ahead of his three pursuers and threw himself into the smoky darkness of the bar.

"Cool it!" barked the bartender, speaking to him and to the three men who had pounded in after him. The bartender, a big black man, reached beneath the bar and brought up a baseball bat. "No shittin' aroun' in here, honkies," he growled. "You fight it out on the street."

Lucas stood in the middle of the room, halfway down the bar, gasping for breath, sweating, bleeding. He turned. The tattooed man, the bearded man, and the driver all stood in a cluster just inside the door, high on the balls of their feet, bouncing up and down, threatening.

"Call the police," Lucas breathed to the bartender.

"Fuck that. They be twenny mints gittin' here, and I ain't havin' you honkies in here no twenny mints. Take you goddamn fight outside, man. Now!"

Lucas looked around. The black men and women at the bar, at the few tables, regarded him with indifferent curiosity. They were smoking, every one of them, over beer, some over shots of whiskey. The men wore straw hats, though some of them had no shirts. Many wore vest undershirts. Sweat gleamed on their smooth, muscular arms and shoulders. The women, fairly reeking sensuality, stroked men's arms with their fingertips, sipped beer, and regarded Lucas with great almond eyes.

"Uh . . ." Lucas gasped. "One phone call. Need to make one call. 'Kay?"

"Make it quick," grunted the bartender, nodding toward the pay telephone on the wall opposite the bar.

If he didn't have a quarter . . . If the number slipped his mind . . . He glanced at the three men still waiting for him at the door, grinning at him now, slapping their palms with their fists. He dropped the quarter and dialed the number. The number rang. Once. Twice.

"Rainbow Show."

"Sergeant?"

"Hoo, yeah. That you, Lieutenant?"

"Yeah, and I'm in deep shit, Sergeant."

"I can hear you are. Somebuddy hit you in the mouth?"

He used as few words as possible to explain, mumbling through his swollen lips, gasping out the words.

"Whassa name o' that place, Lieutenant?"

Lucas turned to the glaring, impatient bartender. "What's the name of this place?"

"Georgie's. And get with it, honk. Get ready to move ass. I want your buddies out that door."

"I hearn him," said Kilbourne on the telephone. "You tell Burton that Kilbourne wants to speak at him."

Lucas pointed at the telephone. "Kilbourne wants to talk to you."

"Shee-it," growled the bartender as he came around the bar. "Keel—" He grabbed the phone. "Who 'is? Keel-bourne. Shee-it. Huh?" He turned narrowed eyes on Lucas. "Shee-it. Huh? Yeah. Three un 'em. Yeah. Oh, yeah! Yeah. 'Kay, Elvin. You got it."

The huge black man turned once more toward Lucas. He glared past him at the three men in the door, who turned suddenly apprehensive. "Them three," said the bartender, pointing. "Don' let 'em out."

The bartender drew a draught beer for Lucas and sat down with him at a table. A young woman wet a bar rag with cold water and came to dab at Lucas's mouth. The tattooed man, the man with the beard, and the driver remained just inside the door, their eyes fastened on half a dozen knives that had been laid out conspicuously on tables. They had made one backward step toward the door and had stopped when the knives came out.

Lucas remained dizzy. He knew he had taken a severe blow on the back of his head. His head began to ache all over. The bartender slipped in and out of focus. The young woman touched the cool, wet rag to his forehead. The beer seemed to relieve his nausea.

Finally Kilbourne arrived.

"Who dem? An' why?" Kilbourne demanded of Lucas, pointing at the three white men still hovering warily just inside the door.

"Don't know," Lucas muttered.

"Le's fin' out," said Kilbourne. "Back room, Burton. Jus' one of 'em. Which one, Lieutenant?"

"Tattoo," said Lucas.

Two young blacks grabbed the tattooed man by both arms and dragged him into a storage area behind the toilets at the rear of the bar. Kilbourne helped Lucas to his feet and led him back there. The room was stacked with cases of beer and dimly lit by one fly-specked bulb hanging on a wire from the ceiling.

"All we wanna know is what the shit you thought you wuz doin'," said Kilbourne to the tattooed man.

"Muggin' him," snarled the tattooed man.

"Shee-it," said Kilbourne. "Take him in a car, haul him from the East Side all the way over here. Shee-it. Don' gimme that. Pull the bastard's pants down, young men."

Kilbourne held his knife to the tattooed man's belly as the two young blacks jerked down his pants and underpants. The tattooed man heaved and gasped, and his eyes bulged with fear.

"Now," said Kilbourne, touching the sharp tip of his blade to the man's scrotum. "You gone talk . . . or I gone circumcise you right up to your bellybutton."

The tattooed man screamed as Kilbourne prodded with the knife and drew blood. "No!" he yelled. "I'll tell you! Some fucker give us five hundred to take care of the dude for him."

"Kill me?" asked Lucas.

"No, no!" the tattooed man protested. "We were supposed to break you up good and dump you on a road over in Jersey."

"Who gave you the five hundred?"

"We don't know his name. I swear! No, don't! Jesus Christ! No! Listen! We're supposed to get another five hundred when we come back and hand him your billfold. I don't know the address, but we can take you there. I can show you. Hey! Jesus! I mean it! C'mon!"

Kilbourne took the five hundred dollars, which the driver was carrying. ("Wouldn't want you boys to keep no ill-got gains.") They left the driver and the bearded man with Burton, and they took the tattooed man in the Chevrolet, back across Manhattan, letting him hunt out the address where he said a tall, gray-haired man had given them five hundred dollars. They had been called, he said, by a pimp who had told them the gray-haired man was an old customer and good for the money.

Lucas was not surprised when the tattooed man identified the house where he and his two friends had gone for their first five hundred dollars and had received their instructions. It was Matt Fraser's townhouse.

He went home. He told Susannah he had been mugged on the street. He did not mention her father. He never would.

UNI sold its stock in HEST to CONTEKS. So did Lucas Paulson and David Berger—for $50 million apiece. Fraser Tech's cash-out tender offer became a dead issue. It was withdrawn, and the Delaware lawsuit was dismissed.

The stockholders' meeting of HEST, Incorporated was held two weeks later. Thomas Miller announced at the meeting that CONTEKS would invest $100 million in redesigning HEST and launching it into new markets. The new board of directors of HEST was: Thomas Miller, chairman, plus three other directors from CONTEKS, and Lucas Paulson and David Berger.

The board of directors met the next day and elected Lucas Paulson president and chief executive officer. Lucas asked the board to elect James Cahill vice president for administration, and the other vice presidents of HEST in their old positions. Dave Berger, who still wanted to retain his professorship, accepted a consulting contract. He was assigned to develop new ways of using the speech transcriber. Melanie Paulson was given a similar consulting contract and was assigned to work on a plan for redesign of the operating system.

The meetings were held in the Waldorf, and it was not until the day after they were over that Lucas returned to the offices in the Pan Am Building. He walked off the elevator to find his name already on the wall: HEST, INCORPORATED—LUCAS W. PAULSON, PRESIDENT.

He made his way toward the executive suite, through

a throng of employees pressing close to offer their congratulations. They jostled with half a dozen moving men with four-wheeled carts, trying to push loads of big wooden packing crates toward the freight elevator.

"What's all that?" Lucas asked no one in particular.

Lois Levenstein answered. "That's all the Jap crap," she said.